Producer Incentives in Livestock Disease Management

OECD
BETTER POLICIES FOR BETTER LIVES

This document, as well as any data and any map included herein, are without prejudice to the status of or sovereignty over any territory, to the delimitation of international frontiers and boundaries and to the name of any territory, city or area.

Please cite this publication as:
OECD (2017), *Producer Incentives in Livestock Disease Management*, OECD Publishing, Paris.
http://dx.doi.org/10.1787/9789264279483-en

ISBN 978-92-64-27947-6 (print)
ISBN 978-92-64-27948-3 (PDF)

The statistical data for Israel are supplied by and under the responsibility of the relevant Israeli authorities. The use of such data by the OECD is without prejudice to the status of the Golan Heights, East Jerusalem and Israeli settlements in the West Bank under the terms of international law.

Photo credits: Cover © Shutterstock/Clive Watts.

Corrigenda to OECD publications may be found on line at: *www.oecd.org/about/publishing/corrigenda.htm*.

Foreword

This report is part of the OECD work on risk management in agriculture, complementing previous publications on *Livestock Disease Policies: Building Bridges between Science and Economics (2013); Livestock Diseases: Prevention, Control and Compensation Schemes (2012); Managing Risk in Agriculture: Policy Assessment and Design (2011)*, as well as reports focussed on other areas of agricultural risk management, such as climate change and food security.

This report examines the incentives for farmers to manage animal diseases and how government policy can align these incentives with public objectives related to such risks. It discusses the role of private producers and government in the prevention and control of animal diseases. It then examines the micro-economics of disease management decisions and draws on insights from behavioural economics to better understand the influences of personal and social factors on farmer behaviour. Collective action by farmers and industry is considered, as well as the role of other food chain participants. Country case studies for Australia, Chile and Korea conclude the examination.

Olga Melyukhina is the main author of this report, with important contributions from Wonsup Yoon. Carmel Cahill and Frank van Tongeren provided guidance at the scoping phase of this work and reviewed progressive drafts. A consultant paper by Christopher Wolf from Michigan State University, Department of Agricultural, Food, and Resource Economics provided input, in particular to Chapter 2, Chapter 3 (Section 3.3), and Chapter 4 (Section 4.2 and Section 4.3).

Special thanks are due to the governments of Australia, Chile and Korea for their support during the preparation of the country case studies. We also highly appreciate the financial contribution to this project by the Korean government. This work benefitted greatly from the reviews and comments by governments and experts from many other OECD countries, in particular Canada, Italy, France, Germany, Ireland, the Netherlands, Sweden, Switzerland, and the United States. Valuable advice and comments were received from the European Commission and its Joint Research Centre (Foresight, Behavioural Insights and Design for Policy Unit). We thank Mr. Alain Dehove from the World Organisation for Animal Health (OIE) for helpful exchange at the scoping phase of this project.

We are grateful to many colleagues in the OECD: Michael Ryan provided comments on the report, Lihan Wei and Christine Arriola contributed statistical work, and Martina Abderrahmane and Michèle Patterson ensured editorial and publication support. Martina Abderrahmane and Marina Giacalone-Belkadi also provided administrative assistance.

This document was approved by the OECD Working Party on Agricultural Policies and Markets at its March 2017 session and prepared for publication by the OECD Secretariat.

Table of contents

Tables

Figures

Boxes

Acronyms

ABARES	Australian Bureau of Agricultural and Resource Economics and Sciences
ABS	Australian Bureau of Statistics
ACCC	Australian Competition and Consumer Commission
ACHIC	Chilean Meat Association
ADAWR	Australian Government Department of Agriculture and Water Resources
AECL	Australian Egg Corporation Limited
AFECH	Association of Livestock Trade Fairs of Chile
AHA	Animal Health Australia
AHF	Animal Health Fund (the Netherlands)
AI	Avain influenza
ASF	African swine fever
ASPROCER	Chilean Association of Pig Producers
AUD	Australian dollar
Ausvetplan	Australian Veterinary Emergency Plan
BPS	Backyard production system
BSE	Bovine spongiform encephalopathy
bTB	Bovine tuberculosis
CBPP	Contagious bovine pleuropneumonia
CSF	Classical swine fever
CSIRO	Commonwealth Scientific and Industrial Research Organisation (Australia)
CWD	Chronic wasting disease
Defra	Department for Environment, Food and Rural Affairs (the United Kingdom)
EADRA	Australian Emergency Animal Disease Response Agreement
EU	European Union
Expocarnes	Meat Exporters Association (Chile)
FEDECARNE	National Federation of Beef Producers (Chile)
FEDELECHE	National Federation of Milk Producers (Chile)
FMD	Foot-and-mouth disease
HACCP	Hazard Analysis of Critical Control Points

HPAI	Highly pathogenic avian influenza
IBR	Infectious bovine rhinotracheitis
ICT	Information and communication technologies
INDAP	Agricultural and Livestock Development Institute (Chile)
INE	Chilean National Institute of Statistics
KAHIS	Korean Animal Health Integrated System
KOSTAT	Statistics Korea
KRW	Korean won
LBN	Livestock Biosecurity Network (Australia)
LHCA	Livestock Health Control Association (Korea)
LPA	Livestock Production Assurance (Australia)
LPAI	Low pathogenic avian influenza
MAFRA	Ministry of Agriculture, Food, and Rural Affairs (Korea)
MAP	Market Assurance Programme
MLA	Meat & Livestock Australia Ltd.
MVO	Official Veterinarian (Chile)
NACF	National Agricultural Cooperatives Federation (Korea)
NAHIS	National Animal Health Information System (Australia)
NCN	Biosecurity Incident National Communication Network (Australia)
NFAS	National Feedlot Accreditation Scheme (Australia)
NGO	Non-government organisation
NLIS	National Livestock Identification System (Australia)
NPS	National Pension Scheme (Korea)
OECD	Organisation for Economic Co-operation and Development
OIE	World Organisation for Animal Health
PED	Porcine epidemic diarrhoea
PHA	Plant Health Australia
PIC	Property Identification Code
PRRS	Porcine reproductive and respiratory syndrome
QIA	Animal and Plant Quarantine Agency (Korea)
R&D	Research and development
SAG	Agricultural and Livestock Service (Chile)
SAGO	Agricultural and Livestock Society of Osorno (Chile)
SAVAL	Union of Agricultural Producers of Valdivia (Chile)
SCA	Sheepmeat Council of Australia

SEM	Structural Equation Modelling
SIPEC	Livestock Information and Animal Traceability System (Chile)
TB	Tuberculosis
TORA	Theory of Reasoned Action
TPB	Theory of Planned Behaviour
TSE	Transmissible spongiform encephalopathy
UF	Unidad de Fomento (Chile)
UK	United Kingdom
USD	United States dollar
WHA	Wildlife Health Australia
WPA	WoolProducers Australia
WTA	Willingness to accept
WTP	Willingness to pay

Executive summary

Management of livestock diseases has become increasingly important given the concentration of livestock production, large volumes of cross-border trade, and international travel. Many diseases pose threats to humans and wildlife. Farmers are the primary decision-makers in livestock disease management. How can government policy align farmer incentives with public objectives related to livestock disease risks? This report examines various aspects of this broad question and provides recommendations for more effective government policy.

Farmers have clear incentives to prevent livestock disease, but as rational entrepreneurs they trade marginal benefits of efforts against the marginal costs. Farmers may also weigh long-term gains from investments in farm biosecurity against returns to investment in other areas. For their decisions on disease management, farmers need to understand the options which depend on disease biology, prevention techniques, tests for infection and their costs, treatments available, market reactions and other factors. The role of policy then is to:

- *Enable farmers to make better informed decisions on disease management*: facilitate their access to necessary knowledge, skills and information, including the information that could be tailored to particular farm situations, as well as decision-support tools.
- *Encourage the development of technologies and services that decrease the costs to prevent and control disease*, so that private solutions on disease management result in lower disease occurrence and lower public costs.
- *Communicate the potential for economies of scope in biosecurity practices*: when farmers understand that certain practices can prevent multiple diseases, farmer incentives to undertake those practices are strengthened.

Uncertainties and risks add complexity as farmers do not have perfect information when making disease management decisions. Risk perception is an important factor: if a farmer believes there is negligible risk that a disease will be contracted on his farm, he will be unlikely to invest in its prevention. There are biases and risk perception issues that must be addressed in order for farm managers to make adequate livestock disease management decisions. Governments should therefore:

- *Ensure sufficient communication and education on animal disease risks*, so that farmers better understand the risks they are facing and their potential effects beyond the farm.
- *Increase government's own understanding of risk awareness and risk preferences of the farming community* as a necessary input into livestock policy design.

Infection on one farm may cause damage to neighbouring farms, affect the whole sector, or even threaten human health. This is the principal rationale for government involvement in animal biosecurity. However, government policies need to address potential information problems, in particular when it comes to very harmful diseases and compensation for related losses. One problem is moral hazard, where a farmer who expects to receive compensation in the event of a disease outbreak has weaker incentives to avoid risk during "peace time". Another problem is that if a farmer reports a disease, there may be costs incurred related to that reporting, and thus a budget-constrained farmer may be inclined to wait and see without alerting authorities. Compensation schemes for epidemics can address these information problems if they:

- *Induce sufficient effort by farmers to prevent disease*; for example, by shifting part of the risk to farmers through less-than-full compensation of losses, or differentiation of payments according to individual risk profiles; by making payments conditional on farmers exercising certain biosecurity practices, or implementing farm biosecurity plans, or participating in disease programmes.
- *Provide incentives for early reporting of disease*; for example, by denying compensation where there is a failure to report, or applying no or reduced payment for diseased animals.

Whether livestock holders run commercial production or farm for subsistence or as a hobby, changes their incentives to manage disease. Policies designed for commercial farms will likely be a poor fit for non-commercial animal operations and hobby farms. Incentives may also depend on geographical location which affects vulnerability to disease risk and farmer's ability to free-ride on the biosecurity efforts of others.

- *Allowing flexibility in policy design to account for specific characteristics of farms* may improve the alignment of incentives.

Economic motivation is essential, but only partially explains farmer behaviour. The broader values of farmers and their ability to process information and gain knowledge, their habits and social connections also influence disease management decisions. Policy needs to act along the whole spectrum of these behavioural drivers to engage different notions – psychological, social, as well as economic – to have a more broadly shared response within the farming community. Information services, education, advice and communication activate such drivers. Thus, policy makers need to:

- *Build evidence on behavioural aspects to understand the complexity of drivers behind farmer disease management* and integrate that knowledge into policy design.
- *Encourage communication and social connectivity amongst farmers*, understand who the opinion leaders are and the farmer's principal sources of reference in disease management in order to exploit effective communication pathways to deliver policy.
- *Use gentle nudges*, rather than coercive measures, by appealing to preferred values.

Farmers are at once individuals who make individual choices and members of communities having a common interest. Collective action can provide responses to shared concerns in disease risk management, by generating economies of scale and scope that reduce the private cost of management. Collective action can strengthen compliance with norms, develop and enforce industry standards, and support best practices. It can also improve the division of responsibilities between government and private actors. The role of policy should therefore be to:

- *Provide evidence of the benefits of collective action, external facilitation, and information through existing networks.*
- *Foster institutional and financial soundness of producer institutions* through legislation, and address the "free-rider" problem that constrains collective action.
- *Develop the potential for collective action* in areas such as farmer capacity building, risk insurance, surveillance, and responses to livestock epidemics.

Farmers and agri-food industries co-operate to ensure food quality and verification of production practices to consumers, and to maintain market access. These programmes may provide a framework to foster farm biosecurity practices or create positive spill-overs to prevent disease.

Finally, wildlife as a reservoir and vector of disease complicates management. Farmers might be able to manage sporadic risks through biosecurity actions, but continuous disease pressure from a disease reservoir in local wildlife is not manageable at the farm level. Government agencies charged with disease control in livestock and wildlife populations should co-ordinate and complement their efforts.

Country-case studies for Australia, Chile, and Korea conclude this report. They all focus on three topics: i) government's awareness of producer behaviour; (ii) information, education and training for producers; and (iii) epidemic compensation policy. Some of the cross-cutting findings are:

- The degree to which these countries integrate knowledge about farmer behaviour into their policy design is uneven, with Australia being the most advanced in this respect.
- While there is strong communication with farmers on veterinary and sanitary issues, there seems to be less emphasis on the economics of disease management. Such considerations are nevertheless shown to be significant drivers of farmer disease management decisions.
- Approaches to compensation related to epidemic diseases differ across countries: Australia has established effective cost-sharing between industry and government, Korea presents an instructive example of tailoring government compensation to particular farmer profiles, while Chilean regulations do not foresee indemnities to producers in the case of disease outbreaks.
- Small livestock holders are an important constituency that should be targeted by animal disease policy, although designing a policy mix to reach out to this producer group is challenging.

Part 1

Economic, social, and internal factors of farmer decision-making related to animal disease

Chapter 1

Farmer and public roles in livestock disease management

This chapter sets out the roles of private producers and government to prevent and control animal disease based on the OECD framework for risk management in agriculture. It then introduces key issues of aligning farmer incentives with public objectives as these relate to animal disease risks.

Livestock disease management is increasingly important given the concentration of livestock production, and the large volumes of cross-border trade of agricultural products, international travel, and the recognition that many diseases pose threats to humans and wildlife. The economic impact of infectious animal disease outbreaks can be enormous. The World Organisation for Animal Health (OIE, 2014) estimated that disease could reduce food output by more than 20% worldwide and create significant risks for human health and animal welfare. More than 75% of emerging diseases are classified as zoonotics – animal diseases that can be transmitted to humans, while the nature of some other emerging diseases remains uncertain. Livestock epizootics may threaten the economic well-being of farmers and ranchers, safety and viability of the food production system, valuable wildlife resources including endangered species, and human health (Cleaveland et al., 2001; Daszak et al., 2000).

Disease is inherent to animal production and a major concern for farmers with livestock. Although significant economic losses from animal diseases would be greater if not for farm management efforts, producers are unlikely to voluntarily take into consideration all the social costs that disease can have on livestock, wildlife and humans. Disease outbreaks in livestock have repercussions up and down the supply chain. For example, trade losses are of prime importance when considering the economic impact of infectious disease. Private farm disease management behaviour may therefore lead to externalities and a rationale for government intervention (Sumner et al., 2005).

The OECD framework for management of risk in agriculture helps to clarify the roles of private producers and government in risk management (OECD, 2011). This framework classifies risks depending on their probability of occurrence and economic impact (Figure 1.1). Three layers are distinguished: high frequency – low damage normal risks; low frequency – high damage catastrophic risks; and marketable risks with intermediate levels of frequency and damage. A key idea is that a differentiated policy response is required across these risk layers. "Normal" risks should remain the responsibility of the farmer. "Marketable" risks can potentially be managed through market tools, such as insurance, and require institutions for risk sharing – these can be fully private or with public participation. Catastrophic risks are beyond the capacity of individual farmers to cope with. They generate significant negative externalities, and governments are expected to provide assistance.[1]

A challenge for policy makers is to establish an optimal pattern of policy intervention by delineating the different risk layers. This delineation is particularly relevant for catastrophic risks because societies will expect government action with respect to such risks. In the area of animal disease, the frontier of catastrophic risk is relatively explicit due to the formal classification of diseases into the most and least harmful at the international (the OIE) and national levels. All countries have lists of harmful organisms for animals, with the most harmful groups effectively delimiting the catastrophic risk. Such groups are commonly termed "notifiable" animal diseases. Due to the strong cross-border and externality aspects of disease risks, they are the responsibility of national authorities and are governed by international regulations and/or regional biosecurity systems (e.g. within the European Union). The international dimension of animal disease risks is an additional factor that calls for well-developed formal frameworks to prepare for catastrophic risk management. In all countries, national governments have an explicit responsibility with regard to the most harmful organisms: verification of reports about suspected disease, ensuring the response to disease outbreaks through measures such as culling of animals, depopulation, restrictions on animal movement, and vaccination, as well as providing indemnities to farmers to ensure that disease is reported.

Some livestock disease risks can be shared through markets and lie within the "marketable" risk layer. Livestock disease insurance exists in EU countries (Germany, the Netherlands, Spain, Czech Republic, Estonia, Finland, Greece and Italy), Turkey, the United States, Chile, and Korea. These insurances can cover highly contagious notifiable diseases as well as others outside that group. While insurance is well developed for many types of business risks, it is more challenging when applied to livestock disease due to generally insufficient biological and epidemiological evidence, which in turn makes it difficult to estimate the scale and probability of a disease event. But governments can create the general conditions for the development and good operation of risk sharing markets. This could include a subsidy provision where there is a market failure (e.g. public-private insurance schemes or subsidised reinsurance), or some other type of facilitation (e.g. creation of information systems to help the "production" of insurance products).

Figure 1.1. Optimal pattern of risk strategies and policies in livestock disease management

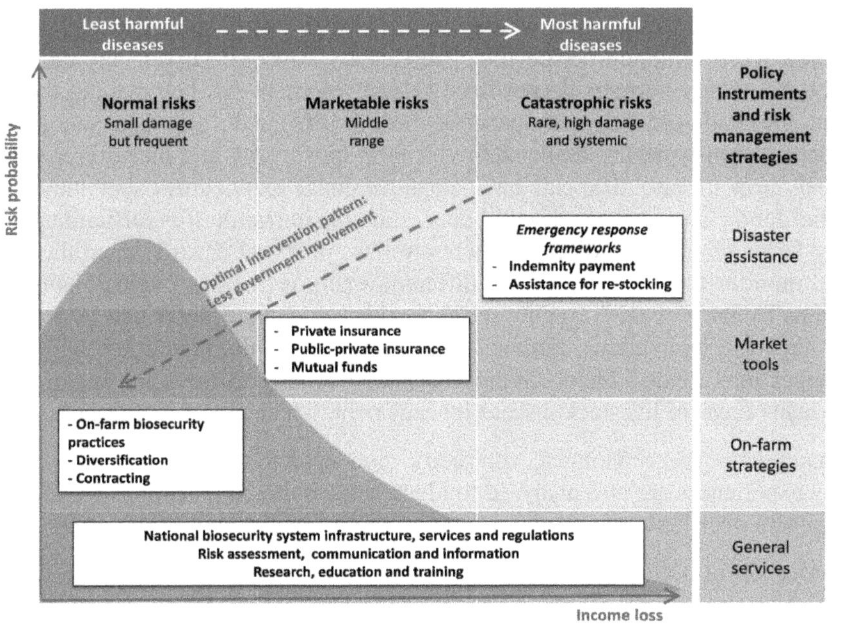

Source: Adapted from OECD (2011).

The "normal" risk layer as applied to an animal disease can be associated with diseases that occur frequently but are not highly harmful. Farmers should be able to manage such risks individually by using on-farm biosecurity techniques, diversification of activity, and other means available to farm households. The government's primary role here should be to support private activity through general economic mechanisms, such as tax, credit or social safety nets. However, some diseases that present a "normal" risk may lead to government programmes, such as those for the eradication of certain endemic diseases.

Finally, governments have responsibilities that cross all risk layers. These are "general services" to enable national biosecurity systems to function as a whole, such as building and maintaining appropriate national veterinary systems for the prevention, control, monitoring of diseases, and supporting regulations. Publicly (co)funded research, risk assessment and communication are other cross-cutting functions of governments. Information is a key element in all risk layers, enabling the detection and evaluation of risks and is a crucial input to decisions of all parties involved in risk management, from government to farmers undertaking biosecurity, to private insurance providers and the food industry. Governments can also be expected to participate in providing training and education that support the whole continuum of animal disease management. However, the boundary between public and non-public provision of such services is intrinsically movable and depends on the nature of the activity, which is not static. Thus, there may be a rationale for collective action by industry in these areas, which can often be undertaken in partnership with governments (Chapter 4).

Farmers are the primary decision-makers and first-incidence parties with respect to animal disease at all layers of risk featured in this framework. This report continues previous OECD work on agricultural risk management by taking a micro-economic perspective that focuses on the incentive-compatible livestock disease management policy. The objective is to examine: a) decision-making by individual farmers with respect to livestock disease prevention and control; and b) relate farmer incentives for animal disease prevention and control to public policies.

This micro-perspective opens a range of issues in animal disease management policy that fall under the broad problem of the compatibility of private incentives with public objectives. Farmers have obvious incentives to prevent livestock diseases due to their negative effects on farm income, farm asset value, and even the viability of the farm enterprise itself. Farm managers take measures against the introduction of diseases and to mitigate the effects of diseases that are present. A rational profit-maximising farmer will invest in disease prevention up to the point where the marginal private benefit from prevention is equal to marginal costs. From a social optimum perspective, even a fully informed farmer may rationally underinvest in disease prevention. Moreover, farmers do not have perfect information when making their decisions: they are uncertain about the trade-off between marginal benefit (avoided loss) and marginal cost of such investment. The financial consequences associated with farm biosecurity and disease reporting are crucially important. Individual farm disease risk can have negative local externalities and may affect the whole livestock industry and food chain, consumer well-being, and human health. It is difficult to perfectly monitor the actions taken by farms to control a disease. There are risks of moral hazard where the government has a role to regulate and monitor the activities of the different actors in the food value chain (Rushton, 2009). Furthermore, decisions by farmers are in reality more complex than those described by traditional economic rationality. Other values and motivations, farmers' ability to process information and build knowledge, their habits and social connections are also factors in their decisions. Finally, farmers are part of groups that have a common interest in many areas of livestock disease management, which creates a rationale to act collectively.

This report synthesises the economics, veterinary, and epidemiology literature that examines these aspects. The country experiences are also analysed to identify the policy implications for incentive compatible farm disease management decisions.

The review proceeds as follows. Chapter 2 considers farm decisions from a viewpoint of standard economic rationale. Various aspects related to farmer decisions and policy incentives are considered, including the trade-off between the economic costs and benefits of disease management, the presence of risk, information asymmetries, and farm size. Chapter 3 extends the perspective beyond the conventional economic rationale and introduces a behavioural economics approach to farmer decision making. It examines how broader values, perceptions, "important others", and social norms influence farmers' decisions. Chapter 4 considers influences and actors beyond the farm, including the role of farmer collective action and other participants in the food value chain. It also looks at the impact that wildlife reservoirs and vectors may have on farm management decisions. Each of these chapters concludes with the implications for animal disease policy. Although each chapter takes a specific perspective on farmer behaviour, there is certain overlap and interdependency among and across these topics. The report concludes with the livestock disease policy experiences in Australia (Chapter 5), Chile (Chapter 6) and Korea (Chapter 7).

Note

1. This framework is an ideal representation of the public and private roles in animal disease management and does not intend to capture the complexity of real-world policy situations. Actual government policy responses may differ from the preferred pattern set out below, reflecting the multitude of influences such as the country's political settings, policy path dependency, and institutional specificities and constraints. The case studies for Australia, Chile, and Korea illustrate such variations in actual patterns of policy responses to animal disease risks.

References

Cleaveland, S., M.K. Laurenson and L.H. Taylor (2001), "Disease of humans and their domestic mammals: pathogen characteristics, host range and the risk of emergence", *Philosophical Transactions of the Royal Society: Biological Series*, Vol. 356, pp.991-999.

Daszak, P., A.A. Cunningham and A.D. Hyatt (2000), "Emerging infectious diseases of wildlife-threats to biodiversity and human health", *Science*, Vol. 287, pp. 443–49.

OECD (2011), *Managing Risk in Agriculture: Policy Assessment and Design*, OECD Publishing, Paris, http://dx.doi.org/10.1787/9789264116146-en

OIE (2014), *Animal Health: A Multifaceted Challenge,* www.oie.int/fileadmin/Home/eng/Media_Center/docs/pdf/Key_Documents/ANIMAL-HEALTH-EN-FINAL.pdf

Rushton, J. (2009), *The Economics of Animal Health and Production*, CABI Publishing, Oxfordshire.

Sumner, D.A., J.E. Bervejillo and L.S. Jarvis (2005), "Public Policy, Invasive Species and Animal Disease Management", *International Food and Agribusiness Management Review*, Vol. 8, pp. 78-97.

Chapter 2

Economic determinants of farmer decision-making related to animal disease

This chapter reviews the major economic and financial issues of farmers' management decisions related to livestock disease. Farmer decisions are first examined from the perspective of cost-minimising or profit-maximising with no risk, uncertainty or information issues, which is most appropriately applied to endemic diseases. The role of risk and uncertainty in farm decisions is then examined, as are farm incentives in the presence of information asymmetries. This analysis provides insights that are relevant to epidemic diseases. Finally, the role of the farm industry structure and spatial effects in disease management are examined.

2.1. Farmer disease management decisions under certainty

- In a basic economic model, farmers prevent and control disease so that expected marginal benefits equal the marginal costs of those activities.
- Expenditures on disease prevention and control have diminishing returns, so it is often not economically optimal to prevent all expected losses from disease.
- Because of the negative externality associated with disease, farmers may under-invest in prevention and control relative to a social optimum.
- Technological improvement and (or) government action to lower prevention and control costs would shift a loss-expenditure frontier, resulting in a private cost-benefit solution with less disease.
- In making decisions on disease management, farmers must be able to understand the options they have related to disease biology and public action on the disease in question.
- One role of policy with regard to farmer profit optimisation is to equip farmers with knowledge and cost-efficient techniques to prevent and control diseases.
- Many biosecurity practices prevent from multiple diseases or vectors to develop; considering these benefits across diseases can lead to greater efforts and investment in biosecurity and surveillance.
- Dynamic relationships between producer choices and disease status may make complete disease eradication a sub-optimal strategy.

Farming as a business enterprise drives food production in OECD countries. The financial aspects of farming include profitability (generating returns), solvency (possessing adequate equity), and liquidity (ability to pay bills as they are due). Animal diseases may decrease profits through market and morbidity losses. Mortality losses of livestock directly affect farm wealth. Lost profitability and wealth can threaten farm financial viability.

Livestock producers continually face decisions with respect to diseases. These management decisions are either *ex ante* to the occurrence of disease, and include prevention measures in susceptible herds, or they are *ex post* and regard control measures when diseases occur (Chi et al., 2002). The probability of infection from a given disease depends on farm practices (prevention) as well as the prevalence rate in host populations (livestock, wildlife, and humans) in the relevant area.

The private benefits of livestock disease prevention and control include higher production as morbidity is reduced, lower mortality or less early culling, and avoided future control costs. With respect to prevention, farmers can allocate operating resources or investments to biosecurity programmes. These programmes often involve limiting livestock contact (e.g. via quarantines and controlling the movement of new livestock), as well as preventing other potential vectors of disease from entering the farm (e.g. wildlife or human contact). In addition, farm biosecurity may involve testing livestock and feed prior to purchase, strict sanitation regarding the possible ways that disease may be introduced on the farm, including via people and vehicles entering the farm, separating new-borns from infected dams, and protecting feed supplies from wildlife. Farmers control disease by monitoring and testing their own herd and reporting relevant infections to authorities. Treating disease is possible in some cases and may involve medicines as well as veterinary visits. In situations where recovery from the disease is impossible or treatment expenses are economically prohibitive, depopulation and culling of animals may be the only recourse. Early involuntary culling has long-term implications for livestock capital stock and significant costs related to animal replacement.

The motivations of farmers to control disease are to avoid livestock mortality and related replacement expenses, livestock morbidity and related production losses, increased veterinary expenses, and potential losses from business interruption when government programmes mandate the slaughter of entire herds or flocks. Farmers' motivations to shirk disease control include time, labour, management, and capital constraints.

The basic economic model of farmer decision-making related to disease management

McInerney et al. (1992) developed a decision model for disease management where the farmer trades off the costs to control disease and avoided losses (Figure 2.1). An output loss implies a benefit that is taken away (e.g. production loss) or an unrealised potential benefit. Losses are reductions on the output side of a process due to livestock morbidity or mortality. By contrast, some economic effects are expenditures (E). They represent resources that have to be allocated either to moderate the impact after a disease occurs or to avoid disease. The negative economic effects of a disease appear in one or other form, so that the total economic effects of a disease occurrence (C) are: $C = L + E$. L(E) is a loss-expenditure frontier that shows the relationship between control costs and avoided losses. If no action is taken to control disease, the losses would equal ($\bar{L}$) on the vertical axis. If expenditure is incurred for control of disease (points M, K and A), this will reduce disease losses (to L_M, L_K or L_A).

This framework employs two key assumptions. First, there is a trade-off between output losses and control expenditures – all other things being equal, higher disease control expenditures result in lower losses. Second, control expenditures have diminishing returns – as they increase it becomes more expensive to reduce losses.[1] One implication of diminishing returns is that economic cost of disease management (C) has optimal level, i.e. the point beyond which adding an additional unit of expenditure would reduce loss by less than a unit.[2] The implication is that it will not generally be economically rational to avoid all expected losses from disease (Dijkhuizen, et al., 1995). As drawn, the frontier, beyond point A runs parallel to the horizontal axis indicating in this example that some positive level of disease loss ($\underline{L}$) is unavoidable. This assumption is justified when diseases are unavoidably present in reservoirs or adjacent to the livestock operations. A new technology that lowers the control cost, public management programmes that reduce the density of disease, or government programmes offsetting the losses with indemnity payments would shift the frontier down and result in a situation with less disease.

Figure 2.1. Farm trade-off between disease loss and control expenditures

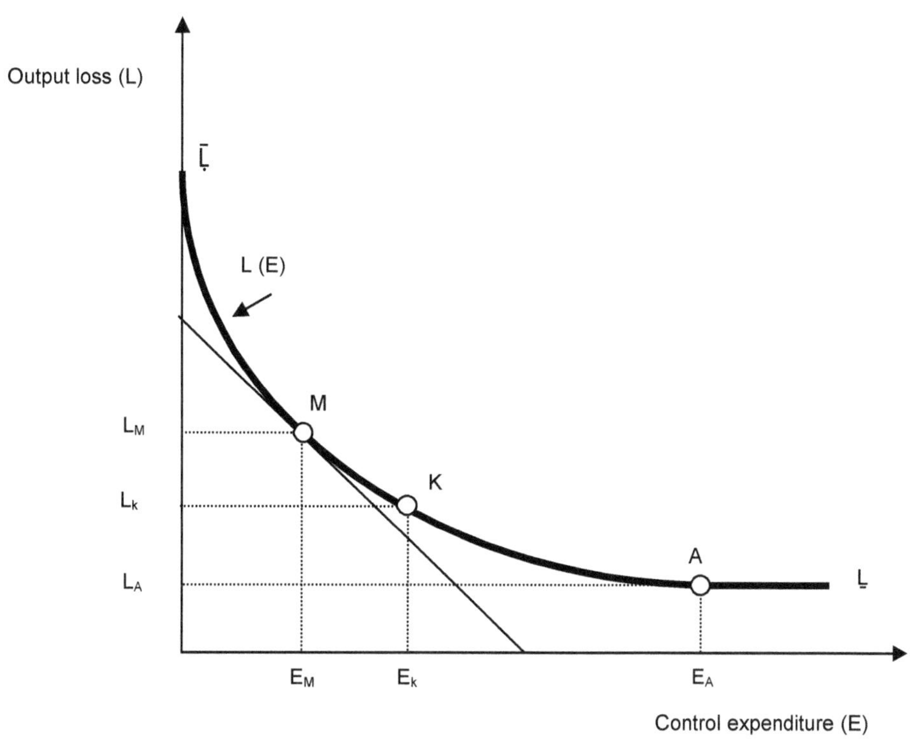

Source: Adapted from McInerney et al. (1992).

Chi et al. (2002) built on ideas of McInerney et al. (1992) and put them into a more formal economic framework of damage control inputs. The authors suggest that the optimal level of disease control, and the consequent disease level, cannot be determined using the same framework as for conventional inputs that tend to increase output levels with higher use. Instead, following Lichtenstein and Zilberman (1986), they consider disease control to be a damage control input because it acts to prevent output from falling, rather than to further enhance production. The farm decision is thus posited as maximising profits by choosing preventive and control measures as inputs in addition to standard production enhancing inputs. Chi et al. (2002) found the standard marginal benefit equals marginal cost for standard inputs, prevention inputs and control inputs.

Producers are concerned about the direct cost of the disease. They will minimise the costs of prevention and curative activities insofar as they pay those costs (i.e. costs are not off-set by government indemnity or disaster payments). These considerations are irrelevant if the producer choice is limited because government programmes mandate a response. This is true in the case of several livestock-borne diseases that pose a direct human health threat or cause large economic damages to the livestock sector or related industries.

The cost-benefit approach also leads to a distinction between the private and social costs of disease management and the existence of disease externalities. Beyond private impacts, animal disease has economic impacts across the wider economic system. This concerns food safety, human health, sanitary reputation to maintain access to export market, and broad spill-overs of disease on business sectors along the food chain. The private cost (C) for farmers does not reflect the full social cost of disease management, implying that private producers do not have inherent incentives to invest in disease management up to the "socially optimal" level which takes into account all externalities of animal disease. The frontier of the social economic cost of disease managements is thus always above the private frontier L(E). The existence of animal disease externalities is the principal economic justification for public investment in animal biosecurity. Furthermore, individual producers may have many objectives when they make investment decisions. Kristensen and Enevoldsen (2008), for example, found that the level of investment in herd health management on Danish dairy farms would never be at the socially optimal level because returns to investment were often better in other areas, and short-term gains were valued more than possible larger long-term gains, i.e. the time value of money and certain pay-off.

To make decisions regarding disease management producers must understand the options they have relative to the disease in question. These options depend on disease biology, prevention techniques, tests for infection and their costs, treatments available, market reactions, as well as industry and government programmes and policies. Disease biology includes transmission modes and rates, disease evolution (e.g. length of time to infectious period), production losses associated with the disease, and mortality rate (where applicable). Preventing the spread of disease often involves movement restrictions and quarantines. Treatment may include medicines and services to assist recovery. Market reaction involves the change in price for infected livestock and livestock products (which may result in a price of zero). Industry and government programmes may include indemnity payments, quarantines, test and cull programmes, or required depopulation and resulting business interruption losses.

Biosecurity economies of scope and preventive spill-overs

It is common practice in the veterinary literature to consider on-farm management on a disease-by-disease basis, in large part because observational or case-control studies are designed to identify management "risk factors" for infection. If each disease is considered as an independent event (i.e. by making biosecurity and health management decisions on a disease-by-disease basis), the full scope of disease management actions are ignored. A preventive spill-over exists whenever a health management or biosecurity practice yields preventive returns for more than one disease, such as control measures that reduce the probability of disease transmission to a facility. For example, improving sanitation practices of poultry production may help prevent both new castle disease and avian influenza.

From an economic standpoint, estimations of disease control functions should take into account the potential for disease management practices to affect the prevalence of multiple diseases, so that resources can be allocated efficiently. Preventive spill-overs may be thought of as either multi-product outputs of individual management practices or as input externalities, which may be either positive or negative. If management practices are viewed as livestock production inputs, then the notion of preventive spill-overs suggests that biosecurity practices are non-allocable factors in the sense that shares of the input cannot be allocated to the prevention of a specific disease or set of diseases and not to others.

Dynamic feedbacks in disease management

The economic analysis also emphasises the interactions between human decisions and epidemiologic state, that is, the feedback between disease management decisions and the evolution of the epidemic. Horan et al. (2010) describe multiple connections of epidemiology with human behaviour: culling rates are determined by a chosen combination of testing and removal efforts, the sub-populations under quarantine are also the result of human choice, domestic animal movements depend on economic activities, such as trade, while densities of wild populations as vectors of disease can also be influenced by wildlife programmes. All these choices appear in epidemiological models as parameters. A further idea is that human choices change as the disease situation evolves. Thus, as herd densities decrease through a density-reducing strategy, producers have fewer private incentives to invest in tests and slaughter of infected animals because of diminishing returns to these investments.

A consideration of dynamic feedbacks in the biosecurity system changes the perspective on optimal disease management strategies. Epidemiological strategies that abstract from these feedbacks generally assume that: (a) the objective is disease eradication, with management metrics based on the disease-free equilibrium, and (b) human behaviours are an external force on the disease dynamics. Alternatively, the bioeconomics approach joins human behaviours and disease biology in one system where human behaviours are endogenous to the analysis. The bioeconomic approach does not impose complete disease eradication as an explicit objective – it uses economic criteria in conjunction with epidemiological modeling to determine the economically optimal level of disease control (Horan et al., 2010). With this approach eradication is only optimal if its marginal benefit outweighs the cost. Fenichel et al. (2010) find that the bioeconomic approach may or may not optimally result in eradication but that in all cases it yields a larger net present value than does the conventional disease ecology approach.

2.2. Risk, uncertainty, and farm decisions

- Farmer decisions depend on their identification of risk; if farmers incorrectly identify risk, they may not act.
- A policy implication is to facilitate risk identification by farmers; better information on the presence, spread and consequences of disease can facilitate farmer decisions.
- Risk-averse farmers are likely to make greater efforts to reduce the probability of disease, leading to lower disease occurrence.
- Disease outbreak changes risk perception, with farmer responses during an outbreak likely being different from their responses during peacetime.
- Insurance can shift the composition of investments towards riskier production activities.

The discussion so far has left aside risk or uncertainty as part of producer livestock disease decisions. This section considers decision-making under risk and uncertainty which most appropriately applies to epidemic diseases. Animal diseases, and in particular epidemics which require a government response, are major sources of risk for farmers. Meuwissen et al. (2001) found that epidemic disease which is viewed as the second largest source of risk is essentially linked to price risk. In that study, non-epidemics ranked 17 out of 22 sources of risk. Baltussen et al. (2006) show that epidemic disease risks are perceived as highly important concerns amongst Dutch dairy, pig and poultry farmers, both in terms of their probability and possible effects. Non-epidemic diseases were typically perceived as less important.

Risks identification and farm risk management strategies

The types of risk faced by an enterprise are important in considering farmer perceptions and decisions. Mikes et al. (2015) define the types of risk as preventable, strategy execution, or external risks. Preventable risks are those that arise from routine operations. Preventable risks should be a focus of routine management and should not be tolerated; one might consider, for example, diseases that can be prevented by vaccination or common animal husbandry practices. Strategy execution risks are those that firms take in order to achieve higher returns; in farming, this might include the risk of infection from bringing in outside livestock during herd expansion. Firm managers can identify and influence the likelihood and impact of strategy execution risks, but some residual risk will remain. External risks arise from events the farm manager cannot influence. An example might be a local outbreak of foot-and-mouth disease due to border protection failure. Farm managers should consider responses and resiliency to external risks. Delineating risks in this way is useful with respect to farm animal disease management decisions because these decisions are primarily concerned with preventable risks. However, this framework suggests that farm managers should consider the potential for disease derived from strategy execution activities. If farmers incorrectly assume a particular disease is external, they will ignore it. Thus, one important job governments can facilitate is risk identification.

As a risk management exercise, animal disease management requires assessing the likelihood of disease. For locally endemic diseases, this is part of standard herd health management. For exotic infectious disease, this assessment will be quite difficult. According to Hardaker et al. (1997), there are many potential psychological pitfalls in making probability judgements. Other pitfalls include avoiding uncertainty instead of managing the situation and incorrectly relating events and likelihoods to past experiences and irrelevant events perceived to be similar. To overcome these pitfalls in assessing probabilities for risky decisions, Hardaker et al. (1997) advocated facilitating subjective probabilities for decision-making by using experts, experiments, past experience, and simulation. All these sources can be used to derive subjective probabilities of exotic disease occurrence on farms. This information could serve as the foundation for farm disease risk information programmes.

At the farm level, risk management strategies can be categorised as collecting information, avoiding risk, selecting less risky practices, diversification, flexibility, and insurance. All these strategies may have relevance to farm animal disease management and information plays a key role as it can help reduce the dispersion of the subjective probability distribution. Information can shift the location of the distribution. Thus, better information on the presence, spread and consequences of disease can facilitate better decisions. Avoiding or reducing exposure to risks includes such potential actions as postponing a decision until more information is available, implementing safety standards until more is known, or taking a decision that is close to the status quo. With respect to farm disease, this might include taking preventive measures prior to confirmation of outbreaks in the area. Selecting less risky practices, such as maintaining a closed herd, would minimise risks of some diseases. Diversification might have less direct relevance to farm animal disease, but one might imagine that diversified farms might be better equipped to deal with consequential losses. Finally, flexibility refers to maintaining options that allow for more responses to risky situations.

Risk aversion and uncertainty

All producers are likely to make certain investments in disease prevention, but their management decisions under risk depend on risk aversion. Rat-Aspert and Fourichon (2010), using a decision-epidemiologic model, found that more risk-averse producers make greater efforts to prevent disease to reduce the probability of such an event, which in turn would lead to lower disease occurrence. Niemi and Heikkila (2011) concluded that a risk-averse producer may be willing to pay advance premiums to reduce unpredictability of disease losses, whereas a risk-neutral producer does not pay attention to the volatility of losses. Risk-neutral producers prefer a financing scheme which collects funds only after an outbreak has occurred, whereas risk-averse producers prefer a scheme which collects premiums both before and after an outbreak.

While it is common to use the concepts of risk and uncertainly interchangeably, economics differentiates between the two. Risk refers to situations where potential states or outcomes are known, along with the probability of their occurring. Uncertainty may be defined as not knowing or having no reasonable approximation of either the outcomes or the probabilities of the event occurring (Hardaker et al, 1997; Mahul and Gohin, 1999). Uncertainty leads to option value and information value literature. Bernanke (1980) notes that uncertainty retards investment. Greiner et al. (2009) analysed the adoption of best conservation practices by farmers and found that option values for unknown events prevented strongly financially motivated farmers from adopting new practices in the absence of external incentives. In the context of livestock disease management where farmers decide whether to invest in biosecurity, the cost of deferred biosecurity is lost output, while the gain is additional information. Bloom (2014) found that uncertainty increases in times of economic downturns. Does risk perception increase during disease outbreak? It seems likely. It is therefore worth considering farmer responses during an outbreak as being different than in "peacetime" with respect to a specific disease.

Elbakidze and McCarl (2006) compared pre-event preparedness *versus* post-event response and asked when it would be economical to protect from infection. Specifically, they highlighted the trade-off between certain pre-event (*ex ante*) expenses for probabilistic events and expenses after (*ex post*) an infectious disease event. For these diseases the probabilities are generally unknown and subject to lack of information and context. They found that the optimal level of investment in pre-event preparedness would increase as an event probability and severity becomes larger and post-event response strategy is less effective and more costly. For potentially low probability of infection, marginal benefits of *ex ante* biosecurity might be quite small. Also, if there are neighbouring farm operations which are not investing in biosecurity or there are wildlife reservoirs nearby, the farmer may believe (justifiably) that their efforts are unlikely to have a significant impact. Thus, one expects farmers to under-invest in prevention of these diseases.

For insurance related to livestock disease – either explicit insurance such as business interruption or implicit insurance such as *ad hoc* compensation schemes—an important issue is the extent to which it can influence farm behaviour. A particular concern is that the presence of insurance may encourage riskier behaviour from farm managers relative to disease management. A risk-averse farmer will reduce the expected financial impact of a loss by reducing the severity of any loss that occurs (self-insurance) and by reducing the probability of loss occurrence (self-protection). Ehrlich and Becker (1972) showed that self-insurance is always a substitute for market insurance, whereas self-protection and market insurance might be complements. OECD (2011) indicates that crop insurance produces a crowding-out effect on production diversification as an on-farm risk management strategy and that farm income has greater variability with a higher share of insured land.

2.3. Farm incentives and information asymmetries

- Information asymmetries exist with respect to farmer actions and risk types.
- Higher indemnities can strengthen the incentive to report, but weaken the incentive to prevent disease.
- There is a lack of empirical studies to verify the predictions from analytical models in this area, but some empirical evidence finds that disease reporting is "price-elastic" in relation to the indemnity received.
- To align incentives with policy goals, any indemnity plan should shift part of the risk to farmers.
- Insurance for interruptions in farm business may increase incentives to report, but is difficult to put into place.

Animal disease management as a principal-agent contract with hidden information

There is a relationship between governments and farmers or livestock industries in preventing and controlling livestock disease. Governments control borders, negotiate trade agreements, and establish eradication and surveillance programmes. Farmers are responsible for their own herd health management and must disclose reportable diseases. For many contagious diseases, particularly those with human health or trade implications, the government will purchase condemned animals as a form of indemnity. Such compensation can also involve further assistance to clean and disinfect farms, or even payments for consequential losses (e.g. business interruption).

These relationships between farmers and government might be thought of in terms of a contract (Gramig et al., 2009; Hennessy and Wolf, 2015). Theoretically, this contract foresees that the farmer will make an adequate effort to prevent disease or – failing that – report the presence of disease, while the government will make efforts to prevent the introduction of the disease, provide surveillance at and within country borders, and organise responses should a disease occur.

A principal-agent framework applied to government-paid indemnities to farmers for diseased livestock can be set up as a government principal wishing to minimise expected disease costs, subject to getting farmers to invest appropriate efforts into disease prevention and control. There are many instances where farmers might have relevant information about disease in his herd, as well as information about their efforts to prevent disease (the likelihood of disease) that are unknown to the government. This can create two types of information problems: moral hazard and adverse selection.

Moral hazard refers to a situation where the agent(s) can undertake actions that affect the value of the transaction with the principal but that the principal cannot monitor or enforce perfectly. If the agent can put in less effort without detection – and less effort decreases the likelihood of a desirable outcome – then one would expect shirking on the part of the agent. That is, if others are willing to pay for mistakes you make, then you are less likely to consider the negative repercussions of your behaviour. The solution might be to make the potential farm loss under disease – that part which is not covered by indemnities – significant enough so that the farmer has an incentive to put time and effort into an effective biosecurity action.

Adverse selection applies to situations where the agent has information pertaining to a relevant transaction but which is unknown to the principal. With respect to insurance, this may lead to customers who are at a relatively high risk *vis-à-vis* others to be relatively well insured (Baltussen et al., 2006). Adverse selection leads to the crowding out of low-risk customers by those who are at high risk, leading to a potential failure of the insurance market. The solution to adverse selection in insurance has been to structure the set of contracts available so that the customers' choice of contract terms signals their risk profile (i.e. high or low risk).

Adverse selection may occur with respect to reporting disease and epidemic indemnification. If the farmer reports a disease, he will incur costs related to that reporting. If the farmer perceives, perhaps incorrectly, that the expected costs are smaller when disease is not reported, one can expect that behaviour to occur. Although most informed farmers would report the disease, in the case of highly contagious diseases, significant economic damage can occur with only a few bad outcomes, even just one (Hennessy and Wolf, 2015). For example, Enright and Kao (2015) using a game-theoretic simulation, suggest that even a small number of non-cooperating farms could make a difference in the prevalence of disease, with this contribution becoming greater if the disease is easily transmissible.

Private costs and economic incentives for disease reporting

The farmer is expected to maximise net profits (or utility as a function of expected profits) by choosing appropriate disease prevention and control practices. A standard optimisation results in a first order condition that equates the decline in marginal expected loss from disease to the marginal cost of control measures (McInerney, 1996; Chi et al., 2002). The decline in expected losses is a benefit from farmers' efforts to manage disease. It may include a lower probability of many diseases on the farm which may also spill-over to benefit neighbours by reducing the incidence of disease on their farms; it may also reduce the possibility of wildlife disease and risks to human health. The desired behaviour is that the farmer should report the disease quickly to limit its spread.

The consequences for an individual farmer of reporting disease, however, provide many disincentives to report. If the animal has a disease for which there is mandatory control or eradication programmes, the herd or flock will be depopulated. This results in lost genetics, potentially lost capital value (depending on indemnity payments relative to actual market value), and losses from business interruption as fixed costs must be covered. In addition, depending on the disease, other herds in the region or even the entire country might be subject to quarantine or movement restrictions. These restrictions result in losses for other herds and perhaps even an entire industry. The slightest suspicion of a diseased animal can shut down international trade for some diseases, e.g. bovine spongiform encephalopathy. The potential for consumers to associate – perhaps incorrectly – human health risks with the presence of disease can result in reduced demand. For diseases with mandatory control and eradication programmes, government and media scrutiny is also unpleasant and potentially costly. Thus, the farmer may be inclined to respond by waiting to see if recovery is possible, quickly marketing the suspect animal, or destroying the animal without alerting the authorities.

The amount required to incentivise reporting is a function of current market conditions and a number of potentially farm-specific factors, but several considerations can frame the problem. In order to align incentives, farmers must be compensated for reporting at least as well as they would be in the next best alternative. For example, if the farmer believes the alternative is to quickly market the animal and avoid business interruption, then the indemnity must be at least at the level that can be achieved on the market. Should depopulation be needed and the farmer to abstain from livestock production for a quarantine period, then business interruption is a relevant consideration for the farmer. Losses from business interruptions include foregone revenues net of avoided costs. To understand business interruption losses, a distinction between variable and fixed costs is useful. When a cattle enterprise is removed, many – and perhaps most – variable costs of production are not incurred. For example, there is no need to purchase feed for cattle. Fixed costs, in contrast, cannot be avoided or varied when production ceases (over the time period considered). The standard list of fixed costs includes interest on investment, depreciation, property taxes, and insurance. Because the depopulated farms are expected to resume operation, the fixed costs must be covered during the interim period.

Finally, the study by Sheriff and Osgood (2010) is interesting in that it adds a temporal perspective, suggesting that incentive compatibility constraint is more restrictive in the multi-period model than in a single period model. By revealing disease exposure today, sellers of livestock signal a higher chance of future exposure. If they believe the buyer will use this information against them, sellers with unhealthy animals must be compensated for future income loss in order to be willing to truthfully reveal disease today.

Compensation effects on disease prevention and reporting

Barnes et al. (2015) undertook a comprehensive review of the literature related to the effect of animal health compensation on farmer disease prevention and reporting. They note that economic insights into this issue are largely based on theoretical or simulation modelling that use stylised situations and simplifying assumptions rather than empirical data (e.g. Jin and McCarl, 2006; Beach et al., 2007a; Hennessy, 2007a; Gramig et al., 2009; Boni et al., 2013; and Hennessy and Wang, 2013). They also conclude that there is a general lack of comparative evaluations based on actual rather than modelled outcomes under different policies.

The basic premise of economic analysis is that all else being constant, the higher the indemnity the greater the likelihood of disease reporting. While compensation encourages reporting, it can also reduce the privately optimal preventive investment (Beach et al., 2007b). Hennessy (2007a) and Hennessy and Wang (2013) find that indemnity payments are likely to reduce producer incentives to protect herds, as do Bicknell et al. (1999). Beach et al. (2007a) found that there was a bigger deviation between private and social optima in regions with greater disease externalities and smaller farms, especially when high compensation was independent of preventive actions.

The study by Kuchler and Hamm (2000) is notable in that it examined 41 years of experience with indemnities as a natural experiment on the incentives created by prices. They studied US farmers reporting of sheep infected with scrapie, a prion disease for which the US government had an indemnity-based eradication programme from 1952 through 1992. It was then replaced by a voluntary flock certification programme. The authors recognised the potential for moral hazard as farmers could essentially manufacture diseased animals if it was profitable to do so. While the market price for sheep moved in response to supply and demand, the indemnity payment was fixed. Relative prices are important in this case and when the fixed indemnity was higher than the market price for sheep, farmers "produced" or found more diseased animals. Similarly, when the indemnity was lower relative to market price, fewer animals were turned in for indemnity. The authors found that not only was the supply of diseased animals upward sloping, but that it was price elastic, i.e. a 1% increase in indemnity payments relative to the market price for lambs yielded a greater than 1% increase in the number of confirmed scrapie cases.

The further logic is that compensation can provide adequate incentives to producers to prevent and report disease if it is designed to account for moral hazard and adverse selection problems. Within this logic, design characteristics of compensation, such as eligibility criteria, payment rates and schedules become essential. The basic principle is that farmers should share risks (and costs) of disease epidemics. Full compensation will not encourage preventive behaviour; indeed, "why bother if all costs are covered?" (Gramig et al., 2009; OECD, 2012; Barnes et al., 2015).

Gramig et al. (2009) suggest an indemnity scenario to deal with both moral hazard and adverse selection problems. A farmer's investment in biosecurity is modelled as an *ex ante* moral hazard problem and farm reporting as *ex post* adverse selection. The authors argue that a one-size-fits-all indemnity payment cannot deal with both information problems. Two distinct mechanisms are needed for each: an indemnity to address moral hazard and help achieve the desired levels of biosecurity, and fines to induce early disclosure of disease status and address adverse selection problem. By combining two distinct policy instruments, each designed to deal with a single information problem, it is possible to create incentives for farmers to behave consistently with government objectives. Comparing this to a simple indemnity reveals an important difference: while standard indemnities increase with disease prevalence in a herd (i.e. pay the farmer for each diseased animal), the solution here is that the indemnity decreases over a range of disease prevalence which reflects how long the disease was present on the farm before it was reported. This scenario represents a differential indemnity schedule based on reporting the disease and employing the deductible principle in order to shift some of the risk to farmers.[3]

Hennessy and Wolf (2015) further develop that if the costs of reporting depend on market, industry, and farm specific factors, behaviour will depend to some degree on those factors. For example, if reporting results in an indemnity payment that is set at an average market price, one might expect farms with inferior quality livestock to be more amenable to reporting than those farms with superior quality livestock. Similarly, if reporting results in mandatory depopulation and business interruption, one might expect that those farms with relatively higher fixed costs (which must be borne during business interruption) to be more reticent to report than those with lower fixed costs (Wolf, 2005).

Making indemnities contingent upon farmer reporting assumes that a reasonable manager would and could notice the disease, so this condition makes more sense for diseases with readily identifiable symptoms. Livestock disease control systems are often based on ways of detection which expand vulnerability. First, detection often uses visual observation of clinical signs; thus disease can be present and spreading before detection. Second, the clinical signs of some important (dangerous) diseases are indistinguishable from signs of other diseases and could be misidentified (Bates et al., 2003; Elbakidze, 2008). Studies reveal that farmers, and sometimes even veterinarians, experience difficulty in identifying reportable diseases (Box 2.1).

Farmer incentives for disease prevention could be increased if indemnities are made conditional on farmers exercising certain biosecurity practices, implementing farm biosecurity plans, or participating in disease programmes. This, however, imposes high monitoring efforts on governments, but country experiences show that this effort could be shared with or performed by industry groups (Chapter 5)). Another way to address incentives for prevention is to differentiate indemnities according to farmer risk profiles, for example, the disease outbreak history of the farm (Chapter 7). Meuwissen et al. (2006) also considered that classifying farms based on their epidemic disease risk and use of deductibles was important in order to align incentives with policy goals. This approach is also demanding in terms of administration: beyond the challenge of defining the risk status and differentiating farms accordingly, it requires the establishment of the relevant information systems.

Consequential losses are typically outside the scope of compensation schemes for epidemics and regarded as entrepreneurial risk. Some of these losses are a consequence of compulsory measures to control the epidemics, such as protective vaccination[4] and livestock movement restrictions. Consequential losses influence the farmers' incentives to disclose a disease as they have strong implications for the longer-term operation of farms.

Livestock insurance may be one solution to market risks related to livestock epidemics (Meuwissen et al., 2000; Meuwissen et al., 2006; Meuwissen and Asseldonk, 2013). However, such insurance is in practice limited because of the significant difficulty to estimate the scale and probability of livestock epidemics risk, classify and price it accordingly, and because this risk tends to be systemic. As a result, the actual supply of livestock insurance is limited, while its uptake from producers is low due to high premium costs. This may indicate a market failure in provision of livestock disease insurance and can be an argument for a policy action (e.g. creation of information systems to facilitate the 'production' of insurance products) to make such insurance more operational. Other market instruments to manage livestock price risks are forward-, futures- and options contracts, but the degree to which these can deal with prolonged market effects is unclear, while only limited groups of livestock producers use futures and options contracts. There exist industry risk pooling arrangements, such as industry funds, but they are rare and typically created to deal with direct epidemic losses. Thus, the approach to consequential market losses from disease epidemics remains a largely open policy issue.

Financial considerations are not the only drivers of farmer reporting behaviour. Farmers may experience difficulty in identifying a reportable disease, dissatisfaction with, limited awareness, or uncertainty about reporting procedures, farmers may also feel guilt and shame about reporting a disease. These aspects are the focus of Chapter 3 which draws on the behavioural literature. It is nevertheless important to stress here the complexity of farmer reporting behaviour (Box 2.1).

In this respect, Barnes et al. (2015) observe that the economic literature concentrates on financial incentives, while the behavioural literature is mostly concerned with non-financial drivers. These two research streams are weakly integrated and there remains scope for investigating the extent to which the performance of compensation arrangements might depend on behavioural influences. The suggestion by Elbers et al. (2010b) well exemplifies the problem – they point out that increasing compensation may be ineffective as a means of encouraging reporting if a disease is not perceived by farmers as a serious problem. Here they notice the interaction between a financial incentive and behavioural driver such as farmer's risk perception. Thus, a range of financial, regulatory and nudging policies are required to match farm response with socially desired outcomes, although empirical and theoretical evidence to discern the optimal mix of interventions is limited.

Box 2.1. Non-financial determinants of farmer-reporting behaviour

Producers' level of knowledge about diseases and their likely consequences informs their risk assessment and responses. The inability to identify clinical signs of disease quickly, or to identify the signs which need to be reported and at what threshold, hampers reporting (Wright et al., 2016; Delgado et al., 2014; Elbers et al., 2010a).[1] The situation may be further complicated if there have been no disease occurrences in a long time, so both producers and veterinarians may not be prepared to quickly identify disease (Elbers et al., 2010b). This could be coupled with the fact that some farmers (and veterinarians) feel that raising a false alarm would be worse than missing a possible emergency (Elbers et al., 2010a; Elbers et al., 2010b). Producers' beliefs about the extent to which they can efficiently control the event may also determine behaviour. Those who feel they can themselves control the outbreak do not tend to report it immediately (Wright et al., 2016).

Risk perceptions are a factor in farmers' reporting behaviour (Wright et al., 2016; Elbers et al., 2010; Delgado et al., 2014). For example, Bronner et al. (2014) studied the brucellosis surveillance system in France based on mandatory notification of bovine abortions. They note that despite the epidemiological rationale to detect a brucellosis outbreak early, most farmers viewed it as an externally-imposed tool concerning an externally-imposed issue that created few worries for them.

The behavioural literature reveals that community opinions influence farmer reporting behaviour. Some sources refer to guilt and shame and "farmer stigma" related to disclosures of disease.[2] Farmers may feel that if they report, in particular if they are the first to do so, they will be negatively viewed by their social network (Elbers et al., 2010b; Delgado et al., 2014). A cross-country study by Vergne et al. (2016) showed that farmers and hunters who did not immediately report suspected cases of disease were more likely to believe their reputation in the local community would be adversely affected if they were to report. However, social influence can also be propulsive to reporting if this constitutes an existing social norm, i.e. if farmers believe that the persons whose opinion matters for them expect them to report and that others would also report if disease occurs on their farms. Delgado et al.,(2014) find, for example, that US cattle producers indicated they would experience social pressure from all the external groups included in the survey (e.g. family, veterinarians, business partners, neighbours, professional organisations) to report cattle with clinical signs consistent with FMD.

Box 2.1. Non-financial determinants of farmer-reporting behaviour *(cont.)*

The transactions costs of disease reporting appear to be a significant factor. Dissatisfaction with procedures – "long and tedious", not transparent, or leaving uncertainty about the outcomes of reporting – are found to be among the deterring factors (Elbers et al., 2010b). Delgado et al. (2014) observed that any uncertainty associated with compensation was likely to influence producers' willingness both to report disease and comply with response measures. Some surveillance actions based on disease notification can be seen by farmers as time-consuming, impractical or compensating for bureaucrats who are not doing their part (Gunn et al., 2008). Consideration of costs and benefits of investigating clinical signs of disease is also identified as a factor of producers' reporting decision-making: if an animal is worth less than the cost of veterinary service, it makes more economic sense to kill it than pay for a veterinarian visit. The service infrastructure, e.g. proximity of a veterinarian, has been identified as a factor in the reporting disease by Australian farmers (Wright et al., 2016).

The general acceptance of reporting frameworks, a sense of ownership of the rules, and overall trust in government play a role in the reporting behaviour of farmers. Although farmers expect to cede some of their autonomy for improved biosecurity, they can feel frustrated at the prospect of losing control of their business if a disease is identified on their property (Wright et al., 2016). Farmers may view control measures as inappropriate and be unwilling to comply with them (Elbers et al., 2010b; Bronner et al., 2014)[3]. Trust-building, involvement in decision-making regarding surveillance and reporting frameworks, a two-way and clear communication about future actions would help increase collaborative behaviour with producers (Wright et al., 2016).

---

1. The study of Dutch farmers by Elbers et al. (2007) showed that Dutch pig farmers had limited knowledge of clinical signs of classical swine fever (CSF): 33% of pig farmers could mention at maximum three clinical signs associated with this disease (all in the late stages of this disease) and 7% were not able to mention a single clinical sign and said they were entirely dependent on the veterinary practitioners' ability to judge a clinically suspect situation. The study by Delgado et al. (2014) of cow-calf producers in Texas showed that less than 20% of respondents strongly agreed they knew the clinical signs associated with serious cattle diseases such as FMD, and less than 30% strongly agreed they knew which cattle were at greater risk of disease introduction.

2. For example, a representative of the Australian Meat and Livestock Association notes that "producers are often reluctant to report disease on their properties for a variety of reasons. In some cases certain diseases create a certain amount of stigma in society. I've been in a situation where a farmer was acutely embarrassed when a certain parasite was diagnosed in his sheep, and he was too ashamed to show his face in the local town for months afterwards" (ABS Rural, 2016).

3. For example, in the Netherlands, specific rules were set on reporting an AI-suspect situation after the epidemic of highly pathogenic avian influenza in 2003. According to Elbers et al. (2010b), poultry farmers indicated that they did not agree with these rules. Farmers did not see why they should report clinical signs that they interpret as being linked to other diseases or other causes. The authors state this is an indication of a lack of ownership of the surveillance system on the part of the poultry farmers.

2.4. Farm size, industry structure and spatial issues

- Industrialised production can be associated with increased disease prevention and control efforts, but also with large impacts of disease if it breaks out.
- Hobby/lifestyle residential farms are likely to be more motivated by factors other than financial.
- Hobby producers are likely to underinvest in biosecurity because they do not consider effects of disease on professional producers.
- Policies designed with consideration of commercial farms only are likely to be a poor fit for non-commercial operations.
- Biosecurity efforts of neighbours affect producer incentives to prevent and control disease.

While the proportion of livestock, dairy and poultry products from large, commercial operations has increased over time, smaller operations exist in the form of part-time, hobby, life-style farms, and, in some countries, as subsistence farming segments. There are many ways to divide or segment farms by type based on the motivation of their operator. Primary motivations include business, such as profit and equity, but also family values, lifestyle, and hobbies. While specific categories depend on the context and method of analysis, it is clear that those who make decisions within farm enterprises vary in their mix of values and motivations that drive their decisions, including those related to disease control and prevention. It should also be noted that in addition to farm livestock, pets and other backyard animals can affect disease occurrence and spread. This section considers the implications for disease management from this diverse set of farming structures. It concludes with the discussion of spatial issues of disease management.

Industrialised agriculture

With changes in technology, reform of long-time agricultural support policies, and the subsequent integration into world markets, livestock agriculture has undergone significant structural change. Commercial farms are becoming larger and more specialised. The prototypical example is contracting in the US poultry and pork industries where large corporations own the livestock which are raised by contracted farmers. This leads to important disease management and liability questions. Disease prevention and control is expected to depend on farm size, available resources and production technology, all of which are jointly determined (Hennessy et al., 2005; Hennessy, 2005).

As livestock operations increase in size, production technology usually dictates a movement towards confinement operations. Animals spend less energy on foraging, defence against predators, and temperature regulation (Wang and Hennessy, 2014). Confining animals also involves physical protection against infection and other diseases. Therefore, the animals' environment is under greater control. At the same time, control technologies are also required as animal and or farm density can be a factor in increased disease risk.

How do incentives to guard against infectious disease risk interact with the scale of production? There should be scale economies in biosecurity, at least in investment in facilities and enclosures. Siekkinen et al. (2012) studied the cost of biosecurity on Finnish poultry farms. They found economies of scale, i.e. costs decreased as size (number of birds) increased. This effect was largely driven by decreasing labour costs. However, Wang and Hennessy (2014) found that because biosecurity is a technical complement to scale, a unit cost decline in biosecurity can reduce optimal scale.

Larger commercial operations (poultry or pig meat) are less likely to become infected because of their larger resources and more stringent biosecurity measures; see for example Beach et al. (2007b) who analyse highly pathogenic avian influenza. However, to the extent that infections do occur in these sectors, the impact is likely to be very large, with many animals killed by disease and depopulated. Mintiens et al. (2003) considered risk of classical swine fever (CSF) spread in Belgium and concluded that densely populated livestock areas incorporate an increased risk for epidemic disease spread when outbreaks occur. Rushton (2009) noted that large, industrial livestock operations might capture most of the benefits of livestock disease control and eradication. In general, one would expect increased biosecurity and therefore less potential for disease outbreaks on very large operations because of the level of investment and specialisation of these operations.

Part-time, hobby or lifestyle residential operations and backyard flocks

The risk factors associated with small (backyard) production include reduced hygiene and biosecurity measures, a mixed confinement which increases the probability of disease transmission across species, and free range allowing the interface with wild life (e.g. Whitehead and Roberts, 2014; Conan et al., 2012; Hamilton-West et al., 2012). Other authors highlight the features of small-scale production which may reduce disease risks, such as extensive free-range systems, which in this argumentation is a factor preventing rapid disease spread, spatial dispersion of small producers, and the fact that animals in small establishments may have a more mobilised immune system due to exposure to diverse environmental stress (Behnke et al., 2011).

As far as developing countries are concerned, smallholders are generally viewed as the major weak point in national biosecurity (Grace et al., 2008). As for developed economies, the evidence about the role of smallholdings in the occurrence and transmission of disease is fragmented. This issue has attracted increased attention in recent years in the context of the outbreaks of highly pathogenic avian influenza. Bavinck et al. (2009) found that from an epidemiological point of view, backyard flocks played only a marginal role in the outbreak of the highly pathogenic avian influenza in the Netherlands in 2003. Smith and Dunipace (2011) estimated that the contribution of backyard poultry flocks to the transmission dynamics of highly pathogenic avian influenza epidemics in commercial flocks was "modest at best". However, they also warned against ignoring the contribution of backyard flocks in estimating the efforts to control the disease. Beach et al. (2007b) observe that minimal biosecurity present in nonindustrial production is frequently identified by animal health agencies as a risk to commercial sectors, even in countries where these activities account for a negligible share of output and sales. Conan et al. (2012) present the view that neither system is more to blame for infectious disease spread and that biosecurity levels have to be increased in both commercial and backyard poultry systems.

Understanding the incentives of small holders to protect their livestock is important for the development of policy approaches towards these constituencies. Part-time, hobby or life-style farmers do not depend significantly on agricultural enterprises for their income. Thus, the financial implications of disease may not motivate them to invest in biosecurity measures (Defra, 2008).

Kobayashi and Melkonyan (2011) found that biosecurity actions with own benefits or lasting impact in home communities exhibited a positive relationship with the behaviour of producers from geographically close areas. The number of biosecurity actions taken were positively associated with the number of animals, and varied among commercial and hobby producers and across species and types of commercial production.

Professional farmers have incentives to carefully monitor and manage biosecurity, while hobby farmers derive utility from the value of the farming activity itself (Blank, 2005; Defra, 2008). Ceddia et al. (2008) considered biosecurity in application to invasive crop species by comparing profit-seeking professional producers to utility-seeking hobby producers. Hobby producers are likely to underinvest in biosecurity because they do not take into account the effects of disease on professional producers. Since disease control generates positive external benefits, hobby producers will under-invest in it. While the gains from a socially optimal policy are sizeable, the transactions costs of a corrective policy may be prohibitively high. A pest control subsidy for hobby producers can lead to an increase in hobby production with associated negative impacts. This subsidy also would not recognise that the mere existence of the hobby farms is an important component of the problem. An alternative is a penalty for hobby farms based on the deviation of their pest control from the socially optimal level. However, this would be hardly realistic as it requires monitoring and large transactions costs. Finally, professional and hobby farmers could get together to have a joint surveillance and control programme. The policy implications of this work are that designing policies with commercial farms in mind is likely to be a poor fit for the non-commercial operations. These groups seem to be logical candidates for voluntary assurance and co-operative programmes.

Spatial aspects

The spatial analysis provides insights into how externalities affect farmer's incentives for disease management. Locational characteristics lead to heterogeneity of producer incentives to prevent and control disease, they affect the degree to which producers are both vulnerable to risk and can free-ride on the biosecurity efforts of others (Horan et al., 2010).

Hennessy (2007b) studied spatial externalities of disease across multiple operations in close proximity. He used an illustrative model of agricultural biosecurity where only farm location and production scale were articulated. The author concludes that the nature of spatial interactions matters as it determines the extent of incentives to free-ride on neighbours' actions. For instance, "edge" farmers (with neighbours only on one side) face lower risks than "middle" farmers located in-between two neighbours. The middle farmers thus would invest more in biosecurity, whereas edge farmers may free-ride on these efforts. Another observation is that intensive production, by strengthening private incentives to protect, can reduce the proportion of potential production lost to disease in a region. However, subsidies targeted to smaller production lots may encourage larger farms to invest less in biosecurity, thus reducing the overall economic surplus.

Rat-Aspert and Krebs (2012) examined the collective action to control endemic diseases for which management decisions are left to individual initiative. In their model a farmer decides whether to protect his herd against a particular disease by vaccinating or by adopting biosecurity measures which create a positive spill-over. By lowering the risk of disease occurrence, this would provide benefit to other farmers. Conversely, farmers could be encouraged to behave as a free-rider seeking to benefit from the efforts of neighbours without bearing the costs. This behaviour would generate a negative externality since this behaviour would lead to maintaining the disease within the geographic area considered. This results in strong interrelationships of individual decisions to control animal disease at the area level. For communicable diseases, effectiveness of control measures will often depend on the ability to act in a coordinated manner across a group of operations (horizontal coordination).

Rich et al. (2005a, b) analysed the decisions to control foot-and-mouth disease (FMD) as a spatial model in which behaviour of neighbours influences the payoffs to each individual from control efforts.[5] Producers could choose between high and low effort to control FMD. Low effort results in contracting the disease with certainty. Because of disease spill-overs, the effectiveness of high effort depends on the actions of neighbours. In locations with high prevalence of disease, the rationale to increase control of disease is relatively low, while spatial spill-overs only exacerbate the problem with the result that disease is likely to be endemic. In locations with lower disease prevalence, producers may be more or less inclined to engage in increased disease control depending on neighbours' choices. The authors suggest that for disease control regulation to be effective, private incentives across space need to be aligned and argue for a spatially nuanced policy depending on risk factors and pay offs to biosecurity. Beyond that, policies that promote market development and increase the herd value may be the most effective as they increase private incentives to prevent and control disease.

2.5. Implications for animal disease policy

This chapter framed the farm management decision by focusing on economic and financial aspects of disease management. It can be expected that individual farmers will under-invest in prevention and control as the market does not reflect all costs or all benefits for farm-level disease management. Farmers may also see returns to investment to be better in other areas and value short-term gains more than possible larger long-term gains from investments in farm biosecurity. In this situation farm managers may not be incentivised to behave as policy makers would prefer them to do when making animal disease management decisions. Thus, policy makers must consider actions to more closely align the public and private costs and benefits of such practices. Several areas of public action for reducing the divergence between private and socially optimal outcomes might be justified, especially as some diseases have large social economic costs.

A rational economic decision process assumes that a profit-maximising farmer will invest in prevention up to the point where the marginal private benefit from prevention is equal to marginal costs. Farmers' biosecurity effort thus derives from weighing the costs against benefits of such effort. The trade-offs depend on the nature of the disease, available techniques, the costs involved, market conditions, and other factors. Producer must understand these trade-offs, so knowledge and information is an essential input into individual's biosecurity decisions. The less aware farmer is likely to make inadequate investment decision to prevent disease and this will determine the overall risk of disease entry. The policy role in this regard is to assist farmers in gaining the relevant knowledge, including by tailoring the information to farmers' particular needs and circumstances and providing them with decision-support tools. Development of technologies and services that lower prevention and control costs is an additional area for public action, for example, expenditures to reduce cost and efficacy of disease tests and veterinary services might be in order. Within the basic economic framework, these investments would shift a private loss-expenditure frontier so that private cost-benefit solution would result in less disease.

Economies of scope in biosecurity practices are generally ignored which undervalues these practices. When disease management is considered at the farm level on a disease-by-disease basis, the cost-benefit can be misleading. Often management practices that prevent or eliminate one disease assist in preventing or eliminating many others. Thus, disease prevention and management may exhibit economies of scope. The consideration of potential preventive spill-overs in disease education and information programmes can encourage farmers to take these effects into account in allocating effort and investment to disease prevention and control. Farm level decision tools and aids should account for these benefits. The potential for realising these gains should be actively communicated to farm managers as part of disease risk communication and advice for farm biosecurity practices. Understanding that practices prevent many diseases will strengthen farm incentives to undertake those practices.

Uncertainties and risks are associated with virtually every aspect of disease management, making farmers' risk perceptions important drivers of their decisions. If a farmer wrongly perceives the risk to contract disease on his farm to be negligible, he is unlikely to invest in its prevention. Furthermore, farmers need to understand the probability of disease to optimise investment in disease prevention. There are biases and risk perception issues that must be overcome for farm managers to make appropriate livestock disease management decisions. Thus, governments should facilitate animal disease risk communication, information, and education so that farmers build understanding about their own risks and the links between individual preventive efforts and outcomes for the sector as whole. On the other hand, to design effective policy governments need to understand the risk awareness and risk preferences of farming constituency. For example, the effectiveness of disease reporting frameworks may depend on farmer's perception of associated risk. Despite the fact that the issue of farming risk is increasingly featured in the governments' policy agendas, there is a continued lack of evidence on farmer individual risk perceptions and preferences.

Public policy intervention in livestock disease management can directly impact producer decisions. Diseases where human health is at risk or which have large potential economic effects associated with them are in the domain of public control. Public policies here range from bounties/indemnities for infected livestock to required herd depopulation and farm decontamination.

Farmer actions and relevant information about the farmer and farm operation are not perfectly observable. The presence of information asymmetries related to monitoring behaviour in preventing and reacting to disease outbreaks created an additional challenge for aligning incentives for disease prevention and reporting.

Higher indemnity payments can encourage farmers to monitor and report diseased animals by compensating for the losses in animal value taken for disease eradication. This is particularly appropriate for diseases where timely detection is crucial to minimise damages to the industry, economy or human health. Paying fair disease-free market value is necessarily greater than the true market value of diseased animals culled by the government. This action is often justified as intending to create incentives to report. However, one must be mindful not to provide incentives for farmers to produce diseased livestock. Several natural experiments have confirmed that misalignments in reactions to financial policy incentives occur. Higher indemnity payments can discourage farmers from biosecurity measures to limit the possibility of disease occurrence and spread. If someone else is paying for losses there is less incentive to avoid risky behaviour. A critical aspect of livestock disease policy is to avoid the perverse incentive to produce infected animals.

Animal health authorities have typically relied on a single mechanism – indemnities – to facilitate both *ex ante* biosecurity effort and *ex post* reporting. By using a single mechanism to promote biosecurity and to report simultaneously, the incentives for individual private action are not clear.

Unless farmers face some uncompensated losses as a result of outbreak it cannot be expected that they undertake sufficient prevention and timely report disease. Some countries have implemented policies which move towards risk-sharing in interesting and appropriate ways. For example, if there is no indemnity for dead animals there may be a penalty for waiting to report disease. This policy can help to achieve incentive compatibility with reduced or eliminated monitoring costs. Some of the risk would shift to farmers if the indemnity rate decreases over some range of disease prevalence, or if partial compensation for already-infected animals is provided. An indemnity plan that does not shift risk in this way may actually create incentives for infection.

Furthermore, farmers react to private incentives and the best course of action for an individual farmer will depend on the farm type and size as well as individual financial considerations. For example, one might expect farmers to react differently to the same indemnity rate depending on the individual costs they incur: e.g. farms with superior quality livestock and higher fixed costs would be more reticent to report disease than those with lower quality animals and lower fixed costs. Economic modelling may be instrumental to evaluate how different farmer groups, regions, and market segments respond to the size of incentives.

In deciding whether to report disease, farmers react not only to financial incentives. The ability to identify reportable disease, transactions costs and uncertainties associated with reporting, psychological barriers, social pressure, acceptance of reporting regulations and overall trust in government, also influence the disease disclosure. The degree to which financial and non-financial drivers interact and impact farmer decisions is little researched. Building a holistic view of barriers to disease reporting is a necessary step towards more effective and cost-efficient disease control frameworks. Some countries have progressed in this direction (Chapter 5).

Diverging farm size and specialisation has implications for farm management and policy. Farm size and type are correlated with incentives and behaviour related to livestock disease management. Large, industrialised farms have significant investments in livestock and are more likely than smaller operations to have accompanying disease management systems. The production technology that complements biosecurity practices is more likely to be present on full-time operations. They are also more likely to have full time veterinary services. However, the magnitude of a disease outbreak is also much larger should prevention or containment fail. Part-time and hobby farms may be less aware of disease issues and practices. Keepers of backyard flocks are even less likely to be concerned with disease prevention. Smaller operations may also be less responsive to financial incentives than larger commercial operations. The existence of part-time or hobby farms alongside commercial livestock operations is important because they are less likely to be motivated by consequences to profit or assets from disease outbreaks. To incentivise these groups for increased disease prevention and reporting, a local action is likely required. This may include voluntary surveillance initiatives, awareness campaigns, information and knowledge dissemination adapted to non-professionals, social rewards, and any other action relevant in the local contexts. The experience can be drawn from local environmental initiatives. Policy could potentially play a role in promoting and facilitating such local initiatives.

Spatial analysis demonstrates that locational characteristics lead to differentiation of farms by the degree to which they are vulnerable to risk given the biosecurity effort of neighbours. Farmers' decisions about additional investments in disease prevention are influenced by negative externalities and positive spill-overs from the actions of their neighbours and farmers may free-ride on the biosecurity efforts of others.

Appropriate disease policies, information and education programmes thus must consider the entire spectrum of livestock operations, including size, intensity and geography. To align incentives policy makers need to classify farms based on motivation, resources and constraints. Segmenting policies by farm size and type and location may also assist in aligning incentives.

Notes

1. The trade-off between losses and expenditures is shown by $L_A < L_M$ with $E_A > E_M$, and *vice versa.* Curve L(E) slopes downward at a diminishing rate, i.e. bringing losses down from L_M to L_K would require smaller additional expenditures than reducing them by the same amount from L_K to L_A, i.e. $E_K - E_M < E_A - E_M$. This is the standard economic assumption of diminishing returns. Concerning this assumption, McInerney et al. (1992) state that it has a powerful logical basis in economics and that the nature abounds in processes which display diminishing returns, so there is no reason to suppose this is different in the case of animal disease.

2. This optimum loss-expenditure combination is reached at the point when an additional unit of control cost is equated to the additional unit of reduced loss. This is the "marginal cost" criterion in economics. Graphically, the economically optimal cost of disease management (C) corresponds to the point M on Figure 2.1 where the 45° line is tangent to the L(E) frontier.

3. Gramig et al. (2009) also consider actual indemnification mechanisms in some countries that use the principle of risk-sharing. For example, Belgium and the Netherlands no longer compensate producers for dead animals in the case of epidemic livestock diseases and only partially compensate them for diseased stock. The authors note that while such a mechanism sets no explicit fine for non-reporting, there is a penalty for waiting to report since dead animals fetch no payment. This feature can help achieve incentive compatibility with reduced or no monitoring costs. Partial compensation for animals that are already infected will shift some of the risk to farmers. The authors suggest that an indemnity plan that does not shift risk in this fashion may actually create incentives to allow infections to spread.

4. Under protective vaccination, animals may not be destroyed. However, when marketed, such animals command reduced price as their processing involves higher costs.

5. In fact, this study looked at the coordination problems of FMD control across countries in South America. However, their model is neutral to whether a country or an individual producer is considered – the authors use these notions interchangeably.

References

ABS Rural (2016), "Disease reporting underpins new biosecurity program's success, Meat and Livestock Australia says", *ABS Rural*, 21 July, 2016. www.abc.net.au/news/2016-07-21/disease-reporting-underpins-biosecurity-program/7649086.

Baltussen, W.H.M., M.A.P.M. van Asseldonk and A.J. de Buc (2006), "Risicobeheer in de land- en tuinbouw: Een visie op de rol van de overhead", Rapport 2.06.12, LEI, The Hague, Netherlands.

Barnes, A.P., A.P. Moxey, B.V. Ahmadi and F.A. Borthwick (2015), "The effect of animal disease compensation on 'positive' behaviours towards exotic disease reporting and implementing biosecurity: A review, a synthesis and a research agenda", *Preventive Veterinary Medicine,* Vol. 122, pp.42-52.

Bates T.W., T.E. Carpenter and M.C. Thurmond (2003), "Benefit-cost analysis of vaccination and preemptive slaughter as a means for eradicating foot-and-mouth disease", *American Journal Veterinary Research,* Vol. 64, pp. 805–12.

Bavinck, V., A. Bouma, M. van Boven, M.E.H. Bos, E. Stassen, J.A. Stegeman (2009), "The role of backyard flocks in the epidemic of highly pathogenic avian influenza (H7N7) in the Netherlands in 2003", *Preventive Veterinary Medicine*, V. 88, pp. 247-254.

Beach, R.H., C. Poulos and S.K. Pattanayak (2007a), "Agricultural household response to avian influenza prevention and control policies", *Journal of Agricultural and Applied Economics,* Vol. 39, pp. 301–11.

Beach, R.H., C. Poulos and S.K. Pattanayak (2007b), "Farm economics of bird flu", *Canadian Journal of Agricultural Economics,* Vol. 55, pp.471-483.

Behnke, D., S. Heft-Neal, J. Ifft, R. Soares Magalhaes, J. Otte, D. Pfeiffer, D. Roland-Holst and D. Zilberman (2011), "Smallholder livestock production and the global disease risk", *ARE Update*, Vol. 14, N3, pp. 9-11, University of California Giannini Foundation of Agricultural Economics, http://s.giannini.ucop.edu/uploads/giannini_public/10/48/104885eb-1f45-452a-86ca-ff74421eb9ad/v14n3_4.pdf

Bernanke, B.S. (1980), "Irreversibility, uncertainty, and cyclical investment", *Working Paper* No. 502 National Bureau of Economic Research, Cambridge, MA.

Bicknell, K. B., J. E. Wilen and R.E. Howitt (1999), "Public policy and private incentives for livestock disease control", *Australian Journal of Agricultural and Resource Economics*, Vol. 43, pp. 501-21.

Blank, S. (2005), "The business of an agricultural 'way of life'", *Choices*, Vol. 20, pp. 161-166.

Bloom, N. (2014), "Fluctuations in uncertainty," *Journal of Economic Perspectives*, American Economic Association, Vol. 28(2), pp. 153-76, Spring.

Boni, M.F., A.P. Galvani, A.L. Wickelgren, A. Malani (2013), "Economic epidemiologyof avian influenza on smallholder poultry farms", *Theoretical Population Biology*, Vol. 90, pp. 135–144, http://dx.doi.org/10.1016/j.tpb.2013.10.001.

Bronner, A., V. Hénaux, N. Fortané, P. Hendrikx and D. Calavas (2014), "Why do farmers and veterinarians not report all bovine abortions, as requested by the clinical brucellosis surveillance system in France?", *BMC Veterinary Research*, Vol 10:93.

Ceddia, M.G., J. Heikkilä and J. Peltola (2008), "Biosecurity in agriculture: an economic analysis of coexistence of professional and hobby production", *Australian Journal of Agricultural and Resource Economics*, Vol. 52, pp. 453–470.

Chi, J., A. Weersink, J. Van Leeuwen and G. Keefe (2002), "The economics of controlling infectious diseases on dairy farms", *Canadian Journal of Agricultural Economics,* Vol. 50. pp. 237-256.

Conan, A., F.L. Goutard, S. Sorn and S. Wong (2012), "Biosecurity measures for backyard poultry in developing countries: a systematic review", *BMC Veterinary Research,* Vol 8:240.

Defra (2008), "Bringing Theoretical and Applied Evidence Together from Across Defra and Highlighting Policy Relevance and Implications for Future Research", Defra Agricultural Change and Environment Observatory Discussion Paper, November.

Delgado, A.M, B. Norby, H. Morgan Scott, W. Dean, W. A. McIntosh and E. Bush (2014), "Distribution of cow–calf producers' beliefs about reporting cattle with clinical signs of foot-and-mouth disease to a veterinarian before or during a hypothetical outbreak", *Preventive Veterinary Medicine*, Vol. 117, pp. 505–517.

Dijkhuizen, A.A., R.B.M. Huirne and A.W. Jalvingh (1995), "Economic analysis of animal diseases and their control", *Preventive Veterinary Medicine,* Vol. 25, pp. 135-149.

Ehrlich, I. and G. Becker (1972), "Market Insurance, Self-Insurance and Self-Protection", *Journal of Political Economy*, Vol. 80, pp. 623-48.

Elbakidze L. (2008), "Modeling of avian influenza mitigation policies within the backyard segment of the poultry sector", *Journal of Agricultural and Resource Economics,* Vol. 33, pp.195–211.

Elbakidze, L. and B.A. McCarl (2006), "Animal disease pre-event preparedness versus post-event response: When is it economic to protect?", *Journal of Agricultural and Applied Economics*, Vol. 38, N 2, pp.327-336.

Elbers, A.R., M.J. Gorgievski-Duijvesteijn, P.G. van der Velden, W.L. Loeffen and K. Zarafshani (2010a), "A socio-psychological investigation into limitations and incentives concerning reporting a clinically suspect situation aimed at improving early detection of classical swine fever outbreaks", *Veterinary Microbiology*, Vol. 142, N 1, pp. 108-18.

Elbers, A.R., M.J. Gorgievski-Duijvesteijn, P.G. van der Velden, W.L. Loeffen and K. Zarafshani (2010b), "To report or not to report: a psychosocial investigation aimed at improving early detection of avian influenza outbreaks", *OIE Revue Scientifique et Technique*, Vol. 29, pp. 435-449.

Elbers, A.R., M.J. Gorgievski-Duijvesteijn, P.G. van der Velden and W.L. Loeffen (2007), "Non-specific clinical signs in pigs and use of exclusion diagnostics for classical swine fever: a survey among pig farmers and veterinary practitioners". *Tijdschr. Diergeneeskd*, Vol. 132, pp. 340-345.

Enright, J. and R.R. Kao (2015), "A Few Bad Apples: A Model of Disease Influenced Agent Behaviour in a Heterogeneous Contact Environment", *PloS One,* 10.3, https://doi.org/10.1371/journal.pone.0118127.

Fenichel, E. P., R. D. Horan, G. J Hickling (2010), "Management of infectious wildlife diseases: bridging conventional and bioeconomic approaches", *Ecological Applications*, Vol. 20, pp. 903–914.

Garforth, C.J., A.P. Bailey and R. B. Tranter, (2013), "Farmers' attitudes to disease risk management in England: a comparative analysis of sheep and pig farmers", *Preventive Veterinary Medicine,* Vol. 110, pp. 456-466.

Grace D., C. Jost, G. Macgregor-Skinner and J.C. Mariner (2008), "Participation of Small farmers in Animal health Programmes", OIE, Compendium of technical items presented to the International Committee or to the regional commission, Vol. 2008, 19-34, http://www.oie.int/doc/ged/D6055.PDF.

Gramig, B. and C. Wolf (2007), "Estimating Within-Herd Preventive Spill-overs in Livestock Disease Management," *American Journal of Agricultural Economics,* Vol. 89, pp.1219-1225.

Gramig, B., R. Horan and C. Wolf (2009), "Livestock Disease Indemnity Design When Moral Hazard is Followed by Adverse Selection", *American Journal of Agricultural Economics*, Vol. 91, pp. 627-641.

Greiner, R., L. Patterson and O. Miller (2009), "Motivations, risk perceptions and adoption of conservation practices by farmers", *Agricultural Systems,* Vol. 99, pp. 86-104.

Gunn, G., C. Heffernan, M. Hall, A. McLeod and M. Hovi (2008), "Measuring and comparing constraints to improved biosecurity amongst GB farmers, veterinarians and the auxiliary industries", *Preventive Veterinary Medicine*, Vol. 84, N3, pp. 310-323.

Hamilton-West C., H. Rojas, J. Pinto, J. Orozco, L.P. Hervé-Claude and S. Urcelay (2012), "Characterization of backyard poultry production systems and disease risk in the central zone of Chile", *Research in Veterinary Science*, Vol. 93, pp. 121–124, http://dx.doi.org/10.1016/j.rvsc.2011.06.015.

Hardaker, J., R. Huirne, J. Anderson and G. Lien (1997), *Coping with Risk in Agriculture,* CABI publishing, Oxfordshire.

Hennessy, D.A. (2007a), "Behavioral incentives, equilibrium endemic disease, and health management policy for farmed animals", *American Journal of Agricultural Economics*, Vol. 89, pp. 698–711.

Hennessy, D.A. (2007b), "Biosecurity and Spread of an Infectious Animal Disease", *American Journal of Agricultural Economics*, Vol. 89, pp. 1226–1231.

Hennessy, D.A. (2005), "Behavioral Incentives, Equilibrium Endemic Disease, and Health Management Policy for Farmed Animals", *Working Paper 05-WP 418*, Center for Agricultural and Rural Development, Iowa State University, Ames.

Hennessy, D.A., J. Roosen and H.H. Jensen (2005), "Infectious disease, productivity, and scale in open and closed animal production systems", *American Journal of Agricultural Economics,* Vol. 87, pp. 900–917.

Hennessy, D. and C. Wolf (2015), "Asymmetric Information and Externalities in Animal Disease", 24 April, online version of record, *Journal of Agricultural Economics*.

Hennessy, D.A. and T. Wang (2013), *Strategic Interactions Among Private and Public Efforts when Preventing and Stamping Out an Highly Infectious Animal Disease*, Working paper No. 13-wp541, October, Center for Agricultural and Rural Development, Iowa State University, Ames.

Hogarth, R. (1987), *Judgement and choice: The psychology of decision* (2nd ed.), John Wiley & Sons, Oxford, England.

Horan, R. D, E. P. Fenichel, C. A. Wolf and B. M. Gramig (2010), "Managing Infectious Animal Disease Systems", *Annual Review of Resource Economics*, Vol. 2, pp. 101–124.

Jin, Y. and B.A. McCarl (2006), "Animal disease related pre-event investment andpost-event compensation: a multi-agent problem", in: *Selected paper at 2006Annual Meetings of American Agricultural Economics Association*, Long Beach, California.

Kobayashi, M. and T. Melkonyan (2011), "Strategic Incentives in Biosecurity Actions: Theoretical and Empirical Analyses", *Journal of Agricultural and Resource Economics*, Vol. 36, pp.242-262.

Kristensen, E. and C. Enevoldsen (2008), "A mixed methods inquiry: How dairy farmers perceive the values of their involvement in an intensive dairy herd health management program", *Acta Veterinaria Scandinavica*, Vol. 50, pp. 1-12.

Kuchler, F. and S. Hamm (2000), "Animal disease incidence and indemnity eradication programmes", *Agricultural Economics*, Vol. 22, pp. 299-308.

Lichtenberg, E. and D. Zilberman (1986), "The econometrics of damage control: Why specification matters", *American Journal of Agricultural Economics, Vol.* 68, pp. 261–273.

Mahul, O. and A. Gohin (1999), "Irreversible decision making in contagious animal disease control under uncertainty: an illustration using FMD in Brittany", *European Review of Agricultural Economics,* Vol. 26, pp. 39–58.

McInerney, J.P. (1996), "Old economics for new problems – livestock disease: Presidential address", *Journal of Agricultural Economics,* Vol. 47, pp. 295-314.

McInerney, J.P., K.S. Howe and J.A. Schepers (1992), " A framework for the economic analysis of disease in farm livestock", *Preventive Veterinary Medicine,* Vol. 13, pp.137–54.

Meuwissen, M.P.M. and M.A.P.M. van Asseldonk (2013), "European Union Subsidies: A Catalyst for Epidemic Market Loss Insurance?" in: *Livestock Disease Policies: Building Bridges Between Science and Economics*, OECD Publishing.

Meuwissen, M.P.M., J.R. Skees, J.R. Black, R.B.M. Huirne and A.A. Dijkhuizen (2000), "An analytical framework for discussing farm business interruption insurance for classical swine fever", selected paper, American Agricultural Economics Association 2000 Annual Meeting, Tampa, Florida.

Meuwissen, M.P.M., M.A.P.M. van Asseldonk, J.R. Skees and R.B.M. Huirne (2006), "Designing Epidemic Livestock Insurance", in D. Hoag, S. Koontz and D. Thilmany (eds.), *The Economics of Livestock Disease Insurance: Concepts, Issues and International Case Studies*, CABI press, Oxfordshire, pp. 126-140.

Meuwissen, M.P.M., R.B.M. Huirne and J.B. Hardaker (2001), "Risk and risk management: an empirical analysis of Dutch livestock farmers", *Livestock Production Science,* Vol. 69, pp. 43-53.

Mikes, A., H. Lausanne and R. Kaplan (2015), "When One Size Doesn't Fit All: Evolving Directions in the Research and Practice of Enterprise Risk Management", *Journal of Applied Corporate Finance*, Vol. 27, pp. 37-40.

Mintiens, K., H. Laevens, J. Dewulf, F. Boelaert, D. Verloo and F. Koenen (2003), "Risk analysis of the spread of classical swine fever virus through 'neighbourhood infections' for different regions in Belgium", *Preventive Veterinary Medicine*, V. 60, issue 3 pp. 27-36.

Niemi, J.K. and J. Heikkila (2011), "Impact of risk aversion and disease outbreak characteristics on the incentives of producers as a group to participate in animal disease insurance -A simulation", *Preventive Veterinary Medicine*, Vol. 100, pp. 4-14.

OECD (2012), *Livestock Diseases: Prevention, Control and Compensation Schemes*, OECD Publishing, Paris, http://dx.doi.org/10.1787/9789264178762-en

OECD (2011), *Managing Risk in Agriculture: Policy Assessment and Design*, OECD Publishing, Paris, http://dx.doi.org/10.1787/9789264116146-en

Perry, B., J. McDermott and T. Randolph (2001), "Can epidemiology and economics make a meaningful contribution to national animal-disease control?", *Preventive Veterinary Medicine*, Vol. 48, pp. 231-260.

Ramsay, G.C., P. Philip and P. Riethmuller (1999), "The economic implications of animal diseases and disease control at the national level", in *The Economics of Animal Disease Control*, coordinated by B.D. Perry, *Office International Des Epizooties Scientific and Technical Review*, Vol. 18, No. 2, pp. 343-354.

Rat-Aspert, O. and C. Fourichon (2010), "Modelling collective effectiveness of voluntary vaccination with and without incentives", *Preventive Veterinary Medicine*, 93, pp. 265-275.

Rat-Aspert, O. and S. Krebs (2012), "Individual and collective management of endemic animal diseases: An economic approach", Selected Paper prepared for presentation at the International Association of Agricultural Economists (IAAE) Triennial Conference, 18-24 August 2012, Foz do Iguaçu, Brazil.

Rich, K.M., A. Winter-Nelson and N. Brozovic (2005a), "Modeling regional externalities with heterogeneous incentives and fixed boundaries: applications to foot and mouth disease control in South America", *Review of Agricultural Economics*, Vol. 27, pp. 456–64.

Rich, K.M., A. Winter-Nelson and N. Brozovic (2005b), "Regionalization and foot-and-mouth disease control in South America: lessons from spatial models of coordination and interactions", *Quarterly Review of Economics and Finance*, Vol. 45, pp. 526–540.

Sheriff, G. and D. Osgood (2010), "Disease Forecasts and Livestock Health Disclosure: A Shepherd's Dilemma", *American Journal of Agricultural Economics*, Vol. 92, pp. 776-788.

Siekkinen, K.-M., J. Heikkilä, N. Tammiranta and H. Rosengren (2012), "Measuring the costs of biosecurity on poultry farms: a case study in broiler production in Finland", *Acta Veterinaria Scandinavica,* 2012, 54:12.

Smith, G. and S. Dunipace (2011), "How backyard poultry flocks influence the effort required to control avian influenza epidemics in commercial poultry flocks", *Epidemics*, Vol. 3, pp. 71-75.

Vergne, T, C. Guinat, P. Petkova, A. Gogin, D. Kolbasov, S. Blome, S. Molia, J. Pinto Fereira, B. Wieland, H. Nathues and D.U. Pfeifer (2016), "Attitudes and beliefs of pig farmers and wild boar hunters towards reporting of African swine fever in Bulgaria, Germany and the Western part of the Russian Federation", *Transboundary and Emerging Diseases*, Vol. 63 (April), pp. e194-e104.

Wang, T. and D. Hennessy (2014), "Modelling interdependent participation incentives: dynamics of a voluntary livestock disease control programme", *European Review of Agricultural Economics,* Vol. 41, pp. 681-706.

Whitehead, M. L. and V. Roberts (2014), "Backyard poultry: legislation, zoonoses and disease prevention", *Journal of Small Animal* Practice Vol. 55, pp. 487–496, DOI: 10.1111/jsap.12254.

Wolf, C. (2005), "Producer livestock disease management incentives and decisions", *International Food and Agribusiness Management Review*, Vol. 8, pp. 46-61.

Wright, B., B. Jorgensen and L Smith (2016), *Development of Behaviour Change Strategies for Animal Disease Surveillance and Reporting*, BehaviourWorks Australia, July 2016.

Chapter 3

Insights from behavioural economics into farmer livestock disease management

This chapter adds the insights from behavioural economics into farmer disease management. This research area combines psychology, sociology, and economics to examine the behaviour of economic actors. The theoretical framework of behavioural studies and the mapping of behavioural drivers into different policy areas is presented first, followed by an overview of the key findings of behavioural research applied to livestock farming. The final section presents a summary of the policy implications.

3.1. Theoretical framework for behavioural economics

The intention of behavioural economics is to infuse psychological realism into theories of economic behaviour as opposed to the standard economic model where actors are fully "rational", with perfect control, and consistently act in their own self-interests (Roberto and Kwachi, 2016). Applied to agriculture, the behavioural economics literature emphasises the importance of social and psychological influences in farmer decision-making and suggests that farmers seek to balance economic, social and lifestyle goals (see overview by Howley, 2015). The behavioural approach has been instrumental in examining the issues related to a voluntary change of farmer behaviour, such as sustainable farming, and mitigation and adaptation to climate change (reviewed in OECD, 2012). The rise of animal disease and animal welfare concerns in the 2000s and the recognition that the individual producer plays a key role in addressing these concerns led to a growing behavioural research in livestock farming.

Behavioural economics attempts to find patterns on how people act in ways that classic economic theories may characterise as "irrational". It seeks to build models that can account for behaviour in a psychological and social context (Amir and Lobel, 2008). If behaviour deviates in predictable ways, policy makers can design policies that take into account a range of drivers of human behaviour, including non-economic ones. While there is no unified underlying theory for behavioural economics, there are models that may be used to understand farmer livestock disease decision-making.

A theoretical framework applied in many behavioural studies in agriculture originates in the Theory of Planned Behaviour (TPB) (Ajzen, 1991).[1] It states that behaviour is the product of an intention to perform the behaviour and distinguishes the following determinants of intention (Figure 3.1): the attitude towards behaviour, the subjective norm to engage or not in behaviour, and the perceived behavioural control. These constructs have further determinants. The attitude towards behaviour results from the beliefs about possible effects of performing the behaviour (outcome belief) and the value that is attributed to this effect (outcome evaluation). The subjective norm is determined by how one sees if the "important others" expect him or not to perform a particular behaviour (social normative belief) and one's motivation to comply with these perceived expectations. The perceived behavioural control is determined by one's belief that he (she) has necessary resources to perform the behaviour (control belief strength) and the importance of these resources (control belief power). That is, of two individuals with equally strong intentions, the one who has the confidence to master this activity is more likely to act.

Ajzen (1991: 199) acknowledged that the TPB was open to additional predictors[2] and more developed versions of TPB consider additional factors that explain why intentions do not always translate into behaviours, such as skills, knowledge, and environmental constraints (e.g. Fishbein and Yzer, 2003). Other studies also introduced additional independent variables that could contribute to the intention-behaviour relationship (Figure 3.1). These, for example, include inertia or habit, moral obligation, self-identity, personal normative beliefs, past behaviour, and cognitive skills (Burton, 2004; De Lauwere et al., 2012). Behavioural research related to livestock disease management employs also other theoretical models and methods which use relatively similar behavioural constructs.[3] The TPB is presented here to facilitate further review as the behavioural studies on livestock disease refer extensively to this model.

The TPB presents (farmer) behaviour as a complex interaction of influences where the explanatory power of these influences regarding behaviour depends on specific contexts. In the context of agriculture, this implies that the impacts of individual factors on intention and the transformation of this intention into specific behaviour depends on a farming issue in question, farming type, individual characteristics of a farmer and other contextual parameters. Using the TPB constructs, Garforth (2015: 34) well describes this multifactorial and context-specific nature of farmer behaviour: "... farmers' behaviour in respect of animal disease risk management would be influenced by their knowledge of specific practices; their attitudes to specific practices and to disease risk management in general; their view on the efficacy of specific practices in reducing disease risk (...'outcome beliefs' and hence attitudes) and of disease risk management in general; their previous experience of specific practices and the experience they have heard from others; their perception of their ability to put specific practices into effect and of factors that constrain them (...'Perceived Behavioural Control'....) which may include current habitual behaviour; their perception of what other farmers in similar situations are doing with respect to disease risk management; and their perception of what other people important to them would think about their implementing or not implementing specific measures (…'subjective norms'…)."

Because of the contextual specificity, any generalisations about the relative importance of behavioural drivers, i.e. the degree to which each of them – farmer attitudes, subjective norms, perceived behavioural control, or any additional predictors – lead to certain behaviour, can be only suggestive. Also, the results coming from various studies depend on specific methods of analysis and how the surveys are structured. However, the value of behavioural research, such as TPB and other models, is that it helps to typify the drivers of behaviour. A further step is to establish connections of these behavioural drivers with specific policy actions. The framework developed by Prendergrast et al. (2008) from the Social Market Foundation in London is an example of such a mapping exercise.

This framework groups the drivers of individual's behaviour into external, internal, and social ones and links them with specific policy domains and policy instruments (Figure 3.2). External factors include monetary and effort costs and are influenced by traditional market-based policy interventions, such as taxes, subsidies and regulations. Internal factors concern individual characteristics of decision-makers related to how they cognise reality and the role of habit in their behaviour. Social factors encompass norms and other aspects of social capital.

This framework illustrates that traditional market-based interventions work through only a part of behavioural drivers. They may be necessary but most likely are insufficient and that policy interventions influencing individual and social drivers need to be also engaged to induce preferred behaviour amongst farmers (Prendergrast et al., 2008; OECD, 2012).

Figure 3.1. Theory of Planned Behaviour framework

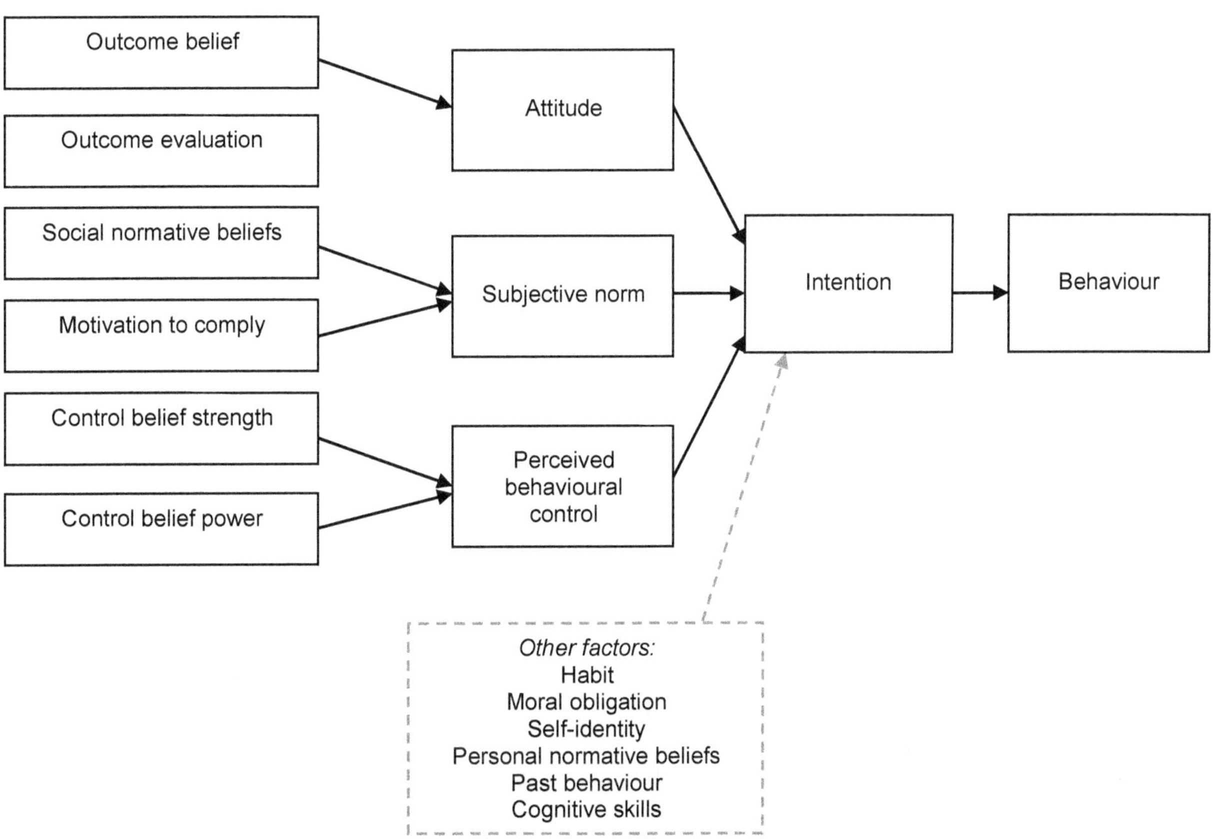

Source: Adapted from Burton (2004); Garforth (2010); and De Lauwere et al. (2012).

Figure 3.2. A framework for policy makers: Behavioural drivers and policy options and tools

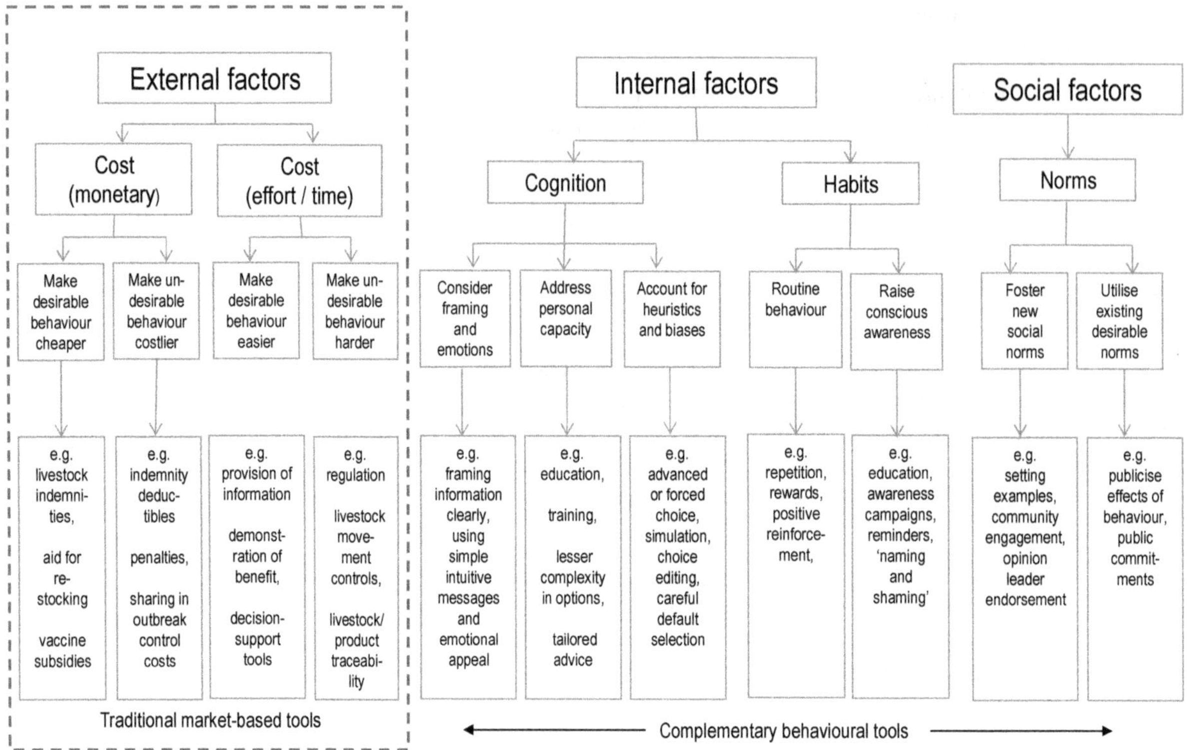

Source: Adapted from Prendergrast et al. (2008).

The following sections are structured along the three axes of the policy framework above: external (economic), internal and social factors of farmer behaviour. The findings from the behavioural economics literature with implications for livestock disease management and policy are discussed. The discussion also draws on general behavioural literature and the studies related to other agricultural issues which are considered of relevance to the disease management. Although the body of behavioural studies in agriculture is increasing, more research is required. In particular, the work focussed on livestock disease and other issues of livestock farming has been less extensive than in the application to environmental and climate change issues. Yet, the available research allows drawing insights that can help livestock disease policies to become more effective.

3.2. Economic considerations: Impact on key determinants of farmer decision making

- Cost-benefit considerations affect all elements of farmer decision-making process.
- Policy can influence farmer beliefs about economic outcomes of their actions and thus facilitate socially desirable private decisions.

Behavioural analysis of livestock farmers demonstrates that economic considerations affect all key determinants of their disease management decisions. Alarcon et al. (2014) studied the decision-making process of pig farmers using the TPB model which includes farmer attitudes, subjective norms, and behavioural control. They found that financial reasons were the most frequent drivers for disease control. In a related qualitative analysis the farmers reported that the observation of ill pigs, reduced production performance, and (or) mortality levels were the most frequent drivers for disease control, the majority of respondents linking these factors with the risk of entering an economically unsustainable situation. Looking further into the subjective norms that affect disease control decisions, the study found that farmers' motivation to comply with external advice depended on their belief that they obtain positive returns. Farmers valued the advice of a veterinarian high because they believed he was able to consider the economics of disease and of possible interventions. The same study also points out that perceived behavioural control as a driver of farmer decisions also had strong economics aspects. Thus, a measurable outcome of a disease measure was shown to be a factor of farmers' control belief, while farmers' perceived inability to employ additional labour or investment to implement a disease measure as a factor of their power to control.

These findings imply that the cost-benefit perspective permeates all elements of farmers' complex decision-making process. There is a role for policy which is to influence farmer perceptions and beliefs about the economic outcomes of their actions. This involves enhancing farmer knowledge and information necessary to assess the cost and benefits of disease management decisions. This also requires providing sufficient evidence on the cost-effectiveness of desired farm practices which can facilitate farmers' decisions to adopt them. The policy objective is to encourage farmers for socially desirable decisions that reduce the overall risks and impacts of diseases. Behavioural approach reveals that economic choices can be influenced by psychological and cognitive factors which policy makers should possibly take into account in formulating and communicating policy.

3.3. Internal factors in farmer decision making: Cognition and bias

- The cognitive process is at the core of farmer decision-making.
- Farmers' overconfidence with respect to biosecurity practices may lead to a lack of action.
- Cognitive biases and habits are defaults that can mislead farm decisions.
- Overcoming these is a role of livestock policy from the behavioural perspective.

Behavioural models regard decision-making mechanism as a cognition process: the process of acquiring knowledge and building understanding by individuals. Thus, farmer decisions depend on whether they are willing to use information, the extent to which they are capable to process it and learn, whether they generally have adequate knowledge, and how they are able to transform it into a decision. Referring to the TPB model, Garforth et al. (2006) state that a significant positive correlation between the attitude, subjective norm, perceived behavioural control, and intention indicates a cognitive driver, while a significant negative correlation indicates a cognitive barrier. In order to induce a desired change in farmer behaviour, policy should reinforce cognitive drivers and address cognitive barriers (Garforth, 2015).

Behavioural research provides insights into perceptions of livestock farmers about their own expertise in disease management and the adequacy of their effort to control disease risks. Based on several collective studies of UK livestock farmers, Garforth (2010) concludes that farmers generally seem to trust their own judgement. Kaler and Green (2013) provide similar observation from their survey of UK sheep farmers who generally consider themselves the experts to manage their complex business. Another study of UK farmers' attitudes to recommended livestock disease practices showed that "farmers felt they were currently doing all they reasonably could do, within the constraints of their farm, to minimise risks and their decisions were appropriate to the level of risk they saw at a time". Farmers typically judged they were making rational decisions and had high level of confidence in their own knowledge and expertise (Garforth, 2015).

The analysis also suggests that although farmers seem to generally feel confident about their expertise and the adequacy of their biosecurity effort, they are susceptible to cognitive biases and failure. Bruijnis et al. (2013), for example, analysed farmer ideas about the cost-effectiveness of various practices related to animal welfare and found that farmer evaluations diverged from the results obtained from models, and in some cases, quite significantly. The authors note that this might be particularly the case of new practices whose cost-effectiveness may be more difficult for farmers to evaluate compared to the well-known techniques. Meuwissen et al. (2001) concluded that farmers were conceptually interested buying insurance for consequential losses of epidemics, but because these epidemics are low-probability/high-consequence events farmers have trouble assessing the probability and potential magnitude of such risks. Due to this cognitive failure, farmer willingness to pay for epidemic insurance is generally less than the actual premium required (Skees and Barnett, 1999).

Biases are defined as systematic error in (farmers') judgments that affects their decisions and behaviour. Some of the relevant biases include the planning fallacy wherein people overestimate the ability to perform future tasks. In application to disease management, such bias could consist of farmers being over-confident in their ability to manage a disease incident without recourse to external expertise, such as testing and consultation by a veterinarian. Optimistic biases may be where people assume they are at below the median risk. For example, although producers may acknowledge disease outbreaks as a high threat at the national level, they may perceive their personal risks as low (Palmer et al., 2016). Present-biased preferences and intertemporal choice where one disproportionately weighs present over future concerns, i.e. farmers may prioritise investments in areas other than increased farm biosecurity because they perceive other business concerns as more obvious concerns (Wright et al., 2016). Finally, the status quo bias results in people sticking to current default options because this involves less effort than switching. Status quo bias routinize behaviour or leads to habits. Even where a new behaviour brings substantial benefits to the individual concerned, breaking habits requires a distinct cognitive effort on the part of the individual (Prendergrast et al., 2008 with reference to Jackson, 2005). Education, training, and awareness campaigns can help establish new behaviour, which should then be reinforced through repetition, awards and continued awareness. Understanding default livestock disease practices and pushing or resetting them is one role for policy. For example, the status quo bias can be overcome by making a programme opt-out rather than an opt-in, which can have a large impact on participation. Habits may have specific aspects in application to livestock disease. Lupo at al. (2014) studied oyster farmers reporting behaviour and observed that "habituation" impeded disease reporting despite the incentive to do so provided by compensation. They described habituation as a consequence of lacking continued alertness and awareness, and the continued involvement by authorities that led to an exotic disease becoming endemic. Barnes et al. (2015) develop this idea by noting more broadly that producers may become accustomed to a situation that was previously stressed as being significant. They highlight the need for persuasion and regular baseline communication between government and producers.

A role of livestock policy from the behavioural perspective is to overcome farmers' cognitive bias and failures. The way in which the policy and disease consequences are presented can factor into overcoming bias (Box 3.1).

Box 3.1. Psychological and cognitive bias affecting economic choices

Problem framing concerns the ways of communicating about the reality. The way a problem is defined determines one's understanding of and approach to that problem. Redefining or reframing a problem can help broaden the range of alternatives and solutions examined. Kahneman and Tversky (1979) developed these ideas in application to economic choices. They pioneered the concept of "loss aversion" which says people care more about losses than gains. Thus, if a problem is framed in terms of potential expenses and costs it will often elicit a different response than the same situation framed in terms of potential gains. Considering loss aversion would suggest that referring to potential losses is likely to be more effective than to gains in encouraging behaviour such as reporting diseases or implementing biosecurity. Bocqueho et al. (2013) confirmed that farmers responded more to penalties than bonuses because of "loss aversion".

The endowment effect occurs when ownership tends to make people overvalue resources because of attachment. The result of the endowment effect is that people's willingness to pay (WTP) is not equal to their willingness to accept (WTA). WTP value is the maximum amount a person would be willing to offer for a good, while WTA value is the minimum amount required for an individual to forgo a good, or to bear some harm. The empirical studies show that the values obtained by WTA are consistently higher than those expressed by WTP, when valuing the same good. The implication of the endowment effect is that policy makers should use willingness to accept values if possible (Shogren et al., 1994). This effect shows up in the willingness of farmers to part with diseased livestock and could affect their intention to report disease in response to the amount of indemnities offered.

The next effect is the reference effect where people tend to judge potential outcomes and actions relative to a previous experience or what they have witnessed even when the current situation has little or no reference. If the farmer has no experience with epidemic diseases, he may fail to understand the potential consequences for their operation.

Another effect can originate with sunk costs which, despite the assertions of economists that these should not influence decisions, often do so. People become psychologically invested when they already have expended money and effort into a project, regardless of the current costs and benefits. Thus, if recommended disease prevention requires a new investment or a move away from current practices, farmers may resist. In this case, demonstration of benefits of alternative practices and setting examples becomes particularly important.

3.4. Social influences in farmer decision making

- Psychological and social factors influence farmer behaviour.
- Opinions of "important others" are factored into farmers' decisions, particularly through subjective norms.
- Veterinarians are the largest outside influence on farm behaviour.
- Social capital is essential to activate norms and collective action.
- Individuals see different values in farming, necessitating a more nuanced rationalising of policy.

The agricultural behavioural literature abundantly demonstrates the importance of the psychological, moral and social aspects of farmer decisions (e.g. Howley, 2015; McGregor et al., 1996; O'Donoghue and Howley, 2012). In a more specific context of livestock disease management, Alarcon et al. (2014: 227-228) report that animal welfare, the image and reputation of the farm, and the pride of being a good manager also acted as motivators of disease control, although these were stated less frequently than the financial ones. Delgado et al. (2012) and Delgado et al. (2014) using the TPB framework examined factors related to Texas cattle producer's intent to participate in FMD detection and control and disease reporting. Moral norms, trust in other producers and social pressure, were among the factors that influenced producer behaviour.

Social influences have been shown to have great effect on decisions. People have a tendency to base actions and beliefs on what others are doing or believing. The probability of an individual adopting certain behaviour increases with the increase in proportion of those who have already done so (Colen et al., 2015). This section discusses social factors of livestock farmer decision-making: social norms, farmers' referents and social capital are in the focus.

Veterinarian, other farmers and government influence on decisions

While farmers generally appear to prioritise their own expertise, the views and opinions of others have been shown to have an effect on farmer decisions. Using the constructs of the TPB model, external opinions influence farmers' outcome beliefs and outcome evaluations and thus, their attitudes towards performing specific behaviour. Opinions of others also affect farmers' behavioural control beliefs. "Important others", or social referents, are at the core of subjective norms as another key construct of farmer behaviour. As a socio-psychological concept, norms represent individuals' basic knowledge of what others do and think they should do. Individuals do not like to feel their actions are out of sync with norms and are motivated to do "the right thing".

A great deal of behavioural research has found that, not surprisingly, veterinarians are the most important source of information and the primary opinion sought by farmers. Garforth (2015: 36), with reference to research in the United Kingdom, notes that veterinarians in private practice are widely seen as credible sources of advice and information by livestock farmers. One reason is that farmers consider veterinarians capable of interpreting and adapting the information according to their farm circumstances. Alarcon et al. (2014) find that the majority of surveyed pig farmers considered their veterinarian's opinion and advice the most valued, while trust in the veterinarian and (or) the acknowledgement of his professional competence was in many cases an important factor to comply with external advice. Garforth et al. (2006: 162) studied the decisions of dairy farmers in South West England to adopt techniques for heat detection in cows. Their respondents indicated the veterinarians as the most important external referents. Elliot et al. (2011), Taylor et al. (2016), Delgado et al. (2014), and Sok et al. (2015) report a similar finding. However, research also contains caveats on the role of veterinarians as farmers' referents. Alarcon et al. (2014: 239) report respondents' negative views that veterinarians "have fashions" and farmers have to be sometimes cautious to take up their advice, importantly also, two respondents in this study saw a conflict of interest of veterinarians as they also sell drugs. Derks et al. (2013) examined veterinarian awareness of farmer goals and attitudes to herd management in the Netherlands and diagnosed veterinarian misperceptions in that area. Hall and

Wapenaar (2012) found that the value that farmers place on discussion with their veterinarians was not matched by a readiness of the veterinarians to initiate discussion.

Research also identifies "other farmers" as key referents of farmer disease management, although the evidence is mixed due to specific contexts. Garforth et al. (2006) found other farmers to be the second important referent after the veterinarians in motivating farmers to act in a specific way. They also measured a considerable gap between the impact of these two referents on farmers' motivation to comply with their views and the impacts of other referents (artificial insemination service, farming press, private consultancy, agricultural universities and internet). Alarcon et al. (2014: 231) similarly report that other farmers' experiences guided some of the respondents' decisions on how to control a disease problem, particularly when the cost issue was of concern to the respondents. In contrast, Bruijnis et al. (2013: 109) studying farmer decisions related to the adoption of dairy foot health techniques found that fellow farmers were not seen as important referents compared to feed advisors, foot trimmers and veterinarians. These authors also found a low "motivational power" on farmers of the animal health service and press.[4]

Farmers' perceptions of government can be drawn from Garforth et al. (2013), who report that the majority of UK pig and dairy farmers in their study judged one or more of Defra's recommended practices for livestock disease management to be either ineffective or inappropriate. In another study of farmers' attitudes towards buying consequential loss insurance, the respondents showed a strong disinclination to comply with the views of Defra on this matter (Garforth, 2015: 34). More generally, Garforth (2015: 36) concluded that a "recurring theme from recent research in the United Kingdom is the view that government departments and agencies are ill-informed about the realities farmers face and are principally interested in regulating and restricting what they can do rather than supporting their farming enterprises". Palmer et al. (2009) also report for Australia a lack of trust in government sources, e.g. scientific institutions linked to the government. This evidence may be partial and reflect a specific country situation at a particular juncture (e.g. an aftermath of a serious disease outbreak), but it suggests that farmers' (dis)beliefs about government may act as barriers to voluntary uptake of policy recommendations.

Overall, these findings underscore the importance for policy makers to understand who the farmers' referents are in order to exploit the most effective "entry points" to communicate and deliver policy. Sok et al. (2016: 118) suggest that social pressure might act as a "catalyst" for policy instruments and leverage the (cost) effectiveness and efficiency of interventions. Veterinarians appear to be the main influence group; in other circumstances, fellow farmers may be also important. Thus, "farmer-to-farmer" or "veterinarian-to-farmer" communication may be more effective in influencing farmer decisions than that of "government-to-farmer". Local and personal contacts have more influence on livestock farmers' intentions than more distant and impersonal sources (Garforth, 2010). Farmer forums should be exploited or promoted where farmers could learn directly from others' views and experiences (Garforth, 2015 with reference to Kilelu et al., 2014).

Social capital and collectivity

Farmers can be viewed not just as individuals making separate choices, but as members of communities which have a tangible interest in common (Defra, 2008). Livestock farmers have an obvious interest in common in discouraging behaviour which causes negative externalities of animal disease. This common interest also serves to address broader societal concerns, such as food safety, various aspects of human health and also food security in less developed countries in particular. Society members identify and pursue common interest through trust, reciprocity, obligations, networks, norms, relationships, values, and informal sanctions. All of these form social capital and determine the quantity and co-operative quality of a society's social interactions. Ahn and Ostrom (2008) distinguish three categories of social capital: trustworthiness, networks, and institutional arrangements. Mutual trust is essential for establishing social relationships. Networks can be described as a set of relationships characterised by familiarity with the others involved through past dealings and repeated interactions with them. Institutions represent more explicit relationships with formalised rules and procedures which often have statutory form, and also tacit rules, but which are sometimes forged over a long history (OECD, 2013). Social capital is important for livestock disease management from several perspectives.

First, social capital helps to promote values and norms that discourage behaviours which cause negative externalities. Because actions outside of social norms are often viewed with disapproval, peer pressure and the need for approval provide incentive to conform. Thus, if social norms include responsible farmer disease prevention and control, the effects are more likely to be lasting than when influenced by authority and less monitoring and enforcement of these practices may be required. If it is normally considered shameful, it might be counter-productive to introduce fines, while if it is normally considered the right thing to do, it might be counter-productive to introduce financial benefits (Dawnay and Shah, 2005).

Second, social capital fosters virtue by encouraging community orientation and co-operation (Defra, 2008). Although farmers are generally in competition with one another, they may in certain situations see collective action as a rational approach to limit or halt disease and to deal with the consequences. Behavioural economics has been applied to examine when and under which conditions collective action occurs. These conditions are largely rooted in social capital, such as responsibility, trust, reciprocity, and information flows through social networks. According to Ostrom (2009), co-operation is more likely to occur in settings where: 1) many of those affected agree on the need for behavioural change and feel joint responsibility for future outcomes; 2) the reliability and frequency of information about the phenomena of concern are relatively high; 3) participants know who else has agreed to change behaviour and that their conformance is being monitored; and, 4) communication occurs among at least a subset of participants. Heffernan et al. (2008: 369), observing UK cattle and sheep farmers, concluded that a lack of trust, or more broadly, a lack of "social connectivity" within the farming community explained a lack of collective action for biosecurity. The primary message is that farmers are much more likely to choose cooperative behaviour if they have social bonds and are aware that others are choosing cooperation as well. Thus, information about costs and consequences from reliable and relevant sources and facilitating communication among farmers may encourage cooperative solutions. Educational and information programmes could utilise well-known examples of preferred behaviour relative to livestock disease prevention and control. These programmes could also utilise veterinarians and industry sources to convey costs and consequences of disease and potential benefits from co-operation across and among farm operations.

Third, social capital is likely to activate interactions between farmers and government. Participation through the existing social networks in discussing issues helps farmers learn about the policy context and act in ways beneficial to the community. Farmers with high linking social capital seem to be inclined to increase interaction with government on specific issues as opposed to farmers with low linking capital (Defra, 2008).

3.5. Farmer values and motivations attached to farming

Rural sociologists have studied farmers' values and their motivations to be engaged in farming. These studies brought into light a concept of farming styles, strongly synergetic with other behavioural analysis. Gasson (1973: 527) distinguished four broad value orientations of those undertaking farming: instrumental: farming is a means of obtaining income and security (e.g. making maximum or satisfactory income and security, safeguarding future income, expanding business); social: farming is for gaining prestige as a farmer (e.g. belonging to farming community, maintaining family tradition); expressive: farming is a self-expression or personal fulfilment (e.g. exercising special abilities, exercising self-respect for doing a worthwhile job, chance to be creative), and intrinsic: farming is an activity in its own right (e.g. enjoyment of work tasks, healthy outdoor life, value in hard work, independence).

These insights led to further research into patterns of farmers' behavioural motivation and the related farm typologies. For example, Rehman et al. (2008) identified several farming styles in England and this work fed into Defra's further development of its Farmer Segmentation Model. Based on a multivariate analysis of responses to a set of 51 statements about farming values and objectives, five farming types were identified: "custodians", 'lifestyle choice", "pragmatists", "modern family business" and "challenged enterprise" (Figure 3.3).

Figure 3.3. Defra's Farmer Segmentation Model

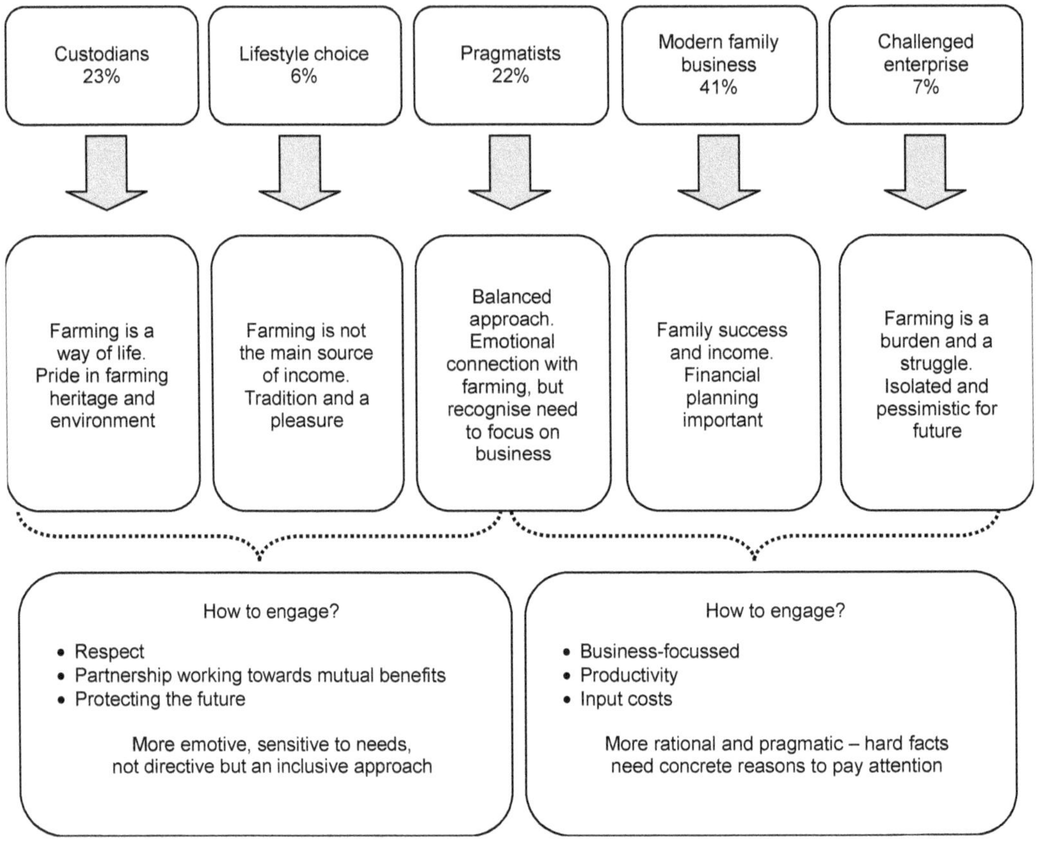

Note: A recent pilot study by Wilson et al. (2011) embedded Defra's segmentation framework within Farm Business Survey for England. 750 Farm Business Survey respondents were interviewed for this study, which established the following distribution of farmers according to segments: custodians (14%), lifestyle choice (7%), pragmatists (53%), modern family business (21%), and challenged enterprise (4%).
Source: Defra (2008).

Notably, this analysis revealed that segments were similar when profiled by "external" descriptors, such as farm size, region and farm specialisation, and it was only when attitudes were included that major differences emerged. Thus, farms can be characterised differently if "internal" characteristics of farm operators are taken into account. A key policy inference is that different farm groups may be less or more reactive to the reasoning based on purely economic rationality (and to economic policy tools). A broader rationale should be employed in incentivising a desired behaviour amongst farmers and different communication and language need to be exercised to influence different farm groups (Defra, 2008). As Defra's Farm Segmentation Model suggests, for some farm groups, a less directive and emotive outreach may be more effective, and which also suggests collective solutions and appeals to public good aspects of farming – these could be benefits of good livestock practices for the local community, animal welfare, human health, or societal welfare more broadly. For other groups, a more pragmatic messaging is required, with reference to cost management, financial consequences of bad or good livestock diseases management, and its impacts on farm productivity.

Certainly, because culture and values differ across societies, the farm segments can have different psychological and social profiles and weights across countries compared to those drawn in the model above. However, a general implication is that differentiating farms also by these features as opposed to conventional criteria of farm size, specialisation, or region, may make policy more effective. Policy communication should engage different notions – psychological, social, as well as economic – to have broader response in farming community. Synergies can be found here with the concept of "nudging" which suggests that policy makers can design policies that improve well-being through gentle nudges rather than through coercive measures by appealing to individuals' more profound values (Box 3.2).

Box 3.2. Nudging approach in policy

Thaler and Sunstein (2008) developed the concept of "nudging" as "any aspect of choice architecture that alters people's behaviour in a predictable way without forbidding any options or changing economic incentives". Nudge is the idea that formal regulations are not required because a small push can get people to change behaviour. In contrast, regulation is "budging" by reducing choice sets (Barnes et al., 2013). Thaler and Sunstein argue that if behavioural economics teaches us that we do not always act in our best interest, then policymakers must rethink the tools of regulatory command to change behaviour and better align our immediate choices and our deeper, truer preferences.

Applied to livestock disease policy, nudging means steering farmers towards better decisions by presenting choices in different ways. For example, it may be the case that presenting biosecurity practices as a form of "production insurance" may encourage adoption more than simply presenting them as livestock health protection. Another example from the research is that that telling someone of their electricity consumption compared to their neighbours prompted them to use less. Perhaps the same applies to livestock disease prevention and control. These types of questions about what language is most appropriate for nudging behaviour could form the core of a rigorous research programme. Economic experiments could be instrumental in this regard (Colen et al., 2015). They allow the identification of relevant behavioural parameters and testing the policy performance against farmer preferences.

3.6. Implications for animal disease policy

Behavioural theory suggests that identification of farmer behaviour is a starting point for policy that aims to influence that behaviour. This theory regards farmers' decisions as an outcome of complex influences which go beyond purely economic and financial factors. Farmers' broad values and motivations, their ability to process information and build knowledge, and their social connectedness also drive farmer decisions.

One implication is that if policy makers desire to see a positive change in farmer behaviour they need to build evidence about it and invest in behavioural research. Beyond monetary cost, this requires joint work between the government and researchers. An important task for the government would be to formulate the policy problem and the objectives sought to be achieved because contexts are essential in any behavioural work. Another implication is that for policy to become more effective, it should act along the whole spectrum of behavioural drivers to constrain those that prevent the desired behavioural change and build upon those that work towards it. Behavioural analysis shows that such interventions lie primarily in the domains of information, education, advice, and policy communication. There is a substantial body of expertise that combines behavioural and communication science which could be applied to livestock disease management (Fishbein and Yzer, 2003).

Livestock farmers generally feel confident about their expertise, but this may reflect overconfidence, cognitive biases and cognitive failure. The role of livestock policy is to understand and offset these through improved risk communication, credible early warning information, and targeted information and advice (Garforth, 2015).

Behavioural economics suggests that information about the disease including its likelihood and consequences, should be framed so as to alleviate or overcome cognitive biases. Establishing a culture of habits and preferred behaviour may strongly influence farmers. The government may wish to use surveys, focus groups and other means of communicating with stakeholders to assess the relevant biases, habits and norms. These actions may have both short- and long-term implications for farmer behaviour.

Perceptions of farmers about trustworthiness of information and advice are highly important. Information from government may be mistrusted and ignored, whereas veterinarians and fellow-farmers may be perceived as reliable referents. Policymakers need to understand who the farmers' referents are to exploit the most effective pathways to communicate and deliver policy. Some evidence suggests that livestock farmers are not particularly proactive in seeking new information (Garforth, 2015). Their willingness to operationalise the information also depends on whether it can be easily adapted to their particular circumstances. Thus, any modes and tools that help farmers to customise general information and evaluate the proposed measures in application to their own business will increase the absorption of information.

Economic considerations permeate farmers' decision mechanism for livestock disease management. Enhancing farmers' knowledge, information, and ability to assess the economic costs and benefits of these decisions should be a permanent policy focus. Providing sufficient evidence on the cost-effectiveness of desired farm practices is integral to that task. To encourage desired behaviour it may be more effective to highlight potential losses than gains, as people tend to focus on losses much more.

While economic motivation is important, farmers differ in how they balance it against other values which are not necessarily connected with farming as business. Farmers may be less or more responsive to the reasoning based on purely economic rationality and, thus, to economic policy tools. Policy should engage different notions – psychological, social, as well as economic – to have broader response in farming community. By appealing to preferred values, policy makers can use gentle nudges, rather than applying coercive measures. Through the use of displaying and communication choices and context, policy-makers can nudge behaviours such as biosecurity practices and reporting of suspect animals.

Social capital – social norms, local networks, professional groups – assists in appropriate decisions by individuals and enables collective action where they see common interest. If policy can change social norms to align with preferred behaviour, the effect is likely to be long-lasting and require less enforcement. Engaging communication and social connectivity amongst farmers should be factored into livestock policy. Building trust between livestock farming and broader society is also important. Raising the general public's awareness on existing biosecurity standards and systems for disease prevention, industry quality assurance, voluntary certification which makes safe products easily recognisable, are ways to reinforce social norms for high biosecurity in livestock farming.

In sum, to integrate a behavioural approach into policy for improved animal disease management decisions the first step is to understand which behaviour is occurring (and by whom). This may result in determining that the behaviour is in line with goals or out of bounds, and identify segments or subpopulations that can be targeted. The second step is to understand why undesirable behaviours are occurring. This information can be utilised in the third step which is to design and implement potential actions to nudge, anchor, or otherwise positively reinforce preferred actions. The policy actions may include information and education programmes, framing desired actions in terms of avoided losses, providing professional or expert information on risks and frequencies of occurrence, or resetting default actions.

Notes

1. Theory of Planned Behaviour is the extension of the Theory of Reasoned Action (TORA) by Ajzen and Fishbein (1980). See Burton (2004) for a discussion of the evolution of TORA model into TPB.
2. De Lauwere et al. (2012: 152), for example, present the views of several authors on the weaknesses and strengths of the TPB model.
3. For example, Valeeva et al. (2011) applied a Health Belief Model to study risk management behaviour of Dutch pig farmers. Palmer et al. (2009) draw on the Social Cognitive Model to research the effect of trust on responses of Australian farmers to infectious diseases. Both of these frameworks originate from behavioural health research. Other authors (e.g. Toma et al., 2013; Sok et al., 2016) employ statistical methods, such as Structural Equation Modelling (SEM) to test and estimate the causality between the *a priori* determinants of farmer biosecurity behaviour. This method is also used in combination with behavioural modelling to test model parameters. Other works (e.g. Elbers et al., 2010 a, b) use a "grounded theory approach" which begins with the collection of qualitative data. These data are then reviewed and codified, and grouped into concepts and categories to constitute a framework of analysis
4. Interestingly, spouses can also be very influential in farmers' decision making. Kuhfuss et al. (2015), for example, report this finding with respect to the adoption by farmers of agri-environmental schemes.

References

ABS Rural (2016), "Disease reporting underpins new biosecurity program's success, Meat and Livestock Australia says", *ABS Rural*, 21 July, 2016, www.abc.net.au/news/2016-07-21/disease-reporting-underpins-biosecurity-program/7649086.

Ahn, T.K. and E. Ostrom (2008), "Social capital and collective action", in *The handbook of social capital,* pp. 70-100, Oxford University Press, Oxford, UK.

Ajzen, I. (1991), "The theory of planned behavior", *Organisational Behavior and Human Decision Processes*, 50, pp. 179–211.

Ajzen, I. and M. Fishbein (1980), *Understanding Attitudes and Predicting Social Behaviour*, Prentice-Hall, Englewood Cliffs, NJ.

Alarcon, P., B. Wieland, A. L.P. Mateus and C. Dewberry (2014), "Pig farmers' perceptions, attitudes, influences and management of information in the decision-making process for disease control", *Preventive Veterinary Medicine*, Vol. 116, pp. 223-242.

Amir, O. and O. Lobel (2008), "Stumble, Predict, Nudge: How Behavioral Economics Informs Law and Policy", *Columbia Law Review* 108, pp. 2098-2137.

Barnes, A.P., L. Toma, J. Willock and C. Hall (2013), "Comparing a 'budge' to a 'nudge': farmer responses to voluntary and compulsory compliance in a water quality management regime", *Journal of Rural Studies*, Vol. 32, pp. 448–459.

Bennett R., C. Garforth, N. Taylor, M. Upton and T. Wilsmore (2007) *Managing the Risk of Exotic Animal Diseases in the UK: Influencing the Behaviour of Key Stakeholders.*

Bocqueho, G., F. Jacquet and A. Reynaud (2013), "Expected utility or prospect theory maximisers? Assessing farmers' risk behaviour from field-experiment data", *European Review of Agricultural Economics,* Vol. 41, pp. 135–172.

Bruijnis, M., H. Hogeveen, C. Garforth and E. Stassen (2013), "Dairy farmers' attitudes and intentions towards improving dairy cow foot health", *Livestock Science*, Vol. 155, pp. 103–113.

Burton, R. J. F. (2004), "Reconceptualising the 'behavioural approach' in agricultural studies: a socio-psychological perspective", *Journal of Rural Studies*, Vol. 20, pp. 359-371.

Colen, L., S. Gomez y Paloma (2015), "(How) can economic experiments inform EU agricultural policy?, *JRS Science and Policy Report*, European Commission, Joint Research Centre, Institute for Prospective Technological Studies, https://ec.europa.eu/jrc/en/publication/eur-scientific-and-technical-research-reports/how-can-economic-experiments-inform-eu-agricultural-policy.

Dawnay, E. and H. Shah (2005), *Behavioural Economics, Seven Principles for Policy-Makers*, the New Economics Foundation (NEF), London, United Kingdom, http://b.3cdn.net/nefoundation/cd98c5923342487571_v8m6b3g15.pdf.

De Lauwere, C., M. van Asseldonk, J. van't Riet, J. de Hoop and E. ten Pierick (2012), "Understanding farmers' decisions with regard to animal welfare: the case of changing to group housing for pregnant sows", *Livestock Science*, Vol. 143, pp. 151–161.

Defra (2010), "Understanding and influencing behaviours: A review of social research, economics and policy making in Defra", *Discussion Paper*. www.defra.gov.uk/evidence/series/documents/understand-influence-behaviour-discuss.pdf

Defra (2008), "Bringing Theoretical and Applied Evidence Together from Across Defra and Highlighting Policy Relevance and Implications for Future Research", *Defra Agricultural Change and Environment Observatory Discussion Paper*, November.

Delgado, A.H., B. Norby, W.R. Dean, W.A. McIntosh and H.M. Scott (2012), "Utilizing qualitative methods in survey design: Examining Texas cattle producers' intent to participate in foot-and-mouth disease detection and control", *Preventive Veterinary Medicine*, Vol. 103, pp. 120-135.

Delgado, A.H., B. Norby, H. Morgan Scott, W. Dean, W.A. McIntosh and E. Bush (2014), "Distribution of cow–calf producers' beliefs about reporting cattle with clinical signs of foot-and-mouth disease to a veterinarian before or during a hypothetical outbreak", *Preventive Veterinary Medicine*, Vol. 117, pp. 505–517.

Derks, M., B. van Woudenbergh, M. Boender, W. Kremer, T. van Werven and H. Hogeveen (2013), "Veterinarian awareness of farmer goals and attitudes to herd health management in The Netherlands", *Veterinary Journal*, Vol. 198, pp. 224–228.

Elbers, A.R., M.J. Gorgievski-Duijvesteijn, P.G. van der Velden, W.L. Loeffen and K. Zarafshani (2010a), "A socio-psychological investigation into limitations and incentives concerning reporting a clinically suspect situation aimed at improving early detection of classical swine fever outbreaks", *Veterinary Microbiology*, Vol. 142, N 1, pp. 108-18.

Elbers, A.R., M.J. Gorgievski-Duijvesteijn, P.G. van der Velden, W.L. Loeffen and K. Zarafshani (2010b), "To report or not to report: a psychosocial investigation aimed at improving early detection of avian influenza outbreaks", *OIE Revue Scientifique et Technique*, Vol. 29, pp. 435-449.

Elliott, J., J. Sneddon, J.A. Lee and D. Blache (2011), "Producers have a positive attitude toward improving lamb survival rates but may be influenced by enterprise factors and perceptions of control", *Livestock Science*, Vol. 140, pp. 103–110.

Fishbein, M. and M.C. Yzer (2003), "Using Theory to Design Effective Health Behavior Interventions", *Communication Theory*, Vol. 13 (2), pp.164–183

Garforth, C.J. (2015), "Livestock keepers' reasons for doing and not doing things which governments, vets and scientists would like them to do", *Zoonoses and Public Health*, Vol. 62 (suppl. 1), pp. 29-38.

Garforth, C.J. (2010), "Motivating farmers: Insights from social psychology", *National Mastitis Council (NMC) Annual Meeting Proceedings.*

Garforth, C.J., A.P. Bailey and R.B. Tranter (2013), "Farmers' attitudes to disease risk management in England: A Comparative Analysis of Sheep and Pig Farmers", *Preventive Veterinary Medicine*, Vol. 110, pp. 456–466.

Garforth, C.J., K. McKemey, T. Rehman, R.B. Tranter, R.J. Cooke, J.R. Park, P.T. Dorward and C.M. Yates (2006), "Farmers' attitudes towards techniques for improving oestrus detection in dairy herds in South West England", *Livestock Science*,Vol. 103, pp. 158–168.

Gasson, R. (1973), "Goals and values of farmers", *Journal of Agricultural Economics*, V. 24/3, pp. 521–537.

Hall, A. and W. Wapenaar (2012), "Opinions and practices of veterinarians and dairy farmers towards herd health management in the UK", *Veterinary Record*, Vol. 170, pp. 441–449.

Hall, C. and F. Burnett (2014), "Will farmers consider collective action to tackle crop diseases?", *Research Briefing*, RPC RB 2014/01, January 2014, Scotland's Rural College Rural Policy Centre, UK.

Heffernan, C., L. Nielsen, K. Thompson and G. Gunn (2008), "An exploration of drivers to bio-security collective action among a sample of UK cattle and sheep farmers", *Preventive Veterinary Medicine*, Vol. 87, pp. 358-372.

Howley, P. (2015), "The happy farmer: The effect of non-pecuniary benefits on behaviour", *American Journal of Agricultural Economics*, Vol. 97/4, pp. 1072-1086, https://doi.org/10.1093/ajae/aau126.

Jackson, T. (2005), *Motivating Sustainable Consumption: A Review of Evidence on Consumer Behaviour and Behavioural Change*, Centre for Environmental Strategy University of Surrey, Guildford, Surrey, www.sustainablelifestyles.ac.uk/sites/default/files/motivating_sc_final.pdf

Kahneman, D. and A. Tversky (1979), "Prospect Theory: An Analysis of Decision Under Risk", *Econometrica*, Vol. 47(1979), pp. 263-291.

Kaler, J. and L.E. Green (2013), "Sheep farmer opinions on the current and future role of veterinarians in flock health management on sheep farms: A qualitative study", *Preventive Veterinary Medicine*, Vol. 112, pp. 370-377.

Kilelu, C.W., L. Klerkx and C. Leeuwis (2014), "How dynamics of learning are linked to innovation support services: insights from a smallholder commercialization project in Kenya", *Journal of Agricultural Education and Extension*, Vol. 20, pp. 213–232.

Kuhfuss, L., R. Préget, S. Thoyer, N. Hanley, P. Le Coent, M. Desole (2015), "Nudges, Social Norms and Permanence in Agri-Environmental Schemes", AES Paper, Agricultural Economics Society 89th Annual Conference, April 13-15, 2015, Warwick University, Coventry, UK, http://ageconsearch.umn.edu//handle/204233

Lupo, C., A.O. Amigo, Y.V. Mandard, C. Peroz, T. Renault (2014), "Improving early detection of exotic or emergent oyster diseases in France: identifying factors associated with shellfish farmer reporting behaviour of oyster mortality", *Preventive Veterinary Medicine*, Vol. 116, 168–182, http://dx.doi.org/10.1016/j.prevetmed.2014.05.002.

McGregor, M., J. Willock, B. Dent, I. Deary, A. Sutherland, G. Gibson, O. Morgan and B. Grieve (1996), "Links between psychological factors and farmer decision making", *Farm Management*, Vol. 9/5, Spring 1996.

Meuwissen, M.P.M., R.B.M. Huirne and J.B. Hardaker (2001), "Risk and risk management: an empirical analysis of Dutch livestock farmers," *Livestock Production Science*, Vol. 69, pp. 43-53.

O'Donoghue, C. and P. Howley (2012), "The Single farm payment: A Basic income for farmers?", *Basic Income Studies,* Vol. 7/1, pp. 1–23.

OECD (2013), *Providing Agri-environmental Public Goods through Collective Action*, OECD Publishing, Paris, http://dx.doi.org/10.1787/9789264197213-en

OECD (2012), *Farmer Behaviour, Agricultural Management and Climate Change*, OECD Publishing, Paris, http://dx.doi.org/10.1787/9789264167650-en

Ostrom, E. (2009), *Games, groups, and the global good, pp.* 207-228, Springer Berlin Heidelberg, Berlin.

Palmer S., F. Fozdar and M. Sully (2009), "The effect of trust on West Australian farmers' responses to infectious livestock diseases", *Sociologia Ruralis,* Vol. 49, pp. 360-374.

Prendergrast J., B. Foley, V. Menne and A. Karalis Isaac (2008), *Creatures of Habit? The Art of Behavioural Change*, Social Market Foundation, London.

Rehman, T., C.J. Garforth, K. McKemey, C. Yates and R. Rana (2008), "Farmers' behavioural inclinations and their influence on the anticipated response to the reform of the Common Agricultural Policy in England", *Journal of Farm Management*, Vol. 13, pp. 281–308.

Roberto, C.A. and I. Kwachi (2015), "An Introduction to Behavioral Economics and Public Health", Chapter 1 in *Behavioral Economics and Public Health,* Oxford University Press, pp. 1-26.

Shogren, J.F., S.Y. Shin, D.J. Hayes and J.B. Kliebenstein (1994), "Resolving Differences in Willingness to Pay and Willingness to Accept", *The American Economic Review,* Vol. 84, pp. 255-270.

Skees, J.R. and B.J. Barnett (1999), "Conceptual and Practical Considerations for Sharing Catastrophic/Systemic Risks", *Review of Agricultural Economics*, Vol. 21, pp. 424-441.

Sok, J., H. Hogeveen, A.R.W. Elbers and A.G.J.M. Oude Lansink (2016), "Using farmers' attitude and social pressures to design voluntary Bluetongue vaccination strategies", *Preventive Veterinary Medicine*, Vol. 133, pp. 114–119.

Sok, J., H. Hogeveen, A.R.W. Elbers and A.G.J.M. Oude Lansink (2015), "Farmers' beliefs and voluntary vaccination schemes: Bluetongue in Dutch dairy cattle", *Food Policy* Vol. 57, pp. 40–49.

Thaler, R.H. and C.R. Sunstein (2009), *Nudge: Improving decisions about health, wealth, and happiness,* Penguin Books, London, UK.

Taylor, M., N. Dhand et al. (2016), "Longitudinal cohort study of horse owners. HHALTER: Horse owners and Hendra virus: A longitudinal study to evaluate risk", *Rural Industries Research and Development Corporation Publication,* No 16/002, RIRDC Project No PRJ-008198.

Toma, L., A.W. Stott et al. (2013), "Determinants of biosecurity behaviour of British cattle and sheep farmers – A behavioural economic analysis", *Preventive Veterinary Medicine*, Vol. 108, pp. 321– 333

Valeeva, N.I., M.A. van Asseldonk and G.B. Backus (2011), "Perceived risk and strategy efficacy as motivators of risk management strategy adoption to prevent animal diseases in pig farming", *Preventive Veterinary Medicine*, Vol. 102, pp. 284–295.

Wilson P., N. Harpur and R. Darling (2011), *Analysis of Farmer Segmentation Across Farms Contributing to the Farm Business Survey: A Pilot Study*, Rural Business Research, The University of Nottingham.

Wright, B., B. Jorgensen, L. Smith (2016), *Development of Behaviour Change Strategies for Animal Disease Surveillance and Reporting*, BehaviourWorks Australia, July 2016.

Chapter 4

Issues of livestock disease management beyond the farm: Collective action, the role of food chains, and influences from wildlife

This chapter considers outside factors that play a role in farmer disease management. It covers how livestock farmers working collectively to manage livestock disease in areas such as risk insurance, surveillance, and in response to livestock epidemics. This collective action often involves partnerships with the government. What influence do actors in the rest of the value chain have on farmer livestock disease management? Responses to food safety and quality, animal welfare and other consumer concerns related to livestock production methods may drive changes in farm practices by aligning incentives with policy objectives. This is followed by a discussion of what the presence of wildlife populations as disease reservoirs and vectors means to disease management and farm decisions. The final section summarises the implications for livestock policy across these issues.

4.1. Producer collective action in livestock disease management

- Livestock disease management functions within a continuum between pure public and pure private goods, which leaves much scope for collective action.
- To act collectively, farmers should perceive an animal health problem as a shared concern.
- The "free-rider" problem is a typical barrier to collective action.
- Many farmers view epidemic disease as a government problem and endemic disease as an individual farm programme which discourages collective action.
- Farmers should see benefits from collective action as greater than costs.

Collective action is defined as "the action taken by a group or an organisation in pursuit of members' perceived shared interests" (Scott, 2014). Collective action in agriculture has been shown to play an important role in supplying farms with inputs, services and marketing agricultural products, risk management (OECD, 2011), and agri-environmental activity (OECD, 2013a; OECD, 2012a).

The premise for collective action in livestock disease management is that the variability and different attributes of related functions place these functions within a continuum between pure public and pure private goods (Box 4.1). The boundary between public and private provision is intrinsically movable and depends on the nature of activity, which in itself is not static and may change, for example as new technology becomes available or new regulation is introduced.[1] In addition, even if the characteristics of activity suggest predominantly a public good nature, this does not necessarily mean that public sector must provide it directly. The government may contract out the service to producer groups and manage it through financing, regulation, taxes, levies, or subsidies. Even if a service is a direct public function, there is rationale for participation of private stakeholders to make the service more effective and efficient, for example, when it concerns risk assessment, building of information systems, design of contingency plans, or implementation of specific disease programmes.

Collective action also depends on the degree to which the societal attitudes of state paternalism *versus* self-reliance are established towards the farming community. It will more likely develop more in the policy environment which creates little expectation amongst farmers that the costs of their business risks will be systematically shared by society. Collective action also depends on farmers' perceptions of particular livestock problems as an individual or collective matter. Heffernan et al. (2008), in their study of bio-security collective action among UK cattle and sheep farmers conclude that they largely considered epidemic diseases as an issue external to individual producer and a matter of border control agencies, national biosecurity policy, and regulations. At the same time, they viewed endemic disease as a problem of "bad" farmers and not of those who manage their stock well. The authors conclude that when a problem is viewed as an individual problem, there is little utility in acting collectively.

The insights from the environmental analysis about the benefits and the barriers to collective action can be projected onto livestock disease management (OECD, 2013a). Collective action can generate economies of scale and scope and reduce the cost of management through sharing and mobilising resources. It can promote norms, industry-specific rules, and best practices. It can enable knowledge sharing among members and increase their technical capacity. Collective action can provide the flexibility to tackle local issues better than in a centralised way. Because disease occurrence and spread has spatial dimensions, disease prevention and control across neighbouring farms can be complements (Hennessy, 2005). In these cases, collective action may allow individual farmers to manage their stock and coordinate farm practices at an appropriate geographical scale beyond administrative borders.

Box 4.1. Theory of public and private goods in application to livestock health

The rationale for public and private roles in the context of animal health is strongly associated with the notion of externalities and public goods. The distinction between public and private goods is based on the criteria of excludability and rivalry. Excludability considers whether the provider or consumer of a service can prevent (or exclude) others from simultaneously benefiting from the service. Rivalry (or subtractability) concerns the extent to which the use or consumption of a good or service by one individual reduces the availability of this good or service to others. High rivalry enables individual consumption, whereas low rivalry permits joint consumption. Holden (1999) applied these criteria to specific veterinary activities and concluded that few of them are purely public, or private goods and most contain elements of each.

Rivalry (or subtractability)	Excludability: Low	Excludability: High
Low	**Public goods** • Epidemic or zoonotic disease control (including surveillance, movement control, quarantine services) • Some extension • Some research • Control of foodborne diseases • Drug quality control	**Toll goods** • Vaccine production • Diagnostic services • Veterinary clinics • Dips
High	**Common pool goods** • Tsetse control on pre-communal land using traps, targets or aerial spraying	**Private goods** • Endemic disease • Sales of drugs and spraying vaccines • Some extension • Some research

Thus, beyond activities with predominantly public and private good properties, some can be qualified as "toll goods", i.e. excludable, but with low rivalry, so that non-paying users can be denied access to the service, but several people may use the service at any one time. An example of a toll good is a cinema - several people can watch the film at the same time, but non-paying users can be denied access to the cinema. Other examples of toll goods are buses, trains and airplanes. Because of the high excludability characteristics, toll goods can usually be financed by the consumer. However, some services with low rivalry may require large initial investment. The investment required might exceed the funds that can be raised by the private sector. The construction costs of a railway line for example may be so great as to deter private sector investment. In certain circumstances, public finance may be justified in order to establish the facilities and resources to produce the service, although the private sector may then finance the operation of these services.

There are also "common pool goods", which on the other hand, have high rivalry characteristics (increased consumption diminishes supply for others) but are non-excludable (i.e. non-paying users cannot be prevented from using the service). An example of a common pool good might be a village water supply: no one can be prevented from using the water, but increased consumption of water by one individual would reduce availability to others. Because non-paying users cannot be denied access to the resource, no incentive exists for the consumer to pay for the service (in this example, to drill more boreholes). Common pool goods, thus, usually require some form of public financing.

Source: Holden (1999).

While yielding potential benefits, collective action also has barriers. A key barrier is the "free-rider" problem. If people cannot be excluded from using a good, they have little motivation to voluntarily contribute to its provision. The issue is then how to limit free riding. Another barrier to collective action is that it requires additional transactions costs compared to individual activity. These include search costs, bargaining costs, and monitoring and enforcement costs. Third, sceptical attitudes to collective undertakings may be a barrier as farmers are used to individual management. As noted in Chapter 3, collective action requires sufficient social capital to create trust and social connectedness that enable potential participants to formulate and pursue shared interest. Fourth, uncertain policy environment including funding, objectives and management can inhibit participation by increasing uncertainty about the future and benefits of the programme (OECD, 2013a).

This uncertainty may be about, for example, potential market effects from trade and movement restrictions or whether *ad hoc* payments for consequential losses will be provided to affected farms.

A distinction of collective action by who leads it is useful for further examination (OECD, 2013a). Collective action may be bottom-up driven and take the form of farmer-to-farmer cooperation. In this case it can typically emerge to deal with issues specific to a particular locality or region. Another type is a top-down collective action led by producer groups when there is a concern for the whole sector. In both cases, collective action may occur without government involvement or may integrate government at different administrative levels and receive government support in various forms. Some countries provide evidence of unique partnerships between farm industries and government in livestock disease management. In Australia, for example, the principle of public-private partnership is at the core of the national on-shore biosecurity system.

Farmer-to-farmer co-operation

- Not much is known about farmer-to-farmer co-operation in livestock disease management.
- Interrelationships of individual decisions to control animal disease can be strong at the area level.
- Farmers are likely to co-operate if there is a shared resource or novel techniques for uptake.
- Mistrust of others' actions and motivations discourages collective action.
- Efforts to support group formation must recognise and address perceptions of social connectedness amongst the communities involved.

OECD (2012a) and OECD (2013) highlight many examples of farmer-to-farmer collective action related to agri-environmental and climate change activities, typically also engaging other rural community stakeholders and local governments. An initial search for such practices in livestock disease management seems to show that they are not well documented and attract less attention of researchers.

Although more investigation is required into the incidence and the scope of farmer-to-farmer cooperation in livestock disease management, some insights can be drawn from a study by Hall and Burnett (2014) who examined whether farmers in England and Scotland would consider collective action for crop disease control. Cooperation was more likely when using new or unknown disease treatments. Farmers were more likely to consider cooperation when there was a shared resource (e.g. a weather station), a third party to facilitate, penalties for free-riders, evidence of benefits from cooperative action, information explaining why cooperation was useful, and financial support to cover cooperative action costs. Factors of mistrust of other farmers that discouraged cooperation were: doubting others would stick to the plan, not wanting to share plans with competitors, likelihood of disagreements, and belief that it was "not in their nature to help each other." One approach to encourage collective action is to utilise existing networks where social capital in the form of mutual trust and reciprocity exists. Farmers were more likely to consider novel cooperative approaches. The authors suggest that policy-makers to encourage collective action should clarify its benefits, provide support including financial support, external facilitation, some form of shared resource, information and evidence of benefit.

Collective action by livestock industry groups

- Industry action is more likely to occur in producer groups that are institutionally and financially sound.
- Country experiences show that the livestock industry can lead in many fields of livestock health.
- Farmer capacity building is a typical area where industry leadership can be exploited.
- Industry co-operation in disease insurance can have advantages over private provision.
- The livestock industry can lead in specific disease programmes, supported by government.

Experiences across countries suggest that the scope for industry-led collective action in livestock disease management can be broad. Such initiatives are most likely to develop if there are strong producer groups, characterised by institutional and financial soundness and the organisation procedures that ensure good connectivity with and among individual members. In some countries producer associations function on the basis of systems where levies are made compulsory by national law for all producers in the industry, and its collection is administered via the national tax systems (Box 4.2).

Box 4.2. Levy systems for producer associations

New Zealand's Commodity Levy Act (1990) empowers producers to self-impose levies through a vote in order to finance the "industry good" activities. Once voted, the levy becomes obligatory for all commercial producers of a commodity and is charged on each unit marketed as a type of sales tax. Levies are collected by downstream operators and transferred to industry good bodies. The obligatory character of the levy is grounded by the necessity to avoid a "free-rider problem": everyone is obliged to pay as it is difficult to exclude non-payers from benefiting from "industry goods" just because they have the characteristics of public goods. However, this compulsory levy is introduced through voting and is therefore self-imposed. There is also a requirement to vote (every six years) the continuation of a levy; it is therefore possible that the levy can be repealed by farmers, which acts as a strong means of farmer control over the association (for example, in 2009 wool producers voted against continuation of a wool levy which happened in the context of substantial economic difficulties that the sector experienced at the time). The activities to be undertaken by the industry good body must be approved by the levy payers.

In Australia, a levy system is operated and administered by the Australian Government at the request of industry. A levy is payable on transactions involving livestock (defined to include sheep, lambs and goats) and/or cattle (defined as bovine animals other than buffalo – there are separate levies on buffalo, deer and pigs). The levy is paid by the trader or the slaughterhouses purchasing the animals. Components of the levy are used to fund: research, development and marketing activities by Meat and Livestock Australia (MLA), programmes conducted by Animal Health Australia (AHA), plus contributions to the National Residue Survey. The Levies Revenue Service (LRS) receives the funds and forwards them to the relevant organisations, in addition to distributing the Australian government's matching research and development (R&D) contributions. Activities funded by levies include R&D, marketing and promotion, plant and animal health programmes, and residue testing.

Source: OECD, (2011); OECD (2012b).

The examination of country practices distinguishes several broad areas of collective action by the livestock industry including: (i) farmer capacity building; (ii) implementation of specific disease programmes; (iii) disease risk insurance; (iv) disease surveillance; and (v) responses to disease outbreaks. In all these areas there is a rationale and examples of partnerships between industry and government.

Capacity building is a typical activity of industry groups, consisting of the provision of general information, training, and education for livestock farmers. This is the case where the benefit of collective action occurs through economies of scale and scope. Funded research on control measures, causes and consequences of disease, as well as co-operative extension and other educational resources are often administered and performed co-operatively between government, university, industry, and private farm organisations. Concrete examples are provided in the country case studies (Chapters 5, 6 and 7).

Industry-led collective action also concerns programmes to control and eradicate specific disease. These are often implemented in cooperation with government: the industries can fully fund the programmes or share the funding with governments and other stakeholders, while government (through its affiliated agencies) can ensure the overall co-ordination and implementation of these programmes (Box 4.3).

Box 4.3. Industry participation in disease control and eradication programmes in Australia

Australia has a long history of industry involvement in livestock disease eradication. At present, livestock industries fund the projects to manage Johne's disease in sheep, cattle and alpaca. These industry-funded projects are co-ordinated by the Animal Health Australia.[1] Technical advice is provided by the National Technical Adviser and, from time to time, Technical Working Groups may be convened at the request of the industries with representatives provided by Animal Health Committee. In addition, to these programmes, Johne's disease Market Assurance Programmes (MAPs) are being carried out for the same types of animals (sheep, goats, cattle and alpaca). They are based on collaboration between the states and the industries concerned. These are voluntary programmes for producers to identify and promote their negative Johne's disease status to clients. Herds and flocks participating in the MAPs are not accredited as free of Johne's disease, but they have a lower risk of being infected compared to non-assessed herds and flocks. Producers can minimise the spread of Johne's disease by sourcing replacement animals from herds or flocks in the MAP assessed. Participating herds or flocks are tested to determine their disease status and managed to reduce the risk of infection (Animal Health Australia, 2016a).

Box 4.3. Industry participation in disease control and eradication programmes in Australia *(cont.)*

Australia carried out a long-standing bovine brucellosis and tuberculosis eradication programme and in 1997 it achieved the status of "TB Free Area". Monitoring for tuberculosis has continued under the five-year Tuberculosis Freedom Assurance Program and measures to further reduce the risk of new cases have been implemented. Radunz (2006) credited the success of this programme to strong industry and government support. Industry supported negative incentives for non-cooperating producers. Industry funding provided financial incentives to accelerate progress such as subsidies for mustering and holding, compensation for exposed stock sent to slaughter or destroyed, low interest loans for cattle yards, fencing, restocking freight rebate and interest subsidies. Funding was provided by the cattle industry (50%), state governments (30%), and the federal Australian government (20%). Funding initially contributed to operational costs and compensation payments for test reactors. Later it was extended to provide compensation for cattle and buffalo exposed to infected animals. Financial assistance was also extended to provide subsidies for low interest loans and other incentives.

1. Animal Health Australia is a not-for-profit public company unifying 32 members and representing Commonwealth, state and territory governments; industry organisations; service delivery and non-programme participants and associate members (feed producers and research institutions). It currently manages more than 50 national programmes related to animal and associated human health, biosecurity, market access, livestock welfare, productivity, and food safety and quality.

Industry-led collective action in the form of mutual funds can also develop in disease insurance. The advantage of mutual funds is that they can provide coverage targeted to specific risks of producer groups which larger and more diversified insurers do not provide. These companies can also better deal with problems of asymmetric information and moral hazard as they tend to have a stronger sense of ownership and trust amongst their stakeholders compared to conventional public stock companies. Mutual funds may also adopt flexible regimes of premium collection, which are better tailored to cash flows of their clients. Governments can provide the initial incentives to create such funds by way of start-up capital and attracting private expertise for product development. However, mutual companies may suffer a lack of financial robustness due to their relatively small size and the small scope for diversification in their risk portfolio, requiring sometimes re-insurance support from the government. Their business decisions may also be more susceptible to stakeholder pressure (Box 4.4).

Box 4.4. Dutch mutual insurance funds for livestock disease

Mutual insurance companies were created for several agricultural industries in the Netherlands, among which two that are specialised in disease risk insurance for poultry and pigs.

Avipol Mutual covers rearing and breeding broiler production farms in the poultry sector against the risk of specified poultry diseases. The point of departure for this insurance was that public assistance was no longer available. Only farmers with an Integral Chain Control and Salmonella Control (ICCsc) certificate can participate in this mutual. Certified flocks are considered to have a lower risk of microbial infections, including the insured salmonella types. In order to obtain a certificate, poultry farmers must take strict measures with respect to: 1) construction, lay-out and cleanliness of the enterprise; 2) manner of keeping poultry; 3) supply of animals, (hatching) eggs and feed; and 4) third party visits. If contamination is detected, strict control measures are applied for treatment or destruction of animals and (hatching) eggs, and removal of the contaminated material and manure.

The Porcopol insurance scheme was created in 2002. It covers consequential losses from swine epidemics (FMD, classical swine fever and Aujeszky's disease) on sow farms. Members of the mutual receive a fixed compensation per sow in the case where (i) sows are infected with Aujeszky's disease and need to be vaccinated; (ii) sows are infected with FMD or classical swine fever and need to be culled; or (iii) sows need to be pre-emptively culled because of an outbreak within a sphere of 1 km. Preventive vaccination does not trigger a payment.

The experience of the Dutch mutuals is instructive in that it shows that specialised insurance funds can fill the market niches that otherwise would not be filled by larger and more diversified insurers. Perils covered by these relatively small-scale companies are generally not covered by large insurers because of expected problems of moral hazard and adverse selection. Small mutual funds can cope with these problems better because they can better address information asymmetries. There is typically good knowledge of the members and their business, involvement of members in mutual control (e.g. as board members of a mutual), and there is direct access to clients. Dutch mutuals also apply specific rules concerning the premium payments, which may provide certain advantages from the perspective of producers. For example, Avipol and Porcopol divide premium payments into advance and adjustment payments, enabling producers to spread premium payments over time. This also creates incentives for risk prevention and to expand the retention level in order to minimise the eventual cost of insurance. If no risk has occurred by the end of the year, the unused premium is allocated to all farmers insured. However, the experience of specialised Dutch mutual also show a lack of financial robustness and that they tend to be dependent on government support (e.g. for re-insurance).

Source: Melyukhina (2011).

Another area where farm industry collective action can play an essential role is the management of disease outbreaks. While the approach in many countries is for the government to operate without direct industry involvement, successful cooperation can occur between government and industry groups. The latter can be instrumental in the assessment of risk and the establishment of the required response measures; they can also play a critical role in ensuring local outreach and feedback. Industry funds to participate – along government – in the cost of livestock epidemics is a potentially important activity, discussed in the following section.

Public-private partnerships in management of livestock epidemics

- Alternative financing to fund disease losses can provide a framework for co-operation and have implications for incentives.
- Some countries have successful long-term cost-sharing arrangements for epidemic diseases.

Public-private partnerships can be created to share the responsibilities and the costs of control of livestock epidemics between government and livestock industries (Box 4.5). Alleweldt (2013) notes that such partnerships are found only in a small number of countries, but where they exist, they have high level of stakeholder acceptance. In the context of this review, it is appropriate to discuss cost-sharing schemes from the perspective of how they help to better align public and private incentives.

Cost-sharing schemes are by definition *ex ante* frameworks and as such, they substantially reduce the uncertainty that individual producers face in the event of disease outbreak. This is achieved through protocols that spell out potential control measures and the procedures to define the sets of measures to be applied in response to a particular epidemic. These schemes can also set in advance the compensation principles, including the scope of compensation (direct losses versus consequential, or types of disease), the formulae to establish compensation amounts, and timeframes for its execution.

Box 4.5. Experiences of cost-sharing arrangements in livestock epidemics

Dutch Animal Health Fund (AHF)

In the Netherlands, producer contributions to direct costs of livestock epidemics are operated through the Animal Health Fund (AHF). The current procedures were developed following the devastating epidemic of classical swine fever (CSF) in 1997/98 when the control measures generated significant expenses for the government. The AHF effectively sets the maximum amount of producer contributions to cover the direct control costs in the case of a disease outbreak. Any spending required beyond this limit is equally shared by the Dutch government and the European Union (the latter through contributions from the EU Veterinary Fund). The AHF covers all primary livestock types: pigs, cattle, poultry, and sheep and goats. The accumulation and use of the Fund is managed by Commodity Boards for Livestock, Meat, and Eggs. Producer contributions occur through levies per slaughtered/exported animal, or per unit of milk sold. The size of the fund and the levy amounts are based on a scientific risk assessment and the evaluation of the financial cost of the control measures. However, the size of contributions is also subject to negotiations between the government and industry. In deciding the size of the Fund, only the risks of major diseases are considered (mainly, CSF, FMD and AI). In the event of other large epidemics, additional assessments are made and additional levies imposed. The combination of measures applied to control epidemics (scope of culling, recourse to preventive vaccination) constitutes part of the budget assumptions. For example, the different control strategies applied in specific epidemic events explain the differences in the amounts of funds for each of the five-year periods since 2000.

German Animal Disease Funds

The main financial arrangement for epidemic diseases compensation in Germany is the animal disease funds (Tierseuchenkassen). In contrast to the Dutch Animal Health Fund it is a more regionally diversified system. The legal foundation for Tierseuchenkassen is the Animal Disease Act which constitutes an overall federal legal framework, but laws in each federal state are also applicable. Fifteen of Germany's sixteen federal states have their own Tierseuchenkasse controlled by a Governing Board whose members are chosen by state agricultural ministries, county veterinary authorities and agricultural organisations. The Tierseuchenkassen compensate livestock owners who suffer financial losses due to epidemic disease outbreaks. Compensation is provided for direct losses due to officially ordered culling, losses from animals that die after destruction was ordered, and when a disease is detected after the death of the animal. Compensation includes the actual value of the animals, and culling and disposing costs.

Box 4.5. Experiences of cost-sharing arrangements in livestock epidemics *(cont.)*

Beyond epidemics compensation, Tierseuchenkassen have a role in prevention and eradication of disease. Prevention measures include surveillance and monitoring for diseases including classical swine fever, bluetongue disease, avian influenza and various cattle diseases, as well as vaccination programmes. Tierseuchenkassen establish and finance actions to eradicate non-epidemic diseases, such as infectious bovine rhinotracheitis (IBR) in cattle. Generally, state governments consult with the Tierseuchenkassen to co-ordinate their respective expertise, experience and financial resources regarding livestock epidemics. Some Tierseuchenkassen voluntarily engage in monitoring and other prevention measures for non-epidemic diseases. Under some state laws, Tierseuchenkassen also implement the mandatory tasks of compensation for rendering and disposing of animal by-products.

These publicly administered funds are supported by mandatory levies paid by livestock operators, as well as by funding from state governments and co-financing from the European Union. Livestock holders' levies are based on the particular species, the number of animals, and possibly other criteria, such as the weight and age of animals, herd size, the commercial use of animals, the risk of disease, and the absence of infectious diseases. They also depend on the expected costs for the general operation of each Tierseuchenkasse for each species. These costs can include prevention measures, the building of reserves or repaying debts stemming from previous reimbursements. Each farmer must annually report data on his/her livestock to the Tierseuchenkasse. Each Tierseuchenkasse's Governing Board determines the levies which are authorised by the state government.

Australian Emergency Animal Disease Response Agreement (EADRA)[1]

The Emergency Animal Disease Response Agreement (EADRA) in Australia is a contractual arrangement between the Australian state and territory governments and livestock industries to collectively ensure preparedness for and response to emergency animal disease. The EADRA covers 61 categorised animal diseases and has 23 signatories (national and state and territory governments and 14 industry bodies).

EADRA is a broad framework that embraces the whole spectrum of activities for prevention, preparedness for, and response to disease incursions. The cost-sharing in the emergency response to disease epidemics is the central component of this agreement. It establishes the formulae for the distribution of burden: (i) between the governments and industry; (ii) the burdens of specific governments within the government part; (iii) and the burdens of specific industries within the industry part. An overall principle to determine the government-industry cost shares derives from the potential externality effects of disease on the overall society: the higher these effects, the higher government's and lower industry's share is, and *vice versa*. For that purpose, EADRA stipulates four categories of animal diseases. The diseases that seriously affect human health and (or) the environment but which may only have minimal direct consequences to the livestock industry are defined as Category 1 diseases (e.g. rabies). The biosecurity measures for diseases in this category are fully funded by governments. Category 2 diseases may have "slightly lower" national socioeconomic consequences, but have significant public health or environmental consequences that result in "very severe" production losses (e.g. BSE, AI, or FMD). The government funds 80% of the cost of measures for Category 2 diseases, while the rest is industry funded. Government and industry share the cost equally of Category 3 diseases, which have "generally moderate" national socio-economic consequences, with minimal or no-effect on human health or the environment, but "severe" production losses (e.g. CSF, Bluetongue, Newcastle disease). Diseases that are not expected to significantly affect the society and for which their main effect is limited to the livestock industry are categorised as Category 4 diseases for which industry pays 80% of the cost (e.g. Aujesky's disease, bovine tuberculosis). Finally, if a disease cannot be characterised under any of the above categories, all costs are borne by the government.

In addition to the proportion of the cost shared between the governments and industry, EADRA sets the specific formula on how the cost is shared between governments of different levels and between different industries. The national and state/territory governments equally share the cost of an emergency disease response. However, the cost that each state shares depends on the disease under consideration. Within the industry, the cost is shared according to the benefit that each industry receives from the emergency disease response. If the disease affects only one species, then the industry related to that species bears the entire cost that falls to that industry. If the disease affects more than one species, the share of the cost contributed by each industry is determined by both the gross value of production and the importance of the specific disease for that industry.

1. See case study on Australia for further discussion of EADRA.

Source: Animal Health Australia (2016); OECD (2012b); Kimura and Antón (2011); Melyukhina (2011).

A cost-sharing approach also inherently incorporates mechanisms to address moral hazard. Because the beneficiaries (farmers through their groups) pay a share of the outbreak response cost, they see an incentive to limit that cost by avoiding disease risk through sufficient preventive effort. An additional lever for prevention can be an inclusion of a requirement for the beneficiaries to be prepared for an outbreak and take recovery measures in order to receive compensation. In the Australian EADRA, for example, there is the requirement for producers to have individual biosecurity plans. These plans contain measures to mitigate the risks of disease entry or spread and can be developed with direct contributions of industries. Thus, grazing industries in Australia have published the National Farm Biosecurity Reference Manual—Grazing Livestock Production as the basis for a farm biosecurity plan. Moral hazard is also addressed through peer pressure: individual producers become eligible for compensation as part of producer groups that can monitor the adequacy of members' practices; this monitoring can also increase pressure for early reporting of disease by individual farmers.

A more fundamental aspect to early reporting is an appropriate level of compensation. While the low level does not incentivise farmer enough to report the disease detection, high level of compensation is likely to reduce farmer's incentive to take an appropriate risk reducing strategy. This is challenging because there is a problem of asymmetric information: government has limited information on the true costs of complying with reporting requirement for the farmers. Cost-sharing schemes can reduce information asymmetries because they involve farmer stakeholders which benefit from and contribute to costs of compensation. These schemes therefore have incentives to generate the information which would lead to an "appropriate and equitable" compensation. Consultations that are part of the cost-sharing agreement enable information sharing, while negotiation procedures between stakeholders provide the flexibility to fine-tune compensation levels and cost-sharing.

Beyond considering the incentives that cost-sharing schemes create for an individual farmer it is also instructive to analyse the factors that make these schemes successful. Based on a comprehensive review of the existing disease compensation schemes (OECD, 2012), Allewedt (2013) suggests several principles for a "pragmatic and manageable" system. One is that such schemes should be mandatory, with those who contribute directly to the overall risk of the disease paying into the schemes. Inclusion of downstream industries does not seem rational as this would add complexity, in particular in the determination of which industries should contribute. Another principle suggested is that all those who pay should receive the benefits if they are directly affected. Cost-sharing schemes should generally cover direct losses related to outbreaks without covering consequential losses. However, it might be warranted to cover business interruption losses in movement restriction zones because if culling is implemented, farmers in such zones may be worse off than those whose herds were culled (this, however, requires further investigation). An additional principle is that schemes should adjust the levies paid according to risks at the individual level; for example, based on the level of biosecurity measures implemented. However, this is hard to apply in practice. Finally, epidemic cost-sharing schemes could incorporate prevention measures, such as financing specific vaccinations.

4.2. The role of other agri-food chain participants

- Other firms in the food value chain are mostly concerned with foodborne illnesses.
- There is increasing public concern with verification and traceability of production practices in food value chains which may encourage other participant to become involved with farm biosecurity and herd health programmes.
- Voluntary insurance programmes are enabled by industry-government co-operation.

Changing public attitudes about livestock and poultry production have made processors and retailers more cognisant about links to farm practices. Specifically, the public in many countries is increasingly aware and concerned about food safety and animal welfare (Waller, 2006). These concerns manifest themselves in food preferences and depend critically on labelling. Agri-food chain firms, including restaurants, food retailers, and processors, are increasing the use of hazard and quality control programmes, traceability, certification, and production contracts. Each of these may play a role in facilitating and encouraging animal disease control either directly, if it affects safety or quality, or indirectly, if the practices spill-over to prevent or control disease (Box 4.6).

Foodborne diseases are a major concern of retailers and processors because of the market effects. Food safety is an over-whelming concern of food marketers. To the extent that disease present at the farm level bears food safety risks, processors and marketers, including retailers, restaurants, grocers, are quite concerned. Government agencies directly deal with most foodborne illnesses from bacterial issues. Many of the practices and monitoring that is performed to prevent and control foodborne illnesses may have spill-over effects to assisting in preventing animal disease. Further, the frameworks that are utilised to monitor and certify practices related to foodborne diseases could be adapted to monitor and certify biosecurity and other measures related to animal disease. An example is the Hazard Analysis of Critical Control Points (HACCP) that identifies risk in food chains. HACCP can point out the risks involved by contacts at markets, the mingling of livestock or poultry, transportation, slaughter, and at preparation points. HACCP can assist in disease control and prevention by providing recommended preventive measures (Edmunds et al., 2013). Edmunds et al. (2013) concluded that adopting the HACCP system could work effectively as a rapid response system to tackle emerging outbreaks of infectious diseases.

Increased vertical integration in many countries and livestock sectors involves increased contracting that explicitly defines management practices and deals with monitoring issues. Contracting and third party verification can certainly involve biosecurity, sanitation, and other practices related to prevention and control of disease. To the extent that these pressures are growing, one might expect the agribusinesses, processors and retailers further down the food chain to increasingly influence farm management decisions. This, in many ways, is captured in the contracting process in the poultry and pork sectors. Market access is also linked to achieving and verifying the practices and standards described in the contracts.

Farm animal welfare is another area of increasing concern related to animal agriculture. Many consumers link farm animal welfare, farm size, and food safety. Pressure to allow traceability and assure the production processes of livestock, dairy and poultry products has led to scrutiny of farm practices. Traceability and certification of origin and practices of food supply is an area of growing importance in food chains (Meuwissen et al., 2003). Specifically, traceability and certification in meat supply chains requires transparency, due diligence and control of livestock epidemics (Meuwissen et al., 2003). In order to encourage and enable these changes, it is important to understand the break-even costs of traceability, liability and recall insurance, and regulatory incentives to motivate adoption by free-riders.

Private agri-food firms as the gatekeepers to market access play a greater role in specifying and verifying farm production practices. In many cases, these firms are concerned with the social license to sell food and, in particular, food safety. Partnerships with government and farm groups may utilise these changes to align farm incentives and encourage practices to prevent and control disease. Thus, the prevention of foodborne illness and the contracts and mechanisms that accompany them could complement animal disease control.

Box 4.6. Livestock traceability systems in Australia

The National Livestock Identification System (NLIS) is the permanent identification and lifetime traceability system in Australia for cattle, sheep and goats. NLIS (Pork) has been also established and NLIS (South American Camelids) is in the process of development for alpaca. All three systems operate as industry–government partnerships.

The NLIS combines three elements to enable the lifetime traceability of animals:

- an animal identifier (a visual or electronic ear tag known as a device)
- identification of a physical location by means of a Property Identification Code (PIC)
- a web-accessible database to store and correlate movement data and associated details

As animals are bought, sold and moved along the supply chain, they must be tagged with an NLIS-accredited tag or device. All animals leaving a property (PIC) must be identified with a NLIS-accredited device before moving off the property, unless a permit is obtained from the state or territory. Each movement they make to a location with a different PIC is recorded centrally on the NLIS Database.

The NLIS is able to provide a life history of animal's residency, and to discern contacts with other animals.

Any device or property statuses that indicate that any animals may pose a biosecurity or health risk are reported to processors to ensure that the affected animals are tested at slaughter. This maintains the safety, quality and integrity standards of Australian red meat and livestock and reduces the impact of a potential livestock disease epidemic or residue incident.

Source: Meat and Livestock Australia (2016); Animal Health Australia (2016b).

4.3. Wildlife relationship to farm animal disease

- Wildlife are increasingly relevant as reservoirs and vectors of disease.
- Farmers consider wildlife as an exogenous force concerning the likelihood of farm infection.
- Biosecurity practices to prevent infection from and to wildlife may be different from standard practices for other disease sources.
- The presence of a wildlife reservoir changes relevant practices and tools for disease control as well as farmer attitudes towards disease management.
- Wildlife diseases are often managed by government institutions different from those dealing with livestock disease, which makes inter-agency co-ordination critical.

The economic risks of wildlife diseases to livestock agriculture are significant. The spread of infectious diseases among and between wild and domestic animals is a major global problem (Daszak et al., 2000; The Economist, 2005). Wildlife can be a disease reservoir as well as a vector of disease transmission. If wildlife are infected, they may become a disease reservoir and the disease can remain present even if it is eradicated in domesticated livestock. The continued presence of many livestock and poultry diseases are caused and facilitated by wildlife such as deer, possums, badgers, ferrets, and elk. Migratory birds may help spread strains of highly pathogenic avian influenza (HPAI) among domestic poultry. Wildlife are also carriers of chronic wasting disease and other pathogens that put livestock and humans at risk of infection (Horan et al., 2010). Another consideration is that the majority of human diseases are zoonotic (Cleaveland et al., 2001), and domesticated livestock and poultry may transmit diseases from wildlife to humans (Pearce-Duvet, 2006).

From the perspective of farm disease management, wildlife are a potentially important source of disease infection that are viewed as exogenous to farm decisions. Thus, when agricultural and environmental agencies are considering the farmer response, they should also explicitly consider the potential for disease pressures from wildlife populations. The presence of wildlife disease reservoirs complicates disease control and eradication both politically and logistically.

Farm biosecurity practices can be divided into those that prevent disease from entering (bioexclusion) and those that prevent disease from leaving (biocontainment) the farm, herd or flock. Farmers often view biosecurity strictly from controlling disease from entering their herd (Liebler et al., 2009). Farmers tend to focus on the bioexclusion aspects of biosecurity rather than biocontainment as they are more concerned about protecting their assets than outside animal populations whether they are livestock or wildlife. The potential for contact—whether direct or indirect—between domesticated livestock and poultry and wildlife that may spread disease means that farmers should be educated and incentivised to consider disease spread from their farm in biosecurity practices.

Livestock population management or biosecurity choices may influence economic damages by affecting disease transmission between wildlife and livestock. Bicknell et al. (1999) modelled multiple populations in a bioeconomic model of bovine tuberculosis (bTB) transmission between brush-tailed possums and dairy cattle in New Zealand. In addition to the standard testing and culling of infected cows, Bicknell et al. suggested managing the possums (i.e. hunting them) to reduce the disease reservoir and potential contacts with cattle. But this was not a true multi-host-pathogen model because possum disease dynamics were not modelled.

Horan et al. (2005) and Horan et al. (2008) analysed the livestock-wildlife problem as a dual-host pathogen where the disease was endogenously determined in both the cattle and deer herds and could move between them. In addition to wildlife management (i.e. feeding and culling deer), biosecurity on cattle farms was a disease management tool. They found that biosecurity in the cattle sector put less pressure to reduce deer stock. If cattle were more profitable, it might become optimal to eradicate deer as a means to eliminate bTB. However, the model demonstrated that it is not always optimal to eradicate the disease particularly if biosecurity can sufficiently separate the two populations. Results indicate there may be benefits to jointly managing the livestock and wildlife populations, but in reality different agencies (or ministries) are often charged with livestock and wildlife disease control. When multiple agencies are involved in managing disease in multiple wild-life and livestock populations, the demands of clients and agendas can lead to conflicts and sub-optimal decisions.

The policy implication of wildlife disease reservoirs and vectors affecting livestock populations are that government agencies charged with disease control in livestock and wildlife populations should coordinate and complement efforts. From the farmer perspective, biosecurity practices should account for the potential for disease to enter and exit the farm via wildlife. Additional management and policy questions should be examined in future research efforts.

4.4. Implications for animal disease policy

The economic theory suggests that the variability and different attributes of specific functions in livestock disease management place them within a continuum between pure public and pure private goods. The boundary between public and private provision is intrinsically movable and leaves much scope for collective action by producers.

Producer collective action in livestock disease management should be given sufficient consideration by policy makers. Collective action can provide more efficient responses to shared concerns by generating economies of scale and scope and reducing private cost of management. It can strengthen compliance with norms, develop and enforce industry standards, promote and support the adoption of best practices. It can improve the division of responsibilities between government and private business in disease risk management and help a better alignment of private incentives with public concerns.

For collective action to occur, farmers should see benefits from it as greater than the costs. Collective action also depends on farmers' perceptions of particular livestock problems as an individual or collective matter. Policy makers should work to build farmers' consciousness about the link between their individual risk management effort and its short-term and long-term effects on livestock markets and the whole food chain, food consumer behaviour, and human health. Livestock policy should integrate as a necessary component the communication and research focussed on the broad spill-overs of farm disease management. Collective action also requires sufficient social capital to generate trust and social connectedness to enable potential co-operators to formulate and pursue shared interest. An initial examination shows that there seems to be little inclination amongst farmers to act collectively at the local level. However, the issue of how strong rationale for such local initiatives may be in disease management requires more research. If there is rationale, policy role would then be to provide evidence of benefit, external facilitation, and information through existing networks.

Industry-led collective action in disease management, in contrast, has sufficient evidence to support its potential as a contributor to disease prevention and control. Collective action in these fields is more likely to develop if strong producer groups exist and are institutionalised around a broad spectrum of shared industry interests. Policy may foster institutional and financial soundness of producer institutions through legislation. In particular, governments can help to address the "free-rider" problem that constrains collective action by making the contribution of all potential beneficiaries obligatory by law. This, however, should be balanced by the flexibility provided to farmers in deciding about the rationale for forming common institutions, their funding priorities, and accountability towards individual members.

Country experiences demonstrate that the scope for industry-led collective action can be broad, spanning from farmer capacity building through disease surveillance, specific control and eradication programmes, risk insurance, to partaking in response to disease emergencies. Through these initiatives, producers obtain a sense of ownership over animal health. In all these areas there is also a rationale for and examples of long-standing partnerships between industry and government.

Public-private cost-sharing in livestock epidemics is an important example and a tool to improve compatibility of public and private incentives in several ways. Cost-sharing between governments and industry, typically involving *ex ante* protocols, can substantially reduce uncertainty for both individual producers and government. It can limit moral hazard and information asymmetries, and thus facilitate early disclosure of disease. Although governments are likely to face strong producer resistance to sharing the financial burden of livestock epidemics, there are examples of long-standing schemes with a high level of stakeholder acceptance. Some experiences show that a strong budget deficit can trigger the introduction of a new system. For cost-sharing schemes to be successful, the responsibilities of parties and where the benefits fall should be clearly determined before establishing the cost-sharing arrangements. Although the advantage of cost-sharing schemes is that they can substantially reduce uncertainties surrounding emergency situations, it is important that they are sufficiently flexible so as to be adaptable to specific circumstances. These schemes need to provide sufficient space for consultation and prior negotiation among the stakeholders.

Industry and farmers co-operate to supply food quality and production practice verification to consumers and maintain market access. These programmes may provide a framework to ensure biosecurity practices or create positive spill-overs to prevent disease.

Wildlife as a reservoir and vector of disease complicate management. Farmers might be able to manage sporadic risks through biosecurity, but a continuous disease pressure from a local reservoir is not manageable at the farm level. It is often the case that different agencies/ministries are tasked with managing wildlife and livestock policies, but lack of co-ordination can exacerbate disease control. Government agencies charged with disease control in livestock and wildlife populations should co-ordinate and complement efforts.

Note

1. For example, the development of drugs and "pour-on" insecticides has changed the control of trypanosomosis in endemic areas from a public good to a private good as the benefits of control can now be limited to those who purchase the drugs or insecticides (Holden, 1999: 428).

References

Ahuja, V. (2004), "The Economic Rationale of Public and Private Sector Roles in the Provision of Animal Health Services", OIE *Revue Scientifique et Technique*, 2004, 23 (1), p. 33-45.

Alleweldt, F. (2013), "Cost sharing in compensation schemes", in: *Livestock Disease policies: Building Bridges Between Science and Economics,* OECD Publishing, Paris, www.oecd.org/tad/agricultural-policies/livestock-diseases-2013.htm.

Animal Health Australia (2016a), "Emergency animal disease activities in Australia", on-line www.animalhealthaustralia.com.au/what-we-do/emergency-animal-disease/.

Animal Health Australia (2016b), "National Livestock Identification System", on-line www.animalhealthaustralia.com.au/what-we-do/biosecurity-services/national-livestock-identification-scheme/.

Bicknell, K.B., J.E. Wilen and R.E. Howitt (1999), "Public policy and private incentives for livestock disease control", *Australian Journal of Agricultural and Resource Economics*, Vol 43, pp. 501-521.

Cleaveland, S., M.K. Laurenson and L.H. Taylor (2001), "Disease of humans and their domestic mammals: pathogen characteristics, host range and the risk of emergence", *Philosophical Transactions of the Royal Society of London, Series B* 356, pp. 991-999.

Daszak, P., A.A. Cunningham and A.D. Hyatt (2000), "Emerging infectious diseases of wildlife-threats to biodiversity and human health", *Science,* Vol. 287, pp. 443-449.

Edmunds, K.L., P.R. Hunter, R. Few, and D.J. Bell (2013), "Hazard analysis of critical control points assessment as a tool to respond to emerging infectious disease outbreaks", *PLoS One*, http://dx.doi.org/10.1371/journal.pone.0072279.

Heffernan, C., L. Nielsen, K. Thompson and G. Gunn (2008), "An exploration of drivers to bio-security collective action among a sample of UK cattle and sheep farmers", *Preventive Veterinary Medicine*, Vol. 87, pp. 358-372.

Hennessy, D.A. (2005), "Biosecurity and Infectious Disease", *CARD Working Paper* 05-WP 413, Center for Agricultural and Rural Development, Iowa State University, Ames, November.

Holden, S. (1999), "The economics of the delivery of veterinary services," OIE *Revue Scientifique et Technique*, 1999, Vol. 18 (2), p. 425-439.

Horan, R.D., C.A. Wolf, E.P. Fenichel and K.H. Mathews Jr. (2005), "Spatial Management of Wildlife Disease", *Review of Agricultural Economics,* Vol. 27, pp.483-490.

Horan, R.D., C.A. Wolf, E.P. Fenichel and K.H. Mathews Jr. (2008), "Joint Management of Wildlife and Livestock Disease", *Environmental and Resource Economics*, Vol. 41, pp. 47–70.

Horan, R.D., E.P. Fenichel, C.A. Wolf and B.M. Gramig (2010). "Managing Infectious Animal Disease Systems", *Annual Review of Resource Economics*, Vol. 2, pp. 101-124.

Kimura, S. and J. Antón (2011), "Risk Management in Agriculture in Australia", *OECD Food, Agriculture and Fisheries Papers*, No. 39, OECD Publishing, Paris, http://dx.doi.org/10.1787/5kgj0d8bj3d1-en.

Liebler, J.H., J. Otte, D. Roland-Holst, D.U. Pfeiffer, R. Soares Magalhaes, J. Rushton, J.P. Graham and E.K. Silbergeld (2009), "Industrial food animal production and global health risks: exploring the ecosystems and economics of avian influenza", *EcoHealth,* Vol. 6, pp. 58–70.

Melyukhina, O. (2011), "Risk management in agriculture in the Netherlands", *OECD Food, Agriculture and Fisheries Papers*, No. 41, OECD Publishing, Paris, http://dx.doi.org/10.1787/5kgj0d5lqn48-en.

Meuwissen, M.P.M., A.G.J. Velthuis, H. Hogeveen and R.B.M. Huirne (2003), "Traceability and certification in meat supply chains", *Journal of Agribusiness*, Vol. 21, pp. 167-181.

Meat and Livestock Australia (2016), *About the National Livestock Identification System*,

OECD (2013), *Providing Public Agri-environmental Goods through Collective Action*, OECD Publishing, Paris, http://dx.doi.org/10.1787/9789264197213-en

OECD (2012a), *Farmer Behaviour, Agricultural Management and Climate Change*, OECD Publishing, Paris, http://dx.doi.org/10.1787/9789264167650-en

OECD (2012b), *Livestock Diseases: Prevention, Control and Compensation Schemes*, OECD Publishing, Paris, http://dx.doi.org/10.1787/9789264178762-en

OECD (2011), *Managing Risk in Agriculture: Policy Assessment and Design*, OECD Publishing, Paris, http://dx.doi.org/10.1787/9789264116146-en

Olson, M. (1965), *The Logic of Collective Action,* Harvard University Press, Cambridge.

Pearce-Duvet, J.M.C. (2006), "The origin of human pathogens: evaluating the role of agriculture and domestic animals in the evolution of human disease", *Biological Reviews*, Vol. 81, pp. 369-382.

Radunz, B. (2006), "Surveillance and risk management during the latter stages of eradication: Experiences from Australia", *Veterinary Microbiology*, Vol. 112, pp. 283-290.

Scott, J., ed. (2014), *A Dictionary of Sociology*, 4th edition, Oxford University Press, New York, NY.

The Economist (2005), "Infection: The usual suspects", Nov. 19, pp. 96-97.

Vanni, F. (2014), *Agriculture and Public Goods: The Role of Collective Action*, Springer, Science and Business Media, Dordrecht.

Waller, P.J. (2006), "From discovery to development: Current industry perspectives from the development of novel methods of helminth control in livestock", *Veterinary Parasitology*, Vol. 139, pp. 1-14.

Part 2

Case studies in livestock disease management

Chapter 5

Case study in livestock disease management: Australia

This case study begins with a contextual overview of the livestock sector and animal health situation in Australia, and then focuses on the following aspects: government awareness of producer behaviour in livestock disease management; information, education and training for producers; and producer compensation policy in Australia. The last section presents the conclusions and policy recommendations.

5.1. Overview of the livestock sector and animal health situation in Australia

Structural characteristics and economic importance of livestock production

About 70% of Australia is arid or semi-arid, and a large part of the land is pastoral and suited only for low-intensity grazing. Livestock farming is thus predominantly an extensive production system with pasture being the principal source of feed. There is a low prevalence of intensive systems although they are becoming more common (DA, 2016; ACCC, 2016; PwC, 2011).[1] Among livestock operations, beef cattle and sheep breeding dominate: 54% of all Australian farms keep meat cattle, 32% sheep and lambs, and only 7% of farms have dairy cattle. Pig and poultry, associated with intensive systems, are relatively rare: only 5% of agricultural establishments are involved in egg production, 1% raise chickens for meat, and 1% pigs (ABS, 2016a).

Livestock production generates about half of agricultural output value and export value. Beef, sheep meat, and wool are the principal exports and accounted for almost three-quarters of the total value of livestock exports in 2014/15 (ABARES, 2016a). In 2014/15, Australia was the third largest exporter of beef, the largest exporter of mutton, the second largest of lamb, and the largest exporter of wool (Whittle et al., 2015). The exposure of these industries to trade is significant. Of the total volumes produced in 2014/15, the exported shares covered 74% for beef and veal, 56% for lamb, 95% for mutton (MLA, 2015a; MLA, 2015b), and nearly the entire production of wool (ABARES, 2016a). Dairy is also an important export sector, but the domestic market absorbs around two-thirds of total milk production (DA, 2016). Other livestock industries – chicken meat, eggs, and pig meat – are oriented at domestic market, meeting most of domestic consumption (USDA, 2016; AECL, 2015).

Livestock production is generally specialised along livestock types with the exception of sheep. Around 86% of total meat cattle are reared on specialised beef farms which generate 84% of all their cash receipts from beef cattle sales. While an average beef farm is estimated to have around 900 heads of beef cattle, the establishments differ greatly in size and can become very large.[2] Dairying is similarly a highly specialised industry: nearly all dairy cattle are concentrated in establishments which receive 87% of their total cash receipts from milk. An average dairy cattle herd is around 284 heads per farm, but there is a steady trend to very large operations of more than 1 000 heads of dairy cattle (DA, 2016). Poultry and egg production are the most specialised and vertically integrated activities. Unlike all other livestock industries, sheep breeding is typically a part of a diversified farming. Specialised sheep farms keep only 37% of total sheep number and receive less than half of their cash receipts from sheep (ABARES, 2016b). Nearly the same share of total sheep number (33%) is on farms with mixed crop-livestock production and another 17% on beef-and-sheep farms. The average sheep herd per farm ranges between around 2 000 heads on farms with mixed livestock production to 3 000 heads on specialised sheep farms (ABARES, 2016b). Structural profile of pig farming is not specifically informed beyond the total farm numbers and inventories (ABS, 2016a). A study of the Sydney region showed that pig production systems were predominantly intensive or semi-intensive (88%), with 69% of the operations being small hobby producers (Schembri et al., 2006).

Livestock farmers are relatively aged, with those at near-retirement (55 to under 65) and post-retirement age (over 65) constituting over half the operators in most livestock sub-sectors (Figure 5.1.A). These two age categories reach nearly 70% in beef, sheep, and beef-sheep farms – the farms constituting the largest part of livestock establishments. As a general trend, the Australian farm workforce has significantly aged – between 1981 and 2011 the proportion of farmers at 55 years and over increased from 26% to 47% (ABS, 2012). It may be assumed that this trend occurred also in the livestock sector. The formal education profile of livestock farmers seems to correlate with the age structure. Over half the farmers in the major livestock sectors have no specialised education, either at technical (vocational) or higher levels (Figure 5.1.B). The predominance of such farmers is particularly high in numerous beef and sheep operations. These features suggest that the livestock policy constituency in Australia is a rather aged and ageing group, most with no specialised education beyond high school.

Figure 5.1. Age and education profiles of livestock farmers in Australia

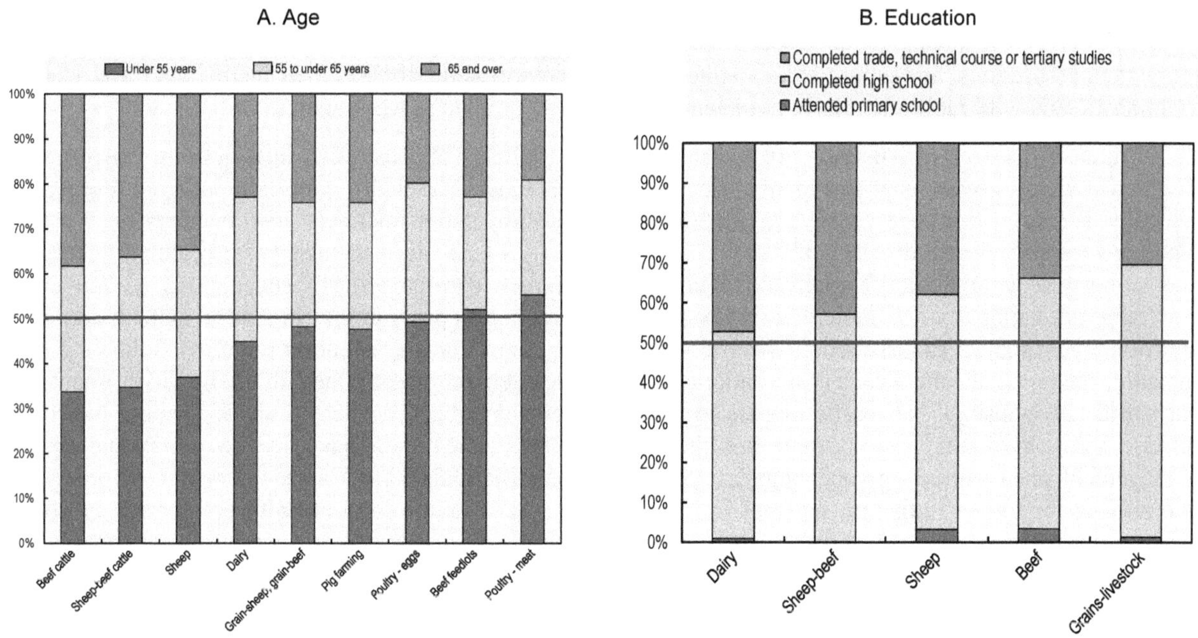

Source: Australian Government (2016) based on data of the Australian Bureau of Statistics.

Beef cattle and sheep breeders operate within a flexible marketing system, with spot deals representing the most frequent type of sales. In 2014/15, almost half of beef cattle and nearly 70% of sheep were sold through saleyard auctions (ABARES, 2016c).[3] The remaining animals are either delivered to abattoirs or sold from paddock, part of these sales also occur on a spot basis. Dairying falls under a more rigid contracting system. Farmer co-operatives handle around 40% of the national milk output and the rest is supplied to various milk processors, including multinationals such as Fonterra (New Zealand), Kirin (Japan), and Lactalis (France). Egg and chicken meat producers are part of highly integrated vertical systems. At the farm level, production is specialised on specific stages of the animal growth cycle and the majority of output is purchased by a small number of processors, who in turn supply a few major supermarkets and restaurant chains. For example, seven processors provide 95% of total chicken meat in Australia, of which the two largest produce 70% and the next five between 3% and 9% (ACMF, 2011). The differences in the marketing systems across the livestock sub-sectors suggest that in beef and sheep farming, where flexible arrangements prevail, on-farm disease management is largely a matter of the individual decisions of farm operators. In vertically integrated sectors, on-farm disease management is based on practices that are largely determined by downstream integrators to ensure the sanitary standards across the vertical production chain.

Overall situation related to livestock and animal disease risk

Australia, as an island, is free of many pests and diseases present elsewhere in the world. This provides the country a significant advantage in access to foreign agro-food markets. Given the high exposure of the livestock sector to trade, biosecurity is an area of particular importance. Considerable efforts involving stakeholders across the biosecurity continuum (pre-border, at the border, and post-border biosecurity activities) are made to maintain the country's good sanitary status.

A range of highly contagious animal diseases have been eradicated in Australia over the past decades. Taking the period since 2005, few outbreaks of OIE-notifiable diseases have occurred. The largest one was the equine influenza in 2007, with nearly 10 000 infected premises. Other occurrences were less widespread: low pathogenic avian influenza was diagnosed in 2012 (one infected premises) and 2013 (one infected premises); highly pathogenic avian influenza 2012 (one infected premises) and 2013 (two infected premises). Certain bluetongue virus serotypes have occurred in Australia, but they were not associated with clinical disease. Outbreaks reported to the OIE as Newcastle disease were caused by a pigeon paramyxovirus and were not eradicated – there have been no detections of this virus in poultry. From 2009, spillovers of the pandemic H1N1 influenza A have been detected in pigs and managed conservatively by quarantine, movement restrictions, and controlled slaughter. Rabbit haemorrhagic disease virus incursions have occurred in domestic and wild rabbits and have not been eradicated (Australian Government, 2016).

Endemic diseases in Australia are managed through policies of Australian jurisdictions, but for some diseases, national government and industry-led programmes exist. Nationally important endemic diseases are typically spread within one or several jurisdictions and some have relatively low occurrence. Australia distinguishes as endemic diseases of national significance (AHA, 2016a): anthrax (with regional occurrence and subject to national notification and compulsory control); carpine arthritis-encephalitis (found across Australia, not nationally notifiable, but with voluntary accreditation programmes in several states); cattle tick and tick fever (subject to jurisdiction-specific surveillance, control, and eradication regimes); Johne's disease in cattle, sheep, goats, and alpaca (with national disease management programmes involving governments and each affected industry); Newcastle disease in poultry (there have been no detections of virulent Newcastle disease virus in poultry since 2001, but the two incidents since then have led to a national disease management plan centred on vaccination); ovine brucellosis (nationally notifiable, but with low prevalence and subject for the accreditation schemes in a number of states); ovine foot rot (with eradication or control programmes in several states); and swine brucellosis (a zoonotic disease that is present in feral pig populations in Queensland and New South Wales with low prevalence, with these states applying accredited herd scheme or movement control).

Figure 5.2. Economic impacts of endemic diseases in cattle and sheep in Australia: Diseases with the largest estimated losses

AUD million

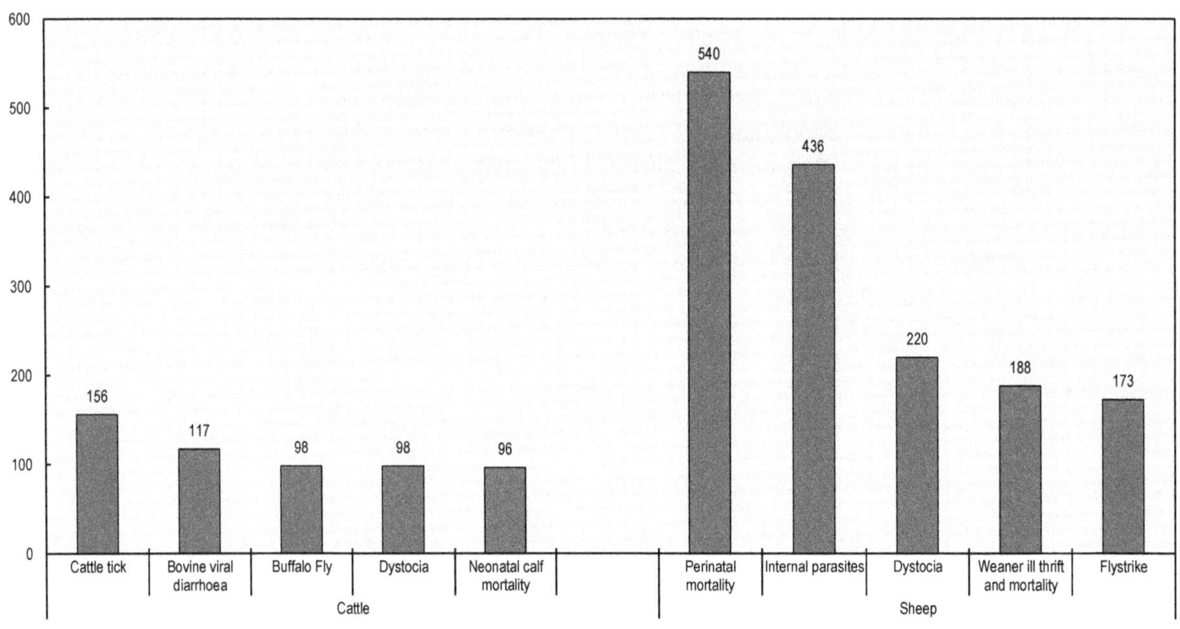

Note: The values shown are based on a model estimating the cost per herd/flock at the farm level for each disease. Costs were calculated for treatment, prevention and production losses. These results have been extrapolated across the regions in which each disease occurs, in line with adopted herd and flock demographics from Australian Bureau of Statistics Agricultural Commodities Statistics for 2010-11 to provide a national total cost estimate.

Source: MLA (2015c).

Research commissioned by Meat & Livestock Australia Ltd. (MLA, 2015c) estimated the economic impacts of endemic diseases. The study used the responses from producer, government and industry surveys, and discussions with the MLA to prioritise 17 most important diseases in cattle, 23 sheep and 9 goat diseases. A model was then used to evaluate the economic costs of these diseases. The five most economically important ones in cattle and sheep are shown in Figure 5.2. The results suggest that endemic diseases in sheep may have potentially the greatest economic impacts on the livestock industry overall.

Key institutions involved in livestock disease issues within country borders

Australia's biosecurity system manages pest and disease risks across a biosecurity continuum with an emphasis on prevention, preparedness and early intervention of pests and diseases with activities undertaken offshore, at the border and onshore. Australia's animal health system is distinctive in that it is based on a partnership between the Australian government, state and territory governments, and private stakeholders. Key institutions dealing with domestic biosecurity issues and interacting with the farmer community within Australia are presented below.

The Australian Government Department of Agriculture and Water Resources represent federal government in the national animal health system. It is responsible for international animal health matters, including biosecurity, export certification and trade, and disease reporting to the World Organisation for Animal Health (OIE). Six Divisions of this Department cover specific areas of biosecurity: Biosecurity Animal Division, Australian Chief Veterinary Office, Biosecurity Policy and Implementation Division, Compliance Division, Exports Division, and Service Delivery Division.

The state and territory governments are responsible for animal health within their borders. They develop and administer legislation relating to surveillance, control, investigation and reporting of diseases; chemical residues and contaminants; and animal welfare. They also deliver services through government-appointed or government-accredited animal health personnel. Nearly 13 000 government and private veterinarians and other health personnel work across the country, together with over a 1 000 stock and meat inspectors (AHA, 2016a).

Animal Health Australia (AHA) is a unique institution underpinning the partnership organisation of the national animal health system. AHA is a not-for-profit public company uniting 32 member organisations (Annex 5.A1):

- The Commonwealth: Department of Agriculture and Water Resources.
- State and territory governments: Departments of Primary Industries or Departments of Agriculture.
- Industry organisations: 14 associations representing relevant livestock sub-sectors.
- Service providers: Australian Veterinary Association and the Australian Animal Health Laboratory of the Commonwealth Scientific and Industrial Research Organisation (CSIRO).
- Associate members: representatives from livestock and milk product exporters, Wildlife Health Australia, and some others.

Animal Health Australia co-ordinates national livestock animal health programmes encompassing areas of disease surveillance, domestic biosecurity services, emergency response to animal disease, endemic disease programmes, and livestock welfare (Annex 5.A2). Most of these activities engage various AHA membership groups in the development and implementation of the measures, and cost-sharing. The Australian government, state and territory governments, and industry parties contribute equal shares to the AHA's core funding, while specific initiatives can be funded through additional stakeholders' subscriptions.

SAFEMEAT is another partnership between the red meat and livestock industry and the state and federal governments; it focusses on standards of safety and hygiene (SAFEMEAT, 2016). SAFEMEAT initiates research, support communication, and monitors the status of meat products. It reviews and promotes the rationalisation of industry food safety regulations and standards, and monitors industry performance in these areas. This partnership covers all stages and actors from the farm to consumer. In what concerns farm and feedlot level, SAFEMEAT is engaged in the development and implementation of programmes such as the Livestock Production Assurance (LPA), LPA National Vendor Declaration and Waybill, National Livestock Identification System (NLIS), and the National Feedlot Accreditation Scheme (NFAS). It is also involved in activities related to the saleyard, transportation and meat processing stages.

Wildlife Health Australia (WHA) is an institution embodying the same partnership principle of biosecurity in the area of wildlife. It complements livestock health activities by investigating and reporting on the health of wild native and feral animals. WHA brings together people, groups and agencies working in these fields at different levels of government, in the private and public sectors (WHA, 2016).

Consultative Committees of the Australian Government Department of Agriculture and Water Resources involve a broad range of stakeholders. They report to the Committee of Agricultural Senior Officials and include the National Biosecurity Committee, Animal Welfare Task Group, Animal Health Committee, and SAFEMEAT. These consultative groups operate to support the cohesion of the biosecurity system and co-ordination between all parties involved in animal biosecurity (AHA, 2016a).

5.2. Government's activity to increase awareness about farmer behaviour

Private operators are the ultimate decision makers of farm enterprises. Evidence about farmer behaviour and their response to policy is thus a necessary input into policy making, including in the area of animal disease.

Availability of information about farmers undertaking livestock activities

As a starting point, governments require sufficient information about the number, structural and social characteristics of the farming community they engage with. This information should have adequate national coverage and consistency. The Australian Bureau of Statistics (ABS) and Australian Bureau of Agricultural and Resource Economics and Sciences (ABARES) are the principal generators of this information. ABS undertakes an agricultural census every five years; it also releases annually updated national data on livestock populations, the number of holdings and other characteristics based on the ABS Agricultural Commodities Survey and the biennium Land Management Practices Survey, which includes collection of livestock numbers, as well as livestock and pasture management.

ABARES carries out extensive farm survey work.[4] Overall, 12 farm surveys are performed, most of them on an annual basis and for specific farm industries.[5]The surveys of broadacre and dairy industries cover grazing livestock producers and provide information on livestock inventories, herd structure, farm financial indicators and receipts, land area, marketing methods, and socioeconomic characteristics, such as age of farm owner and spouse, and hours worked on- and off-farm. ABARES surveys, however, do not include poultry and pig meat industries, which involve only a small proportion of livestock establishments and are not export-oriented sectors. These industries are monitored within the limits of the Australian Bureau of Statistics work plan. No detailed structural studies of these sectors are undertaken on a regular basis, as is done for grazing industries. This may reflect a reduced interest in socioeconomic observation of these sectors due to their highly corporatized structure.

There is a lack of information about farmers undertaking livestock activity not included in the official statistical observation. Both five-year ABS Agricultural Census and annual Rural Environment and Agricultural Commodities Survey cover agricultural businesses with an Estimated Value of Agricultural Operations (EVAO) of AUD 5 000 (ABS, 2016b; ABS 2016c). This leaves the establishments below this threshold – very small businesses and hobby farmers with some livestock – outside official statistical collections. The proportion of beef cattle and sheep on these establishments is estimated to be very small – less than 1%. However, for some livestock types, such as horses, the proportion is likely to be more significant. The evidence about the biosecurity risk that these very small establishments present is limited. However, Beach et al. (2007) note that non-commercial husbandry is frequently identified by health agencies as a risk to the commercial sector even if it accounts for a negligible production share.

Funded research into farmer behaviour

Supporting behavioural research allows the government to build awareness about farmer decision making. Since the mid-2000s, Australian and state governments have funded several studies on animal disease management as well as social rural studies, which, among other issues, examined aspects of livestock farmer behaviour (Annex 5.A3). This work focussed on specific diseases (e.g. FMD or avian influenza), specific geographic areas, and animal types (pigs, horses, or poultry), but provided a number of behaviour-related findings with potentially broader implications:

- Strong influence of risk perceptions on farmers' biosecurity decisions and disease reporting (Palmer et al., 2009; Taylor et al., 2016).
- Poor uptake of recommended practices by (horse) farmers (Taylor et al., 2016).
- Insufficient farmer knowledge on emergency animal diseases or a lack of information (Schembri et al., 2006; Schembri et al., 2016; Hernandez-Jover et al., 2014).
- Reporting by producers can act as a barrier to early identification of (FMD) disease (Matthews, 2011).
- Little knowledge about how farmers obtain information on emergency animal disease (Hernandez-Jover et al., 2014).
- Veterinarians are farmers' trusted sources of information, strongly influencing farmer biosecurity intentions, a finding which is similar to studies in other countries (Taylor et al., 2016).
- A lack of trust in government sources, e.g. scientific institutions linked to the government, a finding which is similar to studies in other countries (Palmer et al., 2009).

A general policy implication from the studies above was the need to adapt communication between government and farmers on biosecurity, including moving from generic messaging towards more specific information to target groups and interacting more actively with veterinarians as policy outreach channels. Other issues were trust building between livestock farmers and government, and increased engagement of local communities in biosecurity. Finally, the gaps in farmers' knowledge about animal disease were diagnosed in specific contexts, which implied the need to identify these gaps more comprehensively, in particular, to adapt the existing extension programmes. Furthermore, the difficulties that farmers demonstrated in understanding the roles of different actors in biosecurity, including emergency situations, indicated the need for better co-ordination and communication about these roles with farmers. Practical steps undertaken since include the creation of a Biosecurity Incident Communication Network and the preparation of a producer guide for planning business risks from emergency disease outbreaks, and the funding for further policy development related to (FMD) vaccination, training for veterinarians, surveillance and community engagement.

In developing the research discussed above, and other feedback (see below), two studies were recently conducted, both funded by the Australian Government Department of Agriculture and Water Resources through the national facilities for priority R&D. The study by BehaviourWorks Australia on "Development of behaviour change strategies for animal disease surveillance and reporting" (Wright et al., 2016) looks at producer risk perceptions, barriers to surveillance, attitudes to surveillance and reporting, knowledge about animal diseases, and trusted sources of information. This research is to be used to review and fine-tune surveillance policy, and create more sustainable partnership-based approaches to surveillance. This project is notable as an effort to develop policy aiming producer behaviour change. It is also instructive in terms of substantive findings and organisation (Annex 5.A4). The other study is the "National survey of agricultural landholders—common established pest animals and weeds", the purpose of which is to measure the level of awareness among the landholders and the community on the benefits of disease management and the costs of inaction. This study is also expected to feed into the development of animal health policy.

Awareness through interaction with industry organisations

Governments at all levels in Australia operate as part of the partnership-based biosecurity system, which creates constant feedback flows from producer groups and other stakeholders to governments. More broadly, this constitutes overall consultative and participatory approach to policy making, open policy reviews, and policy impact assessments in Australia. Formal methods include: industry-government working groups or forums, public consultation (online written submissions), focus groups, stakeholder workshops, and consultations through Animal Health Australia and the Livestock Biosecurity Network. Informal methods include: discussion or email with industry representatives and other stakeholders, monitoring online producer or industry media and participating in social media. An example of how feedback from industry to government is used is the national Ovine Johne's Disease Management Plan (2013-18) which is the result of extended consultations between Sheepmeat Council of Australia (SCA), WoolProducers Australia (WPA), state departments of primary industry and other stakeholders. Another example is the National Sheep Health Monitoring Project where the list of health conditions to be monitored in abattoirs was agreed among the sheep industry peak councils, Animal Health Committee and the Australian Meat Industry Council.

Animal Health Australia interacts with producer and industry organisations to obtain evidence about farmer behaviour and attitudes, and shares this information with the government. Regular Farm Biosecurity Surveys is one such activity, undertaken in co-operation with Plant Health Australia, an analogous institution in the phytosanitary area. The most recent survey in 2013 covered 1 273 producers, but did not include hobby or "lifestyle" farmers (Farm Biosecurity, 2016a). These surveys are an instrument to inform policymaking about actual producer behaviour. They look into farmers' use of different sources of animal health information, how they rank their usefulness and trustworthiness, the preferred ways to access information, and farmers' awareness of key biosecurity information resources. This instrument is also used to identify the employment by farmers of different biosecurity practices, and their attitudes to reporting disease (Annex 5.A5).

Awareness through interaction with veterinarians

Veterinarians are in direct contact with producers and can be key sources for increasing evidence about farmer behaviour. They have an understanding about the adequacy of on-farm disease prevention, farmers' risk perceptions, their awareness about various disease risk management practices and attitudes towards these practices, and what enables or impedes their adoption. Veterinarians can clarify farmers' contact with them and also reasons for no interaction.

There are no routine arrangements for interacting with veterinarians on these issues, e.g. focussed surveys of veterinarians, or regular questionnaires. A range of general means to communicate with veterinarians exists, including working groups, the public consultation process and scientific and media events. Many government-appointed veterinarians have past experience working with producers or work directly with them. Animal Health Australia and the Livestock Biosecurity Network employ veterinarians and animal health officers to formulate and adjust producer and veterinary education and training programmes (e.g. about biosecurity, disease surveillance, emergency disease management), especially for priority target groups (e.g. livestock exhibitors) or to develop policy around specific issues (e.g. swill feeding, the use of antibiotics in livestock and measuring antibiotic use).

5.3. Communication, information and training for farmers

Information and education influence all aspects of farmer decision-making. Appropriate communication and information about disease existence, its identification, consequences, costs and benefits of control and prevention programmes, responsibilities and policies enables farmers to make well-informed decisions and ensure diseases are managed effectively.

Communication and information

According to the 2013 Farm Biosecurity Survey by Animal Health Australia, producers seek and gather information from a variety of sources. Veterinarians are the most frequent source (reported by close to one-third of respondents), followed by the state departments of primary industries (23%), industry bodies (17%), suppliers (17%), and internet (15%). The share of farmers who understand biosecurity as a set of measures to protect farm production has increased notably since the previous survey. However, around one-fifth of respondents indicated, without any prompting, that they did not know the meaning of the term "biosecurity", while almost the same percentage understood it as "border protection or quarantine" (Farm Biosecurity, 2016a). A large share of farmers thus lacked the understanding of biosecurity consistent with how it is currently used by policy makers: as a range of "measures to protect farm production from disease, pest and weeds". This may be due to the fact that this term is relatively recent, but it can also imply that many farmers may not be capable of identifying and using all the information about animal biosecurity that they may actually need.

A variety of national, regional, and industry channels provide information on animal biosecurity. Possibly, the most comprehensive is the Farm Biosecurity website operated as a joint initiative of Animal Health Australia (AHA) and Plant Health Australia (PHA). It is targeted to farmers and includes information about diseases, pest and weed risks, what they can do to reduce those risks and how. It provides materials to help producers implement good biosecurity on their property (Farm Biosecurity, 2016b). Users can create their "biosecurity toolkits" – i.e. the information can be filtered by topic, farm specialisation type, or animal type – as well as receive electronic newsletters. State and territory governments maintain biosecurity pages on the official websites of their departments of primary industries or departments of agriculture; beyond national issues, these pages provide information customised to jurisdictions, for example state-specific disease control policies and state animal programmes. All peak industry bodies include information on animal health in their on-line communication with members. It is typically focussed on areas specific to the profession, i.e. particular livestock diseases, national disease programmes of relevance to industry, or industry disease initiatives (e.g. Livestock Assurance Programme, or National Livestock Identification System).

Thus, many providers at different administrative levels and multiple industry groups are involved in communicating biosecurity information. One issue in this respect is to understand the degree to which farmers use various channels and to identify the most effective ones to communicate with producers. For example, the 2013 survey indicated that 90% of surveyed farmers had access to internet, but that only 48% used it daily and 17% obtained biosecurity information from the internet. Somewhat less than two-thirds of livestock producers did not know about the national Farm Biosecurity website (Farm Biosecurity, 2016a). Another issue is a lack of co-ordinated management, so duplication and lack of harmonisation may occur across the different levels of government, as well as between industry and government, and Animal Health Australia. A co-ordination initiative was the creation of the Biosecurity Incident National Communication Network (NCN). Its purpose is to produce nationally consistent public information about the response to pest and disease outbreaks (biosecurity incidents). The core network consists of communication managers from the broad range of government and industry bodies involved in biosecurity (NCN, 2016).[6]

The content of biosecurity information to best respond to producer needs is another area for consideration. Some evidence about farmer information needs is available from the Farm Biosecurity Surveys by Animal Health Australia. The 2013 survey found that the most frequently sought information by farmers was the "biosecurity warnings and alerts". Disease emergencies and risk awareness are indeed a strong focus of animal health communication to farmers. The National Pest and Disease Outbreaks website provides public information about current emergency animal disease outbreaks and the Biosecurity Incident National Communication Network explains policies and practices. Several state animal health departments distribute newsletters which report notifiable disease cases in their region. Ausvetplan contains detailed emergency guidelines and sets out control and eradication strategies for each disease, operational manuals, and reporting requirements. However, recent research identified the need for further work on information around compensation.

While there is active communication with farmers on veterinary and sanitary issues, there seems to be less emphasis on economic aspects of disease management. Behavioural analysis has demonstrated that economic considerations are often the strongest drivers of disease management decisions and producer views about cost-efficiency of practices can be a principal factor to take up or ignore recommended measures. Communication with producers should include information to help them understand the cost and benefits of disease management decisions. This is facilitated if the information is tailored to farmers' particular circumstances, for example through decision-support tools, e.g. worksheets or web-based tools. An example of tailored decision-support communication is the "Tools and Calculators" offered by Meat & Livestock Australia for red meat producers.[7] Another type of economic information which is important to convey is the one that helps farmers understand the economic impacts of animal disease on farm enterprise. Studies by Productivity Commission (2002), and most recently by ABARES (Hafi et al., 2015), take steps in this direction. The latter study estimated what the authors called "the value of biosecurity at farm gate", or the effect of a disease outbreak on annual farm enterprise profits (or gross margins).[8] It is also important to communicate to farmers the broader effects of potential disease outbreaks – on the livestock sector as a whole, upstream and downstream industries, consumers and local communities. Some research has been undertaken in Australia on these issues, but the base of the impact analysis could be increased to support communication to different groups (specialisations) of farmers on a variety of disease issues. This would likely require going beyond one-time impact studies, and possibly conducting a longer-term research programme that involves research centres and the Australian Department of Agriculture and Water Resources.

Disease related information programmes are currently not comprehensively assessed by government, except that with online information campaigns, the number of website hits/views/shares/comments is counted. Many of these programmes have top-down, one-way communications (rather than collaborative efforts) because this involves relatively low costs in addition to the fact that there is a lack of expertise in engagement and effective communication measurement (Australian Government, 2016). Government-funded research recently undertaken by BehaviourWorks (Wright et al., 2016) has, as one of its themes, improved animal health communication and is expected to be used in communication development (Australian Government, 2016).

Education and training

Producers with good basic competencies, as well as a technical and business education can be expected to make better informed decisions. They tend to look for and adopt new practices (OECD, 2010). There is also evidence of a positive correlation between levels of education and cognitive skills (Pearson, 2016), which implies that those with a better education may be less susceptible to cognitive failure when making decisions.

The share of owner-operators with special education – technical and tertiary – varies between 30% in mixed grains-livestock farms to 47% in dairying. Amongst those who have a high school education, around half only completed one to four years (Australian Government, 2016). This likely compares favourably to similar groups at an international scale, given Australia's overall high education status. Nevertheless, these data also show that owner-operators without special education prevail in Australian livestock industry. Formal education is not the only determinant of managerial capacity and skills, but general concerns about supply of skills are raised by the representatives of the agro-food industry. This challenge is increased by the population outflow from rural areas, particularly among young people, and the rapidly ageing workforce (OECD, 2015).

Education and training in animal health in Australia is decentralised across state and territory governments, Animal Health Australia, as well as industry groups, and the education sector. Topics, financing and organisation vary according to jurisdiction, the type of issue or disease and its priority, the scope of the programme (whether national or regional), and the stakeholders involved. In terms of funding, some programmes, particularly those administered by Animal Health Australia, are financed through levies from the beneficiary industries and contributions are sought from governments and industry. Other programmes are initiatives taken by industry, financed and organised by a peak industry body. The state of New South Wales is unique in that it has a Local Lands Services system which socialises the cost of programmes in regional areas within this state (Australian Government, 2016).

Animal Health Australia carries out training with national outreach. It focusses on emergency animal disease and targets responsible personnel in state and territory governments and the livestock industry, both producers and groups working with livestock. Training includes an online study, work-based tasks, and face-to-face workshops.

Industry groups promote training amongst their members. The majority of peak livestock bodies provide information to members on courses available externally at educational institutions. Some industry bodies develop and deliver their own extension and training programmes. Meat & Livestock Australia Ltd. offers probably the most extensive one. Australian Egg Corporation Limited (AECL) also organises its own training programmes. Other industry bodies operate more simple formats, such as livestock shows, e.g. the Australian Alpaca Association. The Livestock Biosecurity Network (LBN) was recently created as an industry initiative to fill a perceived gap due to reduced government extension services.[9] It represents a network of regional extension offices in four Australian states (Northern Australia, Victoria, Tasmania and New South Wales). LBN personnel give presentations on various topics of animal health at agricultural events across Australia.

An examination of the on-line pages of state agricultural departments shows that only a few contain a rubric on farmer training, suggesting this activity is not a significant focus of the state-level government. However, an example of state engagement is the PROfarm courses delivered by the Department of Primary Industries in New South Wales. Many of these courses are subsidised through the Local Lands Services system mentioned above. On-demand courses tailored to the specific needs of individual groups can also be organised. Another example is the State of Tasmania Department of Primary Industries, Parks, Water and Environment which promotes training through TasTAFE, the largest state-owned vocational education and training provider in Tasmania. In both New South Wales and Tasmania, the training concerns general animal husbandry with no specific courses in animal disease management.

In sum, it is difficult to generalise about the overall structure of programmes and the spending on farmer education and training in animal health. This activity is highly decentralised across a wide range of levels and providers. Training with a national scope focusses on disease emergencies and rapid response. Livestock industry groups provide information on the opportunities available at various educational providers as well as their own training programmes. The involvement of state and territory governments in farmer training, at least at the level of the bodies responsible for agriculture, seems to be limited, except in a few jurisdictions. The training beyond disease emergencies, e.g. related to "peace time" issues of disease prevention and good husbandry, is likely a matter of private initiatives by farmers. The degree to which farmers undertake training requires further examination.

5.4. Current experience with farmer compensation policy

Compensation is the principal economic instrument of livestock policy with a direct impact on producer incentives and actions to manage disease risk. Compensation is understood in this case study to be any payment or reimbursement provided to farmers within the framework of disease control and prevention programmes. This includes (i) indemnity for direct disease losses, such as dead or destroyed animals; (ii) compensation for consequential losses, such as those from business interruption; and (iii) payments for farmer *ex ante* actions, such as subsidising biosecurity investments and operations. This part examines the degree to which Australia's compensation policy stimulates or discourages producers to make adequate efforts to prevent disease and report it in a timely fashion when it occurs.

Owners of livestock in Australia may be eligible for compensation in the case of an animal disease emergency. The response to an outbreak is generally determined and managed by state or territory legislation, processes and procedures; however there is provision in Commonwealth legislation for the Australian government to lead a response under certain circumstances. Compensation is to be paid to an owner of any livestock or property destroyed for the purpose of eradication or prevention of the spread of an emergency disease and any dead livestock that would have been otherwise compulsorily slaughtered. The jurisdictions can share these costs with the parties to the Emergency Animal Disease Response Agreement if compensation falls under the scope of this agreement and provided that it is included in the emergency response plan adopted for a particular outbreak case.

The Emergency Animal Disease Response Agreement (EADRA) is a unique contract between the Australian, state and territory governments and livestock industry groups to prepare for—and respond to—emergency animal disease incursions. It has 23 signatories and covers 61 categorised diseases. It is a comprehensive *ex ante* framework to deal with animal disease emergencies. EADRA embodies a set of government-industry agreements which in broad terms establish the baseline for biosecurity, requirements for disclosure of incursion, standard actions to control and eradicate disease, and financial commitments of the parties to contribute to disease response costs. Detailed modalities underpin these agreements (Table 5.1).

EADRA is an arrangement that explicitly delineates the public, collective (industry), and private roles in disease management. First, it employs the concept of "normal/acceptable business risk" to set the frontier between the costs to be borne by an individual producer, on one hand, and government and producer groups, on the other. Second, the principle of cost-sharing between government and industries is based on the notion of externalities, or the consequences of a farm disease incident on external parties. The externality concept is EADRA's instrument to determine the parties affected by a disease and thus the beneficiaries of any response to this event. The government's financial burden increases as the estimated impact of a disease across the economy and society broadens. This is established through the categorisation of diseases, from those with potentially the broadest human health and socio-economic consequences to those whose impacts are limited to specific industries. Four disease categories are distinguished on this basis, with the government's share of total outbreak response costs ranging from 100% (category 1) to 20% (category 4).

EADRA creates disincentives for moral hazard because producers, if affected, would share the financial burden to control an outbreak. The connection to cost-sharing is straightforward, as the incident would trigger a "disease response levy" on producers (except the case where costs are fully borne by government). Although the largely *ex post* nature of the levy may eliminate some potential for awareness raising amongst livestock holders, there is substantial communication to increase risk awareness (OECD, 2012). Moral hazard is also controlled through regulation, particularly in cases where the government bears the total or the majority of the financial burden (i.e. for disease categories 1 and 2). This includes the formal commitment by EADRA industry parties to risk mitigation, which in practice is implemented through their obligation to develop industry biosecurity plans and the requirement for farmer-members to have individual biosecurity plans. There is also a conditionality attached to compensation of no illegal behaviour or failure to adhere to standards.

There is a strict requirement by EADRA to report diseases: industry parties should instruct their members to notify the applicable authority within 24 hours of becoming aware of an incident. Government parties, on their part, are obliged to give formal notification to the Consultative Committee on Emergency Animal Disease within 24 hours of becoming aware of an incident. Any failure to comply means that a jurisdiction may cease to be eligible for cost-sharing under EADRA. This mechanism establishes a common responsibility for the parties to report early, as well as creating a strong financial incentive to do so. An additional economic incentive is the possibility that a top-up payment beyond the initial compensation will be provided if on the day when the property becomes eligible to be restocked this is more expensive than the payment received for dead or culled livestock. The cost-sharing provides additional economic incentive for disease reporting because farmers are encouraged to report early so as to contain any incursion and resulting levy collection. Animal Health Australia reports there has been no misbehaviour of producers related to disclosure of disease (OECD, 2012).

EADRA does not foresee compensation for consequential losses. In this respect, one group for which negative incentives may potentially be created is livestock owners subject to movement restrictions who are not eligible for compensation for lost animals but may experience consequential loss. Possible negative incentives related to consequential losses are addressed to a certain extent through guaranteeing a rapid response and the requirement that restricted areas should not be larger than is epidemiologically required to prevent the spread of infection (e.g. restricted areas should not simply be determined by administrative borders) (OECD, 2012).

Table 5.1. Key components of Australia's Emergency Animal Disease Response Agreement

Incentive aspects	Modalities
Existence of a framework which sets out potential set of response actions	Australian Veterinary Emergency Plan (Ausvetplan) is a national response plan for the management and eradication of emergency diseases. It contains detailed control and eradication strategies for 35 most significant emergency diseases and policy response briefs for 27 other emergency diseases. It explains policy and rationale, and recommended operational procedures, such as quarantine and movement controls.
Cost-sharing agreement between the parties	1. All parties commit to contribute to funding the eligible costs of response to an emergency by which they are affected. 2. Cost-sharing does not apply to activities: (i) considered "normal" and carried out by a Lead Agency's normal biosecurity commitments; these are considered as a baseline above which other costs can be shared; each state or territory is obliged to define costa that are considered 'normal'; (ii) considered to be part of normal/acceptable business risk; (iii) consequential loss (costs not directly related to the response); (iv) recovery costs related to outbreak; these are managed outside disease control legislation and procedures. 3. Upper cost limit for cost-sharing: each party's proportional share of 1% of the gross value of production of the industry(ies) affected by the emergency (2% in the case of foot-and-mouth disease). Once this threshold is reached, the National Management Group would discuss increasing the limit, continuing the response, changing agreed cost-sharing proportions or revising the emergency animal disease response plan. 4. Costs are covered by government and industry in proportions that change depending on the scale of potential externality effects of disease: the higher these effects are the higher government's share is and lower the industry's share. (see Annex 5.A6 for further detail) 5. Formulae for cost-sharing between governments within the government total share and industries within the industry total share (see Annex 5.A6 for further detail).
Industry arrangements to meet cost-sharing obligation	The Commonwealth may initially meet an industry's cost-sharing obligations, which industry should then repay to the Commonwealth – usually within a ten-year period. At the same time, each industry party must ensure that it meets its cost-sharing obligations. An "emergency animal disease response levy" can be established for that purpose. Usually, it is set to zero and activated only in an incident. This is, however, not the only option, and one industry party has chosen a fixed amount held in reserve, which provides the greatest flexibility in adjusting levy rates to suit particular needs.
Stakeholder-consulted and approved Emergency Animal Disease Response Plan	The Plan is developed by the state or territory chief veterinary officer(s) in whose jurisdiction(s) the emergency incident has occurred. It must be prepared in accordance with a specific schedule and follow certain procedures: in particular, it must be endorsed by a consultative committee of technical representatives of the parties and subsequently approved by a higher level group of affected parties, the National Management Group.
Explicit rules for the scope and valuation of livestock holder compensation (see Annex 5.A7 for further detail)	1. Any livestock or property that is destroyed for the purpose of eradication or prevention of the spread of the emergency disease, and any livestock that has died of emergency disease. Compensation also covers damaged or destroyed farm equipment and destroyed product. 2. The livestock and property for compensation are valued at market value. A "topping-up" provision is also included for livestock: if the livestock prove to be more expensive to be replaced on the day that the property becomes eligible to be restocked, a second payment ("top up payment") may be available.
Disease reporting obligations of parties	The parties to EADRA must notify the relevant government authority within 24 hours of becoming aware of an emergency incident. Failure to do that may trigger no cost-sharing of compensation under EADRA.
Biosecurity obligations of parties	Parties undertake biosecurity obligations to reduce the risk of an emergency incident. Animal Health Australia manages a national biosecurity planning and implementation programme under which industry parties develop industry biosecurity plans. Government parties are obliged to develop biosecurity statements outlining policies and programmes on feral animal, public health and environmental policies.

Source: EADRA (2016); AHA (2016c); OECD (2012).

Protocols and formal procedures are an important pillar of EADRA, influencing producer incentives in several ways. First, they reduce uncertainties for producers, and strengthen their compliance with disease reporting and response plans. EADRA provides clarity to producers about a potential set of response measures, scope and timing of compensation, and commits parties to secure funds for and effectively fund emergency responses. Second, protocols and procedures reduce information asymmetries in outbreak response measures. They ensure that the necessary information is collected, shared and considered by all stakeholders, the decisions follow a consultation process and are agreed amongst stakeholders. These principles are in particular manifest in the procedure of the Emergency Animal Disease Response Plan, which is based on the nationally agreed response policies published in Ausvetplan. The Emergency Animal Disease Response Plan, prepared by the state or territory chief veterinary officer(s), must be endorsed by the Consultative Committee on Emergency Animal Diseases which brings together technical representatives of the parties; it is then submitted to the National Management Group, a higher level group representing each of the parties affected. The Group should approve, or not, the invoking of cost-sharing and manage, on behalf of the affected parties, the national policy and resourcing needs of the Response Plan (AHA, 2016c).

The EADRA was first ratified in 2002, and has been undergoing constant reviews and updates since then, but has not been changed significantly. This indicates its general good performance and acceptance by stakeholders. The cost-sharing has been effectively invoked several times since 2002, most recently in respect of avian influenza outbreaks in 2012 and 2013 (Table 5.2). But the largest event was the 2007 outbreak of equine influenza, which, however, was a special case with respect to EADRA. Although equine influenza is among the EADRA-listed diseases, at the time of the outbreak the affected equine industry had not yet signed on to the EADRA. The cost-sharing mechanism was not officially invoked, but the cost-sharing procedures were essentially applied whereby the Australian government ultimately underwrote industry's share of response costs. Beyond that, the Australian government provided other substantial support to affected businesses and individual workers, essentially for the industry recovery and business interruption. The decision to provide such large-scale assistance through EADRA was first, because the outbreak originated with imported horses, and second, prior to the outbreak the horse industry had already initiated their adherence to the EADRA (OECD, 2012).

As shown above, the EADRA has broad application in terms of livestock industries and the scope of diseases. It is nevertheless worthwhile to highlight the areas outside this framework. First, considering the scope of diseases, although the list of EADRA emergency diseases is long, certain diseases remain outside this framework.[10] EADRA applies only to response measures which have been included in and approved under its Response Plan. Any response measures outside this plan will potentially be left at the discretion of state and territories. Furthermore, EADRA does not extend to livestock holders who are not members of industry bodies participating in EADRA and who are above the minimum industry business threshold (gross value of production below AUD 20 million) – in these cases compensation may be payable under state and territory legislation and could be cost-shared if agreed by all parties.

Second, EADRA does not compensate for consequential losses. As in many countries, these losses are typically outside the scope of compensation schemes for epidemics and regarded as entrepreneurial risk. At the same time, some consequential losses are corollary to compulsory measures applied in response to epidemics, such as protective vaccination and livestock movement restrictions. For example, under protective vaccination animals may not be destroyed, but when marketed, they command reduced price and involve additional costs in processing. Consequential losses thus influence farmers' incentives to disclose disease and to participate in preventive vaccination or movement control. As such, they have strong implications for the longer-term viability of farm businesses and even the entire industry.

Table 5.2. EADRA-shared expenditures on emergency animal disease events

Year	Disease	Species	Response measures	Total expenditure, AUD	*of which* Direct costs of disease control: Total	Direct costs of disease control: *of which* paid to livestock owners	Operational support	Price support	Consumption measures
2002	Newcastle disease in Victoria and New South Wales	Chickens	Stamping out Surveillance Vaccination Zoning	2 342 000	..	..	..	..	..
2007	Equine influenza	Horses and other equids	Movement control Screening Vaccination Disinfection Quarantine Treatment of affected animals	354 298 689	97 700 000	..	256 598 689	0	0
2012	Highly pathogenic avian influenza in New South Wales	Chickens	Movement control Quarantine Zoning Vaccination prohibited No treatment of affected animals	775 800	775 800	261 884	0	0	0
2012	Low pathogenic avian influenza in Victoria	Ducks	Movement control Screening Disinfection Quarantine Stamping out Zoning Vaccination prohibited No treatment of affected animals	1 004 559	1 004 559	..	0	0	0
2013	Highly pathogenic avian influenza in New South Wales	Chickens	Movement control Screening Disinfection Quarantine Stamping out Zoning Vaccination prohibited No treatment of affected animals	5 135 334	5 135 334	2 312 257	0	0	0

.. not available.

Note: Direct costs of disease control include (i) compensation paid to livestock owners for destroyed animals and lost product and (ii) salaries and wages, operating expenses and equipment costs incurred in control and eradication activities. Operational support (in the case of equine influenza) includes hardship fund, business assistance grant, wage supplement to equine workers, commercial horse assistance payment, and grant to non-government non-profit equestrian organisations.

Source: Australian Government (2016); OIE (2015); OECD (2012).

Livestock insurance may be one solution to market risks related to livestock epidemics. In Australia, there is generally no insurance for specific emergency animal diseases, except that valuable stud animals may be insured for death regardless of the cause or type of disease (Australian Government, 2016). Comparing internationally, livestock epidemics insurance is indeed limited because of the significant difficulty to estimate the scale and probability of livestock epidemics risk, classify and price it accordingly, and also because this risk tends to be systemic. Some analysts point to a market failure in provision of livestock disease insurance, and conclude about the need for government subsidy or other action, such as facilitation of the "production" of insurance products to make such insurance more operational (e.g. Meuwissen and Asseldonk, 2013). This facilitation may include creation of an information-sharing system on risks involving insurers, farmers and government, which could help reduce transaction costs incurred by insurers in obtaining the information and facilitate setting actuarially sound insurance premiums for different risk groups. Broadly speaking, subsidised insurance seems unlikely in the context of Australia where there is little public acceptance of intervention in markets and where farmers are viewed as ultimately responsible for assuming their business risks. The country's overall favourable disease status, assumingly reducing potential demand of livestock producers, also puts into question the feasibility of such insurance.

Finally, there is a constituency of non-commercial livestock holders who are not typically incentivised to prevent and report disease through compensation for lost animals but who may present difficulty. For example, the recent avian influenza emergencies drew attention to poultry exhibitors in Australia as a risk group for disease introduction through allowing wild birds to have contact with domestic birds, the high frequency of bird movements and the lack of appropriate isolation for incoming birds (Hernández-Jover et al., 2015). As a result, a range of materials was produced for poultry exhibitors and fanciers by the Australian Government Department of Agriculture and Water Resources. A standard compensation policy towards these groups is unlikely and they should be rather incentivised through local action, such as targeted awareness campaigns at the level of local communities, training to improve the ability to recognise and report diseases, voluntary assurance action, and community pressure for due diligence.

5.5. Conclusions

The official statistical and public research institutions in Australia generate a large body of structural information to support livestock policy development. At the same time, the statistical observation of small commercial livestock producers, particularly in the pig and poultry sectors, is limited and there is also a lack of information about livestock holders below the size threshold of official statistical coverage.

Governments at all levels in Australia recognise the importance of understanding individual producer behaviour for the development of effective animal health policy. The national partnership-based biosecurity system creates interactions with industry stakeholders and feedback flows to government about "on-the-ground" actors of biosecurity. Government and industry also undertake specific efforts to increase their own awareness of private producer behaviour, such as Farm Biosecurity Surveys and government-funded research, with the most recent studies conducted as part of the national priority research. All of these elements are the necessary input into the fine-tuning of policy in response to the knowledge gaps, perceptions, and attitudes of farmers that drive their decision-making processes. The efforts so far have evolved from one-off case studies to broader behavioural research which is intended to feed into policy development. There is, nevertheless, room for a more comprehensive behavioural work related to farm biosecurity, e.g. involving a longer-term research programme and the monitoring of change in farmer behaviour through surveys with possibly higher frequency and larger scope than currently, as well as focussed feedback from veterinarians.

Information on animal biosecurity comes to farmers from multiple channels. It is necessary to build a good understanding about the degree to which farmers use this external information and what their preferred sources are. It is also necessary to improve the co-ordination and harmonisation of biosecurity information. The type of information is also important and there is a need for more emphasis on the economic aspects of biosecurity, such as the cost efficiency of various disease management practices, and the impacts of good (bad) disease management at farm, industry and society levels. Information that is adaptable to specific farm contexts has a higher chance of uptake by farmers, implying that communication should be more targeted and that tools to customise the information to individual conditions are needed. The government has been taking steps in all of these directions, so the issue is to build on and continue these initiatives.

The structure of programmes and spending on education and training in animal health for farmers is difficult to estimate at the national scale as these activities are highly decentralised across a wide range of levels and providers. It is, nevertheless, warranted to investigate the knowledge and skills of livestock farmers and the extent to which they are adequate, to fully understand biosecurity and improve disease management practices. The knowledge and skills gaps that may be identified could help to prioritise extension and training in livestock disease management. Co-ordination of training programmes across various providers seems to be an issue as in the area of information and communication. Finding synergies between different channels of provision and less duplication could help more efficient allocation of public and private resources in farmer training.

Australia's compensation policy, with the Emergency Animal Disease Response Agreement (EADRA) at its centre, is an international example of a well-designed compensation policy. The EADRA creates mechanisms to align private, collective and public incentives. Cost-sharing is the principal mechanism to delimit public and private responsibility in disease emergencies and to control moral hazard and incentivise early reporting. EADRA's economic incentives are coupled with regulatory instruments and *ex ante* written protocols and procedures. These serve to ensure informed and consensual decisions and to commit parties. It is worthwhile noting, however, that an agreement like EADRA largely follows from Australia's specific conditions – the overall tradition of public-private partnership building and the strong institutional organisation of agricultural industries – advantages that some other countries may not enjoy.

The compensation framework in Australia – which combines EADRA and state and territory legislation – has the flexibilities to indemnify small livestock holders on a case-by-case basis, providing, in principle, an incentive to these constituencies to report disease. However, outreach to small livestock holders, particularly hobby farmers, needs to be diverse so as to include direct and targeted actions at the local level. This includes awareness campaigns, information and knowledge dissemination adapted to non-professional recipients, publicising and awarding positive behaviour, or any other initiatives appropriate in the local contexts. Policy could potentially play a role in promoting and facilitating such local initiatives.

Notes

1. For example, between 1992 and 2015, the share of cattle slaughter sourced from feedlots rose from 8% to 30% in response to strong growth in demand, including the demand for marbled beef from external premium markets, in particular from Japan (ACCC, 2016).

2. Anna Creek Station in South Australia is the world's largest working cattle station. The North Australian Pastoral Company Pty Limited (NAPCO) is one of the largest country's beef cattle producers, with a herd of over 180 000 cattle and 14 cattle stations in Queensland and the Northern Territory. The Australian Agricultural Company (AA Co) manages a cattle herd of more than 585 000 heads. Heytesbury Beef Pty Ltd owns and manages over 200 000 heads of cattle across eight stations in Northern Australia.

3. Producers using this channel transport cattle to saleyards to sell it to the highest bidder. Beyond the sites for physical deliveries, there is also an online platform AuctionPlus: in this case cattle are assessed prior to sale by accredited personnel and the seller outlines sale terms, including bidding and collection conditions, prior to the auction (ACCC, 2016). The use of auctions as a marketing channel differs in the south and north of the country. For example, in 2014/15 almost 80% of beef cattle in South Australia and only less than 2% in the Northern Territory, were sold through saleyard auctions (ABARES, 2016c). According to ACCC (2016), beef cattle herds in South Australia are small, the farms are often located close to saleyards and trade relatively small lots composed of mixed types of cattle. In contrast, the average beef cattle herd in the Northern Territory

is large, which makes it possible to form greater lots of livestock with similar quality and avoid losses due to handling in saleyards. Also, some breeders in these areas face long distances to saleyards.

4. Farm surveys undertaken by ABARES are funded by the Australian Government Department of Agriculture and Water Resources, with some either co-funded or fully financed by industries. For example, the ABARES broadacre industry survey, *Australian Agricultural and Grazing Industry Survey* (AAGIS) is mainly funded by the Australian Government Department of Agriculture and Water Resources with some co-funding by the Grains Research and Development Corporation and Meat & Livestock Australia. ABARES's *Cost of Production Supplementary Survey* (COPSS) is fully funded by the Meat & Livestock Australia (ADAWR, 2016).

5. Four surveys of specific farm industries are conducted on an annual basis and include: broadacre, dairy, and vegetable and irrigation farms in the Murray-Darling Basin. Broadacre surveys cover five farm types: wheat and other crops, mixed livestock-crops, sheep, beef, and sheep-beef farms.

6. These bodies include Australian, state and territory (agriculture/biosecurity), departments, Plant Health Australia, Animal Health Australia, CSIRO's Australian Animal Health Laboratory, Australian Government Department of Health, and the Australian Local Government Association. Wildlife Health Australia and the National Farmers' Federation are the observers in this Network.

7. Six different calculators are available on-line for specific themes. One of them is the Health Cost Benefit Calculator to determine the benefit and marginal rate of return of applying an animal health treatment to a herd for bloat, clostridial diseases and grass tetany. The Tool is downloadable on a personal computer and requires a limited amount of farm-specific information, e.g. herd size and structure, and price data (MLA, 2016).

8. The study considers six potentially significant biosecurity threats: foot-and-mouth-disease, Mexican feather grass, citrus greening, highly pathogenic avian influenza, Karnal bunt and red imported fire ants. The value of biosecurity is approximated by the on-farm costs and losses avoided as a result of biosecurity activities that target the pathways through which pests, diseases and weeds enter, become established and spread throughout Australia. Without an effective biosecurity system, the likelihood of a pest, weed or disease incursion is expected to be significantly higher and, in the event of an incursion, pests, weeds and diseases are expected to become endemic. As a result, farm profits may be lower because of: (i) direct production losses; (ii) additional expenditures on control measures; and (iii) export market losses. The analysis estimates that the profits of typical broadacre farms are AUD 12 000 to AUD 17 500 a year higher than they would be in the absence of an effective biosecurity system, in terms of the on-farm costs and losses avoided as a result of Australia's biosecurity activities that reduce the risk of an incursion (Hafi et al., 2015).

9. In 2016, Animal Health Australia took over the management of the Livestock Biosecurity Network.

10. The EADRA, however, provides guidance on how other diseases, including the previously unknown emerging ones, could be included in an emergency.

References

ABARES (2016a), *Agricultural Commodities: June Quarter 2016*, Australian Bureau of Agricultural and Resource Economics and Sciences, www.agriculture.gov.au/abares/publications.

ABARES (2016b), *Agsurf Data*, Australian Bureau of Agricultural and Resource Economics and Sciences, http://apps.daff.gov.au/AGSURF/.

ABARES (2016c), *Farm Survey Data for the Beef, Slaughter Lambs and Sheep Industries*, http://apps.daff.gov.au/MLA/.

ABS (2016a), *Agricultural Commodities, Australia*, 2014-15, cat. No.7121.0, Australian Bureau of Statistics, Canberra.

ABS (2016b), *Agricultural Census*, Australian Bureau of Statistics, Canberra, www.abs.gov.au/AUSSTATS/abs@.nsf/DOSSbytitle/AD7C6DD1D14FB809CA256BD000272737?OpenDocument.

ABS (2016c), *Rural Environment and Agricultural Commodities Survey*, Australian Bureau of Statistics, Canberra, www.abs.gov.au/ausstats/abs@.nsf/dossbytitle/26975048871D6352CA257D380080B38C?OpenDocument.

ABS (2016d), *Value of Agricultural Commodities Produced, Australia*, 2014-15, cat. No. 7503.0, Australian Bureau of Statistics, Canberra.

ABS (2012), *Australian Social Trends: Australian Farmers and Farming*, December 2012, cat. No. 4102.0, Australian Bureau of Statistics, Canberra.

ACCC (2016), *Cattle and Beef Market Industry – Interim Report*, Australian Competition and Consumer Commission, Canberra, www.accc.gov.au/system/files/1128%20Beef%20and%20cattle%20report_D08.pdf.

ACMF (2011), *The Australian Chicken Meat Industry: An Industry in Profile*, Australian Chicken Meat Federation (ACMF) Inc., North Sydney, NSW, Australia.

ADAWR (2016), *Statistical Activities Calendar 2016*, Australian Government Department of Agriculture and Water Resources, Canberra.

AECL (2015), *Australian Egg Corporation Limited. Annual Report 2015,* https://www.aecl.org/assets/About-us/Annual-Report-2015.pdf

AHA (2016a), *Animal Health in Australia 2015*, Animal Health Australia, Canberra, Australia, www.animalhealthaustralia.com.au/wp-content/uploads/2015/09/AHiA_REPORT_2015_WEBVERSIONFINAL.pdf.

AHA (2016b), Animal Health Australia on-line, www.animalhealthaustralia.com.au/.

AHA (2016c), *EADRA Frequently Asked Questions*, Animal Health Australia, Canberra, Australia.

Australian Government (2016), "OECD project on producer incentives in livestock disease management: Country case questionnaire", Responses to the OECD received from the Australian Government.

Beach, R.H., C. Poulos and S.K. Pattanayak (2007), "Agricultural household response to avian influenza prevention and control policies", *Journal of Agricultural and Applied Economics*, 39, pp. 301–11.

DA (2016), *Australian Dairy Industry in Focus 2015*, Dairy Australia, www.dairyaustralia.com.au/~/media/Documents/Stats%20and%20markets/Australian%20Dairy%20Industry%20In%20Focus/Australian%20Dairy%20Industry%20In%20Focus%202015.pdf.

EADRA (2016), "Government and Livestock Industry Cost Sharing Deed in Respect of Emergency Animal Disease Responses", Version 16/01, January 29, 2016, www.animalhealthaustralia.com.au/wp-content/uploads/2015/09/EADRA_Version_16_01-290116_Final.pdf.

FAO (2016), *FAOSTAT database*, FAO Publications, Rome, http://faostat.fao.org/.

Farm Biosecurity (2016a), *2013 Producer Survey Summary*, www.farmbiosecurity.com.au/.

Farm Biosecurity (2016b), Farm Biosecurity homepage, www.farmbiosecurity.com.au/.

Hafi, A., D. Addai, K. Zhang and E. M. Gray (2015), *The Value of Australia's Biosecurity System at the Farm Gate: An Analysis of Avoided Trade and On-Farm Impacts*, ABARES research report 15.2, Department of Agriculture, Canberra, June.

Hernandez-Jover, M., V. Higgins, M. Bryant, L. Rast and C. McShane (2014), "Farm Biosecurity Practices and the Management of Emergency Animal Disease", www.csu.edu.au/research/ilws/research/summaries/ps/managing-emergency-animal.

Hernández-Jover, M., K. Schemann, I.J. East and J.-A.L.M.L. Toribio (2015), "Evaluating the risk of avian influenza introduction and spread among poultry exhibition flocks in Australia", *Preventive Veterinary Medicine*, V. 118, pp. 128-41.

Matthews, K. (2011), *A Review of Australia's Preparedness for the Threat of Foot-and-Mouth Disease*, Australian Government Department of Agriculture, Fisheries and Forestry, Canberra. www.agriculture.gov.au/pests-diseases-weeds/animal/fmd/review-foot-and-mouth-disease.

Meuwissen, M. and M. A.P.M. van Asseldonk (2013), "European Union Subsidies: A Catalyst for Epidemic Market Loss Insurance?" in: *Livestock Disease Policies: Building Bridges Between Science and Economics*, OECD, Paris, www.oecd.org/tad/agricultural-policies/LivestockDiseasesPolicies_Proceedings2013.pdf.

MLA (2016), Health Cost Benefit Calculator, Meat and Livestock Australia on-line, www.mla.com.au/extension-training-and-tools/tools-calculators/health-cost-benefit-calculator/.

MLA (2015a), *Fast Facts: Australia's Beef Industry*, Meat and Livestock Australia, September 2015.

MLA (2015b), *Fast Facts: Australia's Sheep Industry*, Meat and Livestock Australia, September 2015.

MLA (2015c), *Priority List of Endemic Diseases for the Red Meat Industries: Final Report*, prepared by GHD Pty Ltd for Meat and Livestock Australia, March 2015.

NCN (2016), Biosecurity Incident National Communication Network on-line, www.outbreak.gov.au/about/biosecurity-incident-national-communication-network.

OECD (2015), *Innovation, Agricultural Productivity and Sustainability in Australia*, OECD Publishing, Paris, http://dx.doi.org/10.1787/9789264238367-en.

OECD (2012), *Livestock Diseases: Prevention, Control and Compensation Schemes*, OECD Publishing, Paris, http://dx.doi.org/10.1787/9789264178762-en.

OECD (2010), *Measuring Innovation: A New Perspective*, OECD Publishing, Paris, http://dx.doi.org/10.1787/9789264059474-en.

OIE (2015), *The World Animal Health Information System*, The World Animal Health Organisation, www.oie.int/en/animal-health-in-the-world/the-world-animal-health-information-system/the-oie-data-system/.

Palmer, S., F. Fozdar and M. Sully (2009), "The effect of trust on West Australian farmers' responses to infectious livestock diseases", *Sociologia Ruralis*, Vol. 49/4, pp. 360-374, http://onlinelibrary.wiley.com/doi/10.1111/j.1467-9523.2009.00495.x/pdf.

PC (2002), "Impact of a Foot and Mouth Disease Outbreak on Australia", *Research Report*, AusInfo, Productivity Commission Canberra, www.pc.gov.au/inquiries/completed/foot-and-mouth/report/footandmouth.pdf.

Pearson (2016), *The Learning Curve*, http://thelearningcurve.pearson.com/index/index-ranking.

PwC (2011), *The Australian Beef Industry*, PricewaterhouseCoopers, www.pwc.com.au/industry/agribusiness/assets/australian-beef-industry-nov11.pdf.

SAFEMEAT (2016), SAFEMEAT homepage on-line, http://safemeat.com.au/.

Schembri, N., K. Hart, R. Petersen and R. Whittington (2006), "Assessment of the management practices facilitating the establishment and spread of exotic diseases of pigs in the Sydney region", *Australian Veterinary Journal*, V. 84, N 10, October 2006, pp.341-348.

Schembri, N., M. Hernandez-Jover, J.-A.L.M.L. Toribio and P.K. Holyoake (2015), "On-farm characteristics and biosecurity protocols for small-scale swine producers in eastern Australia", *Preventive Veterinary Medicine*, Vol. 118/1, pp.104-16.

Taylor, M., N. Dhand, J.-A.L.M.L. Toribio, A. Wiethoelter, N. Schembri, K. Sawford, N. Kung, H. Field, B. Moloney and T. Wright (2016), "Longitudinal cohort study of horse owners. HHALTER: Horse owners and Hendra virus: A longitudinal study to evaluate risk", *Rural Industries Research and Development Corporation Publication* No 16/002, RIRDC Project No PRJ-008198, https://rirdc.infoservices.com.au/downloads/16-002.

USDA (2016), Production, Supply and Distribution Online (database), https://apps.fas.usda.gov/psdonline/.

WHA (2016), Wildlife Health Australia on-line, www.wildlifehealthaustralia.com.au/AboutUs.aspx.

Whittle, L., K. Zhang, K. Mazur, M. Skirtun, D. Addai, E.M. Gray and A. Davidson (2015), "Australia's cost recovery arrangements for export certification: implications for Australian agriculture", ABARES research report 15.8, Canberra, October. CC BY 3.0.

Wright, B., B. Jorgensen and L. Smith (2016), *Development of Behaviour Change Strategies for Animal Disease Surveillance and Reporting*, BehaviourWorks Australia, July 2016.

Annex 5.A1

Members of Animal Health Australia

Governments	Industry associations
Australian Government Department of Agriculture and Water Resources	Australian Alpaca Association
State of New South Wales (NSW) Department of Primary Industries	Australian Chicken Meat Federation
State of Queensland (Qld) Department of Agriculture, Fisheries and Forestry QLD	Australian Dairy Farmers
State of South Australia (SA) Department of Primary Industries and Regions SA	Australian Duck Meat Association (no website)
State of Tasmania (Tas.) Department of Primary Industries, Water, Parks and Environment	Australian Egg Corporation
State of Victoria (Vic.) Department of Primary Industries	Australian Horse Industry Council
State of Western Australia (WA) Department of Agriculture and Food WA	Australian Lot Feeders' Association
Australian Capital Territory (ACT) Department of Territory and Municipal Services	Australian Pork
Northern Territory (NT) Department of Resources	Cattle Council of Australia
	Equestrian Australia
	Goat Industry Council of Australia
	Harness Racing Australia
	Sheepmeat Council of Australia
	WoolProducers Australia
	Service providers
	Australian Veterinary Association
	CSIRO – Australian Animal Health Laboratory
	Associate members
	Australian Livestock Export Corporation (LiveCorp)
	Australian Racing Board
	Council of Veterinary Deans of Australia and New Zealand (no website)
	Dairy Australia
	National Aquaculture Council Inc.
	Wildlife Health Australia
	Zoo and Aquarium Association

Source: AHA (2016b).

Annex 5.A2

Animal health Australia: Main activity areas and nationally co-ordinated projects

Animal Health Australia (AHA) currently manages more than 60 national projects which fall under four principal areas: disease surveillance, domestic biosecurity services, emergency response to animal disease, endemic disease programmes, and livestock welfare (Figure 5.A2.1).

Figure 5.A2.1. Activities and projects under co-ordination of Animal Health Australia

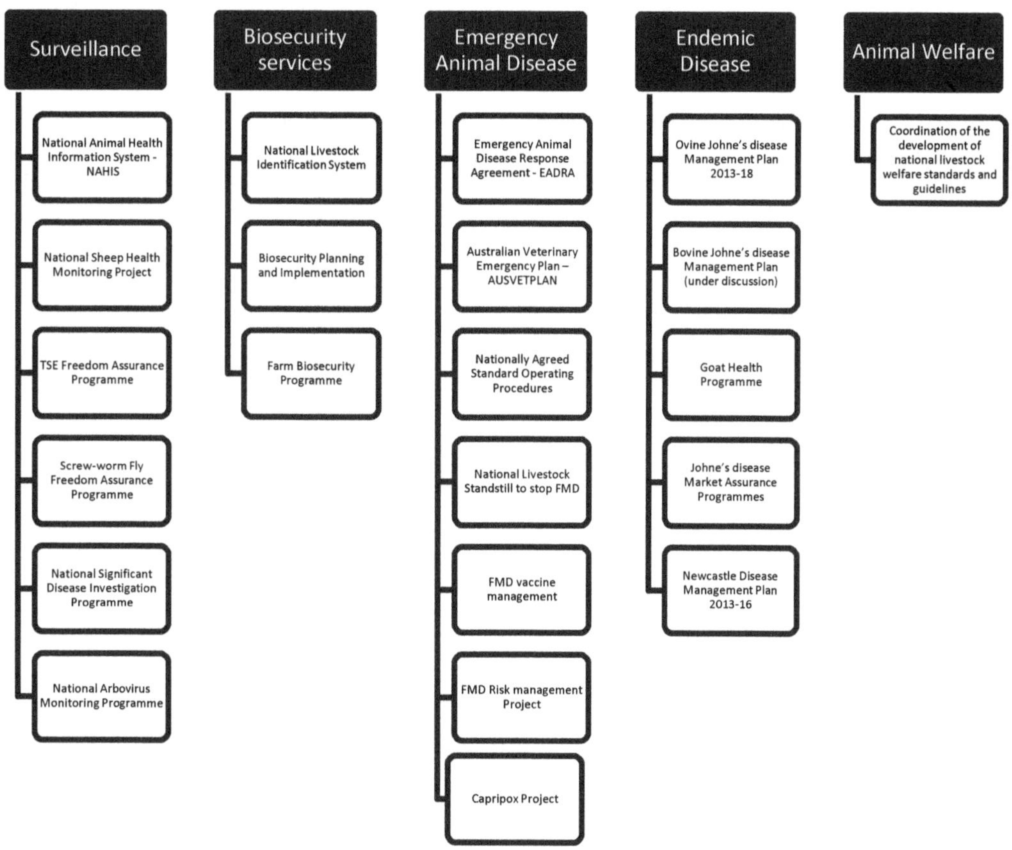

Source: AHA (2016b).

All AHA's projects operate on the principle of partnership in the development, implementation and funding of animal biosecurity activities. Selected examples of the partnership principle in the activities under AHA's co-ordination are presented below.

Australia's National Animal Health Information System (NAHIS) is probably one of the most developed animal health information systems. It combines information from laboratory network, national animal health programmes (e.g. TSE freedom assurance programme and Johne's disease market assurance programmes), veterinary investigations, altogether forming more than a dozen of information channels and databases. AHA is tasked to collate these data and provide an overview of animal health in Australia (OECD, 2012).

The National Sheep Health Monitoring Project monitors lines of adult sheep in abattoirs (groups of animals purchased from a single location, but sourced from different vendors) for a number of health conditions. The list of the monitored conditions was agreed among the sheep industry peak councils, Animal Health Committee and the Australian Meat Industry Council. Fourteen domestic and export processing plants located in all states are monitored. The data are stored in the national database which is maintained by AHA. The information is processed and can be used by governments, producers, and processors. Some state jurisdictions provide producers with individual animal health status reports on the lines inspected. Industry associations Wool Producers Australia and Sheepmeat Council of Australia fund this project, while each state department of primary industries has a state co-ordinator to facilitate the return of data to producers and provide extension advice about the conditions that are monitored.

The Ovine Johne's Disease Management Plan (2013-18) has been developed through extended consultations between Sheepmeat Council of Australia (SCA), WoolProducers Australia (WPA), state departments of primary industry and other stakeholders. It is funded by sheep meat and wool industries and draws on the R&D programme managed by Meat & Livestock Australia. The main objectives are to minimise the risk of infection for properties and regions that currently appear to be disease free and to reduce the adverse effects of the disease on individual flocks, and on the sheep industry as a whole. A similar Johne's Disease Management Plan for cattle is currently under stakeholders' review process.

Australia is a country with "negligible risk" for bovine spongiform encephalopathy (BSE) and free from classical scrapie – the types of transmissible spongiform encephalopathies (TSEs). TSE Freedom Assurance Programme is a nationally integrated management of animal-related TSE activities, including ruminant feed-ban scheme (a total ban on feeding meat and bone meal), surveillance of imported animals, national surveillance programme, and R&D. The objective of the national surveillance programme is to demonstrate the country's ability to meet the requirements for a BSE negligible risk and classical scrapie–free country, and provide early detection of these diseases should they occur. It receives funding from ten industry stakeholders (livestock and associated industries), the Australian Government, and the state and territory governments.

Annex 5.A3

Studies into livestock producer behaviour co-funded by Australian and state governments

1.	Study title	*Development of behaviour change strategies for animal disease surveillance and reporting* (2016), http://www.ava.com.au/sites/default/files/AVA_website/pdf/BWA-Final-Report-Animal-Disease-Surveillance-September-2016_0.pdf
	Motivation for study	The independent review "Australia's Preparedness for the Threat of Foot-and-Mouth Disease" by K. Mattews (2011) identified surveillance gaps (in particular, reporting by producers) acting as a barrier to the early identification of disease. The research was undertaken as part of priority work under a funded policy initiative to optimise the allocation of resources to surveillance needs.
	Issues	Risk perception, barriers to surveillance, attitudes to surveillance and reporting (or contacting a veterinarian), knowledge about animal diseases, and trusted sources of information.
	Performer	BehaviourWorks Australia
	Funding	Research consultancy funded by the Australian Government Department of Agriculture and Water Resources. A limited tender process was undertaken to procure providers.
	Use in policy development	The findings of the research are being used to review and fine-tune surveillance policy, and create more sustainable, partnership, approaches to surveillance (e.g. producer-based syndromic surveillance networks).
2.	Study title	*Pest Animal and Weed Management Survey: National Landholder Survey Results* (2016), http://www.agriculture.gov.au/abares/research-topics/social-sciences/pest-animals-weed-management-survey
	Motivation for study	The Australian Government is investing AUD 50 million through the Agricultural Competitiveness White Paper to improve the way pest (including feral animals) and weeds are managed and increase the capacity of farmers to deal with these threats. The primary purpose of the survey is to measure the level of awareness among the landholders and the community on the benefits of management and costs of inaction.
	Issues	Pests and weeds, knowledge and attitudes, risk perception, pest and weed management.
	Performer	ABARES (a division within the Australian Government Department of Agriculture and Water Resources).
	Funding	Government funding through the Australian Government Department of Agriculture and Water Resources.
	Use in policy development	Extension activities.
3.	Study title	Schembri N., M. Hernandez-Jover, J.-A.L.M.L. Toribio, and P.K. Holyoake (2015) "On-farm characteristics and biosecurity protocols for small-scale swine producers in eastern Australia", *Preventive Veterinary Medicine*, V. 118, N , pp.104-116. http://ac.els-cdn.com/S0167587714003985/1-s2.0-S0167587714003985-main.pdf?_tid=14b8aaf2-80d7-11e6-a5c0-00000aab0f26&acdnat=1474557373_c2b93cd586fbff51de51760ec2c62f23.
	Motivation for study	Following an independent review of Australia's preparedness for managing an FMD outbreak by K. Matthews (ibid.), enforcing the ban on swill feeding was identified as a 'gap' requiring more government and industry intervention.
	Issues	Farm characteristics of small-scale swine producers, biosecurity practices (on farm and at sale yards).
	Performer	University of Sydney, Victorian Department of Primary Industries, Graham Centre for Agricultural Innovation.
	Funding	Australian Biosecurity Cooperative Research Centre – a consortium of government and research institutions.
	Use in policy development	The specific practices and concerns of small-scale swine producers (and the differing management practices and motivations within this group) were used to inform industry and government extension programmes.

4.	Study title	Schembri, N., K Hart, R. Petersen, R. Whittington (2006) "Assessment of the management practices facilitating the establishment and spread of exotic diseases of pigs in the Sydney region", *Australian Veterinary Journal*, V. 84, N 10, October 2006, pp. 341-348, www.researchgate.net/publication/6448665_Assessment_of_the_management_practices_facilitating_the_establishment_and_spread_of_exotic_diseases_of_pigs_in_the_Sydney_region.
	Motivation for study	Since the UK outbreak of FMD caused by swill feeding, enforcing the ban on swill feeding in Australia has been viewed as a priority. However, to inform any intervention, research was first required to identify on-farm characteristics and biosecurity practices among Australian pig producers, and to assess the disease risk level of groups within the industry.
	Issues	Farmer biosecurity practices and risk perceptions (especially around swill feeding), farmer awareness of risks and their potential effects, awareness about exotic diseases and risk management practices, and attitudes towards these practices.
	Performer	Vale Rural Lands Protection Board. Lead researcher is an employee of the latter and was also a research student at the University of Sydney.
	Funding	New South Wales Department of Primary Industries and Moss Vale Rural Lands Protection Board
	Use in policy development	Peri-urban backyard farmers have been identified as a key (high risk) group for intervention. Industry and government have worked together to increase awareness of the swill-feeding ban, pig traceability and preventing the provision of swill by supermarkets and restaurants. However, non-English speaking backyard owners are still recognised as a difficult group to reach.
5.	Study title	Hernandez-Jover M, V. Higgins, M. Bryant, L Rast L, and C. McShane (2014) *Farm Biosecurity Practices and the Management of Emergency Animal Disease* www.csu.edu.au/research/ilws/research/summaries/ps/managing-emergency-animal.
	Motivation for study	Following an independent review of Australia's preparedness for managing an FMD outbreak (Matthews, 2011), government (at the Australian and state levels) was tasked with enhancing communication with farmers about how emergency disease threats (FMD, in particular) should be recognised, reported and managed. The research was to fill a gap in understanding about beef producer behaviour.
	Issues	How farmers obtain information on emergency animal disease, the ways in which they understand and manage disease risks, and whether current communication strategies are effective in improving farmer understanding and knowledge of how to deal with disease threats.
	Performer	Charles Sturt University
	Funding	Research consultancy funded by the Australian Government Department of Agriculture and Water Resources. A limited tender process undertaken to procure providers.
	Use in policy development	In its approach to communication and engagement, the Australian Government Department of Agriculture and Water Resources is moving away from broadcasting messages to generic, anonymous group of "livestock producers" and instead providing more specific information to target groups. Attempts to improve co-ordination and collaboration between stakeholder organisations are proving more difficult. A Biosecurity Incident National Communication Network has been formed to assist with this aim.
6.	Study title	M. Hernández-Jover, K. Schemann, I.J. East, and J.-A.L.M.L. Toribio (2015) "Evaluating the risk of avian influenza introduction and spread among poultry exhibition flocks in Australia", *Preventive Veterinary Medicine*, V. 118, pp. 128-41, www.ncbi.nlm.nih.gov/pubmed/25496909.
	Motivation for study	The Australian commercial poultry industries have long identified backyard poultry as a biosecurity threat. With the outbreak of zoonotic highly pathogenic avian influenza, and research confirming its spread through wild birds, industry and government supported further research to evaluate the risk posed by backyard poultry and shows.
	Issues	Exhibition poultry enthusiasts' biosecurity practices and risk perceptions (especially around contact with wild birds and commercial flocks).
	Performer	University of Sydney with support from the Australian Government Department of Agriculture and Water Resources
	Funding	Government funding was provided for the study and staff from the Australian Government Department of Agriculture and Water Resources provided data and epidemiological input.
	Use in policy development	There is little evidence of contact between commercial poultry and show/backyard poultry. However, the government worked directly with exhibitor groups to develop traceability measures and biosecurity guides. Measurement of the impact of these activities is not available, however.

7.	Study title	Taylor, M., N Dhand, J.-A.L.M.L. Toribio, A. Wiethoelter, N Schembri, K. Sawford, N Kung, H. Field, B. Moloney, and T Wright (2016) "Longitudinal cohort study of horse owners. HHALTER: Horse owners and Hendra virus: A longitudinal study to evaluate risk", *Rural Industries Research and Development Corporation Publication* No 16/002, RIRDC Project No PRJ-008198, https://rirdc.infoservices.com.au/downloads/16-002.
	Motivation for study	This report summarises the findings of a three-year mixed methods research study designed to capture factors that influence horse owners' practices on mitigation of Hendra virus (HeV) risks.
	Issues	Horse owners' knowledge, attitudes, and risk mitigation practices, i.e. uptake of vaccination, property management, and biosecurity practices.
	Performer	Biosecurity Queensland, Department of Agriculture and Fisheries and New South Wales Department of Primary Industries
	Funding	The study was funded by the Australian government and the states of New South Wales and Queensland under the National Hendra Virus Research Program.
	Use in policy development	The study has recently concluded. It is expected that results will lead to alternative approaches to engagement of horse owners around Hendra virus prevention activities.
8.	Study title	Palmer S., F. Fozdar, and M. Sully (2009) "The effect of trust on West Australian farmers' responses to infectious livestock diseases", *Sociologia Ruralis,* V. 49, N. 4, pp. 360-374, http://onlinelibrary.wiley.com/doi/10.1111/j.1467-9523.2009.00495.x/pdf.
	Motivation for study	Globalisation means that more new animal diseases have been identified in Australia since 1994 than in any previous equivalent period. To protect its relatively disease-free status (which is of economic value) and leverage additional resources (funding for agricultural extension continues to shrink), the Australian policy is to treat biosecurity as a shared responsibility across government and industry. While farmers are perfectly placed to provide surveillance data and enhance the capacity for early detection and response to exotic diseases, lack of government engagement with this group means that little is known about their behaviours and attitudes towards biosecurity.
	Issues	Farmer trust of government, farm biosecurity practices, attitudes to disease surveillance and reporting, farmer risk perception.
	Performer	Murdoch University
	Funding	Australian Biosecurity Cooperative Research Centre for Emerging Infectious Disease – a consortium of government and research institutions.
	Use in policy development	Since a lack of trust in government was identified as a key issue, government (at all levels) is now relying on trusted messengers (i.e. industry members and veterinarians) to deliver education, and investing more in training these trusted messengers (and less on pamphlets, ads, etc.).
9.	Study title	Buetre B., S. Wicks, H. Kruger, N. Millist, A. Yainshet, G.Garner, A. Duncan, A. Abdalla, C. Trestrail, M. Hatt, L.-J. Thompson, and M. Symes (2013) *Potential Socio-Economic Impacts of an Outbreak of Foot-and-Mouth Disease in Australia*, ABARES Research report 13.11, October 2013. http://apo.org.au/resource/potential-socio-economic-impacts-outbreak-foot-and-mouth-disease-australia.
	Motivation for study	The independent review of Australia's preparedness for managing an FMD outbreak (Matthews, 2011) recommended a programme of FMD biosecurity work for government and industry. This led to an economic study commissioned to investigate the costs of a foot-and-mouth disease incursion in Australia.
	Issues	Information needs, community impacts, household impacts, personal impacts, community involvement in outbreak response.
	Performer	Australian Government Department of Agriculture and Water Resources
	Funding	The work was undertaken internally by the Australian Government Department of Agriculture and Water Resources (then known as the Department of Agriculture, Fisheries and Forestry).
	Use in policy development	The study resulted in funding being granted for policy development around FMD vaccination, training for vets, surveillance and community engagement. To increase producer knowledge and resilience, a guide for producers to plan for risks to their business (posed by emergency animal disease outbreak) was created.

10.	Study title	*Managing Complex Systems* - The findings from Grain and Graze are available in the June 2008 report. www.wool.com/globalassets/start/on-farm-research-and-development/production-systems-eco/whole-farm-systems/grain-and-graze/managingcomplexsystemsfinalproduct1.pdf.
	Motivation for study	Improve the profitability and sustainability of mixed farms, focusing on cropping, pastures, livestock, profitability, whole-farm economics, farming systems, social issues and natural resources such as soil, water and biodiversity.
	Issues	Social research into the trade-offs influencing mixed farming decisions
	Performer	Australian Government Land & Water Australia and three R&D corporations
	Funding	Collaborative partnership between government and R&D corporations.
	Use in policy development	The programme expanded the scope of R&D and extension related to farming systems in Australia through explicit recognition of the triple bottom line and development of formal and informal approaches to integration across these dimensions.
11.	Study title	*Livestock Movement in Australia and Emergency Disease Preparedness* www.agriculture.gov.au/animal/health/livestock-movement-australia.
	Motivation for study	To gather information essential for planning for and managing infectious disease (e.g. drafting Ausvetplan manuals).
	Issues	Biosecurity practices, movement of livestock.
	Performer	Various consultants contracted by the Australian Government Department of Agriculture and Water Resources.
	Funding	The Australian Government's "Securing the Future" initiative was used to fund Department's project 'Emergency Animal Disease/Emerging Disease Awareness' (within this project, various contractors were each commissioned to report on a particular livestock industry).
	Use in policy development	Affected disease management policy, as captured in Ausvetplan, www.animalhealthaustralia.com.au/our-publications/ausvetplan-manuals-and-documents/.
12.	Study title	*Research Portfolio Summary 2005-2012. Invasive Animals Cooperative Research Centre, Canberra* www.invasiveanimals.com/wp-content/uploads/2012/12/ResPortfolioSumm_2005-12.pdf. Understanding stakeholders attitudes towards the adoption of new pest control strategies. (p.13) Social implications of managing deer. (p. 90) Public attitudes to pests and methods for their control. (p. 134)
	Motivation for study	Invasive/pest animals in Australia impose significant commercial losses on livestock producers and also pose disease threats to humans, livestock and native fauna.
	Issues	Public and landholder attitudes to pests and pest control.
	Performer	Invasive Animals CRC (a consortium of government, industry and research institutions) www.invasiveanimals.com/research/.
	Funding	Co-operative research centre comprising government, industry and research organisation funding and resources.
	Use in policy development	Unknown.
13.	Study title	Various social studies by ABARES www.agriculture.gov.au/abares/publications/pubs?url=http://143.188.17.20/anrdl/DAFFService/pubs.php?topic=SocialIssues%26sort=date%26sortOrder=desc%26outputType=list%26showIndex=true%26indexLetter=_.
	Motivation for study	Trade or agricultural productivity concerns.
	Issues	Issues involving the survey of farmers about: pest management, land management, agricultural workforce, illegal logging, farmers' response to weather variability, social impacts of drought, water use, animal welfare, sustainability, natural resource management, lifestyle farmers
	Performer	ABARES
	Funding	Work undertaken by ABARES researchers.

Source: Australian Government (2016).

Annex 5.A4

Project on development of strategies for farmer behaviour change in Australia: methods and findings

The Australian Government Department of Agriculture and Water Resources (ADAWR) sought to change the perception of livestock producers regarding the risk of emergency animal diseases and to encourage them to participate in surveillance activities. There had been concern that farmers did not prioritise disease surveillance amongst other more urgent issues: for example, debt or drought. Another consideration was that further top-down awareness campaigns would not be effective and would not be a desirable way forward. To provide evidence for alternative strategies, BehaviourWorks Australia undertook the project "Development of Behaviour Change Strategies for Animal Disease Surveillance and Reporting".

Structure of the project

The project had four phases, each employing a specific study method that provided input into the subsequent phase:

1. *Literature, policy and practice review* to understand the problem, the behaviours of interest, and the target audience.
2. *Focus groups* to investigate common themes and issues that were pertinent to how producers related to surveillance and reporting of animal disease. Three focus groups were organised: the first one with sheep-and-cattle producers in rural South Australia who formed a community group to discuss collective issues; the second one was conducted as part of the Wool Producers Australia meeting, with participants from all states and territories; and the third one used individual interviews with pig producers.
3. *Online farmer survey* to collect behavioural data and perform a predictive analysis of behaviour on that basis. A questionnaire was developed based on the themes identified by the focus groups. It was reviewed against established questionnaires and theoretical frameworks (notably, the Reasoned Action Approach) so as to ensure there was sufficient coverage and detail for the areas of interest. A computer-assisted telephone interview was then conducted with 200 producers from the sheep, cattle and pig industries. Based on the data collected, a cluster and multiple regression analyses were undertaken to identify predictors of the behaviours of interest.
4. *Design workshop* with key stakeholders to plan potential targeted interventions based on the findings from the data analysis. This workshop sought to facilitate collective decisions, which is important to appropriate, realistic and achievable design approaches. Nine stakeholders, in addition to the staff of BehaviourWorks Australia, attended the design workshop. These additional stakeholders included seven staff members from the Department of Agriculture and Water Resources, one representative from state government, and one representative from the Livestock Biosecurity Network.

Project outputs

The project outputs include: (i) the findings from the review of the existing sources and from the discussions in the focus groups; (ii) predictors of Australian farmer behaviour resulting from the analysis of the survey data; and (iii) the themes identified for potential policy development.

Following the review of the existing sources and discussions by the focus groups, a range of topics were identified to study surveillance and reporting by Australian farmers. The subsequent farmer survey was based on these topics. Its findings include:

- *Past experience and intentions related to disease outbreak*: A minority of producers (12%) had experienced an emergency disease. Asked what they would do if they experienced an outbreak, 99% of farmers responded they would talk to someone, the vast majority (86%), to a veterinarian; 65% of respondents would report suspicious signs within 24 hours, 18% would get a second opinion, 15% would watch animals before reporting, and only 1% said their action would depend on the severity of the disease.
- *Confidence in the ability to identify the disease*: When asked as a general question, confidence was rated at 7 points on a 10-point scale, but ranged between 2 and 5 points when asked in relation to a specific disease. This may indicate an over-confidence of producers in their general ability to recognise diseases, but may also mean that although they are able to recognise suspicious symptoms, they are not able to associate them with a specific disease.
- *Competency to deal with outbreaks*: Farmers scored local veterinarians highest (8 points on a 10-point scale), followed by themselves (7 points), followed by an industry organisation, Animal Health Australia, state departments, other farmers in the region, and the Australian Department of Agriculture and Water Resources, which ranked lowest (5 points).
- *Responsibility of different stakeholders*: Producers rated themselves as having the greatest responsibility for both surveillance (9 points out of 10) and dealing with emergencies (nearly 9 points).
- *Attitudes towards the Australian Department of Agriculture and Water Resources*: This was rated highest in terms of providing easily accessible and useful information (7 points) and lowest in terms of making good management decisions and dealing with producers (6 points).
- *Perceived risk*: Producers perceived the impact of disease outbreak on their farm to be high, but saw the risk of it developing on own farm to be lower than on other farms.
- *Social norms*: Producers perceive a social norm to exist for monitoring and reporting disease, and that this behaviour is expected of them by the community. These expectations are not perceived by farmers as being unreasonable.

A further analysis of the data collected points to the following significant predictors of Australian farmer behaviour related to disease monitoring and reporting:

- *Government as a source of credible and clear information:* Producers who trusted the government (ADAWR) to follow the best available science and to communicate this effectively were more likely to report disease emergency. This implies that producers need to trust the accuracy of information, and the method and time of communication. Including producers in developing strategies to monitor their stock is a starting point to build collaborative relationships that are effective.
- *Personal responsibility:* Producers who felt responsible for dealing with disease emergencies in their livestock were more likely to engage in monitoring behaviour. Farm trials of surveillance actions and providing access to additional information resources may assist in this.
- *Perceived behavioural control*: Producers who reported they knew what they should do were more likely to monitor their livestock and work with a private veterinarian.
- *Proximity to preferred veterinarian*: The greater the distance, the less likely producers monitor disease and report it to their veterinarian. Increasing skills and resources of producers to levels that

do not require recourse to consultation in the first instance, and using communication technologies to connect remote farmers with veterinarians, could be ways to address this issue.

- *Social norms*: Social rewards of approval and the attribution of social sanctions are likely to be effective.

The design workshop subsequently prioritised three areas for intervention: (i) changing producer perceptions of risk; (ii) building relationships between producers and veterinarians; and (iii) supporting producers with poor access to veterinary services. The next step foreseen is to refine these interventions with producers and develop a framework to evaluate the effects of intervention on producer behaviour. Overall, this project highlighted the importance of clear communications, the necessity to engage stakeholders, and to align the understanding of behavioural drivers with interventions.

Source: Wright et al. (2016).

Annex 5.A5

2013 Farm Biosecurity Survey in Australia: Main findings

Question category	Summary of producer responses
Understanding of biosecurity	
The overall level of understanding of biosecurity amongst Australian producers was improved in 2013	• Without any prompting, almost half of all producers surveyed related the term "controlling diseases, pests and weeds" to biosecurity, a substantial increase from 37% in 2010. • A further 24% thought, without prompting, that biosecurity meant "border protection/quarantine". This was the same result as reported in 2010. • While there was also a reduction in the proportion of producers surveyed who responded "nothing" or "don't know" when they hear the term "biosecurity", these still accounted for 20% of all responses in 2013. • When prompted with four different statements to choose from, around 90% of all respondents identified "Measures taken to protect farm production from disease, pests and weeds" as the best definition of biosecurity. This has increased from around 80% in 2010.
Current practices undertaken to protect crops and livestock	
Most producers surveyed continued to implement the same practices they reported in 2010, with some increases in the practices of weed control and livestock monitoring.	• 35% of respondents said they control weeds, when asked the question, "What biosecurity practices do you currently undertake to protect your property from pests or diseases and weeds?" • Overall, the practice of monitoring livestock saw the biggest increase over 2010 results, with 20% of all producers listing "monitoring livestock" as a biosecurity activity in 2013 compared with only 14% in 2010. • Of those producers surveyed that did undertake a biosecurity activity, controlling weeds was the most prevalent (35%), followed by controlling livestock pests and diseases (33%). There were predictable differences for plant and livestock producers consistent with their operations.
Sources of agronomic, animal health and biosecurity information	
Producers seek and gather information from a wide variety of sources	• Agronomists were the most typical source of information on farm management issues for 26% of all respondents. • Information on animal health, crop protection and biosecurity was most commonly provided by a vet (31%) followed by an agronomist (23%), state department of primary industries (23%) industry bodies (17%) and suppliers (17%) and the internet (15%). • When asked what specific information they wanted to be able to access regarding biosecurity, 26% of all respondents replied "biosecurity warnings and alerts". The producers surveyed reported email as the preferred way to receive information on biosecurity (48%), with hard copy in the mail being the next preference (32%), followed by websites (18%). • Around 90% of all producers surveyed have internet access on their property. • Overall, around 48% of all respondents used the internet daily with just under 20% of all producers using the internet less than every two-three weeks.
Association membership	
Around two-thirds of all producers say they belong to a crop or livestock industry association	• A total 64% of all respondents belong to a crop or livestock industry association. • Of livestock producers surveyed, 63% said they belong to an industry group or association compared with 56% of grain growers who said they belong to an industry group or association.

Awareness of the Farm Biosecurity programme (1)

Awareness of the Farm Biosecurity programme is highest amongst plant producers

- A total 36% of respondents had heard of the Farm Biosecurity programme with awareness highest amongst plant producers (37%) compared to livestock producers (33%).
- Awareness of the programme amongst livestock producers was highest for alpaca producers at 67%.
- The largest increase in awareness between 2010 and 2013 results was amongst grain growers. In 2013, 34% had heard of the programme compared to 23% in 2010. Most respondents reported hearing about the programme in their local newspaper (37%), whilst 25% had heard about it through their industry association.

On-farm biosecurity monitoring

When asked who monitors crops or livestock for disease or pests, most producers identified themselves or their family or staff

- More than 80% of producers did their own monitoring, while 31% relied on family or staff.
- While grain producers reported similar levels of self/family/staff monitoring, more than half also used an agronomist or cropping consultant.
- The amount of producers surveyed who used their family and/or staff rose from 25% in 2010 to 31% in 2013.
- In 2013, approximately 1 in 10 producers surveyed identified cropping groups as monitors of their crops. In 2010 no producers, at all, identified cropping groups monitoring their crops.
- Half of all producers monitored daily but it varied from 34% of grain producers to 56% of livestock producers. Monitoring daily increased, compared with 2010 from 41% to 50% overall.
- Grain producers were less frequent monitors than other groups and as likely to monitor weekly as daily.
- 60% of producers kept records of their monitoring, with similar levels across all groups. In 2010, only 46% kept records.
- Close to 80% were willing to share the records of their monitoring.

Identifying and reporting new or unusual pests and diseases

Almost all producers surveyed said they would do something to try to identify an unusual pest or disease on their property.

- Almost half of the producers surveyed would seek advice from their state department of primary industries or the Department of Agriculture. Two-thirds of grain growers would ask a private agronomist or advisor and 50% of livestock producers would consult a vet. Both of these options increased in 2013.
- 97% said they would report a new pest or disease found on their property
- The same sources (state department of primary industries or the Department of Agriculture, vet and agronomist) were the most cited places to report a new pest or disease. Again, government agencies were less used than in 2010, while more would notify an agronomist.

Benefits of implementing biosecurity practices

"Freedom from diseases, pests and weeds" and "protection of incomes and livelihoods" were the most often cited reasons to implement biosecurity practices.

- "Freedom from diseases, pests and weeds" was the main benefit, reported by 57% of producers.
- The next most reported benefit was "protect livelihood/income".
- While the levels of reported benefits of biosecurity were similar to 2010, there was an increase in the proportion who cited "protect livelihood/income" (40% in 2013 compared to 29% in 2010).

1. Farm Biosecurity programme is an awareness campaign through a joint initiative of Animal Health Australia and Plant Health Australia on behalf of their members. Its core is a website hub of farm biosecurity information, which includes information to help producers understand disease, pest and weed risks, what they can do to reduce those risks, and how to go about it. It provides materials to help producers implement good biosecurity on their property.

Source: Farm Biosecurity (2016).

Annex 5.A6

Cost-sharing scheme in Australia's Emergency Animal Disease Response Agreement

I. Cost-sharing between government and industry

Category of disease	Government funding	Industry funding
Category 1: 5 diseases Predominantly seriously affecting human health and (or) the environment (depletion of native fauna) but which may only have minimal direct consequences to the livestock industries	100%	0%
Category 2: 13 diseases Potentially causing major national socio-economic consequences through very serious international trade losses, national market disruptions and very severe production losses in the livestock industries that are involved. This category includes diseases that may have slightly lower national socio-economic consequences, but also have significant public health and/or environmental consequences.	80%	20%
Category 3: 16 diseases Potentially causing significant (but generally moderate) national socio-economic consequences through international trade losses, market disruptions involving two or more states and severe production losses to affected industries, but have minimal or no effect on human health or the environment	50%	50%
Category 4: 27 diseases Mainly production loss diseases: while there may be international trade losses and local market disruptions, these would not be of a magnitude that would be expected to significantly affect the national economy. The main beneficiaries of a successful emergency response to an outbreak of such a disease would be the affected livestock industry(s).	20%	80%

II. Cost-sharing within government funding

Government funding is shared between the Commonwealth, the six states and the two territories. For each disease, the Commonwealth share is 50% of the total government share.

The split between states and territories is based on a set of detailed formulae. For Category 1 diseases, the formula uses figures from the latest human population census. For all other diseases, the formula is based on the relevant livestock population and on Gross Value of Production data of the industry(ies) affected by the disease.

III. Cost-sharing within industry funding

The split of costs eligible for sharing between the industry parties where disease affects more than one species, or concerns more than one industry party for a species, are similarly determined on the basis of the Gross Value of Production of each industry.

Source: AHA (2016c).

Annex 5.A7

Compensation rules in Australia's Emergency Animal Disease Response Agreement

Scope of compensation	Cost-sharing under the EADRA applies to several types of expenses: 1. Compensation to livestock holder is payable for livestock or property destroyed to control an emergency animal disease, as well as for dead animals that, had they not died of the disease, would have been ordered slaughtered. 2. Salaries and wages; operating expenses; and capital costs which result directly from disease response plan implementation and exceed the implementing agencies' normal commitments. Neither routine biosecurity expenses nor consequential losses incurred by communities within affected states/territories are cost-shared.	
Consequential losses	No allowance is to be made for loss of profit, loss occasioned by breach of contract, loss of production or any other consequential loss whatsoever.	
Eligible beneficiaries	Commercial holders of livestock represented by one of the industry organisations that are EADRA signatories	Compensated for animals and property destroyed during a disease response and for dead animals which would have been culled
	Small industries	Can be compensated even if not represented by an EADRA signatory, if their industry gross value of production (GVP) is less than AUD 20 million.
	Animal Health Australia	Can be reimbursed for non-normal costs incurred during a disease response
	Commonwealth and state/territory governments	Can be reimbursed for non-normal costs of salaries and wages; operating expenses; capital costs; and compensation payments
Rules for valuation	For destroyed property, the value is assessed immediately prior to destruction. For livestock, the market value of animals destroyed and dead as a result of the disease is based on farm-gate price. If applicable, a second, top-up payment compensates for the difference between the market value of the equivalent livestock on the date restocking eligibility is granted and the previous compensation.	
Conditionality	Unless in a sector with GVP less than AUD 20 million, a livestock owner must be represented by one of the industry organisations that are EADRA signatories to be compensation eligible. Industry parties must advise their members to notify authorities within 24 hours of an incident. Also, a state/territory may lose its claim to cost-sharing through failure to notify the Consultative Committee on Emergency Animal Diseases of an incident within 24 hours. Livestock holders must notify the appropriate authority within 24 hours of dead animals or about "the occurrence of a confirmed or reasonably held suspicion of an emergency animal disease (not including a disease investigation where the provisional diagnosis is that the disease is endemic although it is known that the disease may be an emergency animal disease)". Industry parties have also committed to development of biosecurity plans.	
Timeframe for compensation	A holder's initial compensation claim must not follow livestock death or destruction by more than 90 days; a request for a valuation of restocking cost needs to be made within 30 days of notification of restocking eligibility; and a claim for a second compensation payment has to be made within 21 days of receipt of the second valuation's results. Compensation payments are made in short order by the states/territories	

Source: OECD (2012).

Chapter 6

Case study in livestock disease management: Chile

This case study begins with a contextual overview of the livestock sector and animal health situation in Chile, and then focuses on the following aspects: government awareness of producer behaviour in livestock disease management; information, education and training for producers; and producer compensation policy in Chile. The final section presents the conclusions and policy recommendations.

6.1. Overview of the livestock sector and animal health situation in Chile

Structural characteristics and economic importance of livestock production

Chile has a unique geography occupying a narrow strip along the Pacific coast of South America whose width at maximum reaches only 420 kilometres. The long extent from north to south leads to the desert climate in the extreme north of the country evolving into Antarctic climate in its southernmost part. Most of the agricultural activity occurs in the depression between the Andes and lower Coastal range running parallel to the Pacific Ocean (FAO, 2006). Such a landscape creates natural barriers to disease transmission, although coastal wetlands with migratory birds present a risk for disease introduction. Livestock farming is concentrated in the South plains and Patagonia, the regions rich in grasslands and pasture. The husbandry is largely pastoral, with low livestock densities and dispersed herds, which also reduces the risks of disease spread. Confined poultry, pig meat and dairy intensive systems exist in the central zone and intensive dairying is also present in the southern regions.

The livestock sector generates 37% of Chilean agricultural output (OECD, 2016). Total livestock production more than doubled between 1990 and 2013 and rose by almost 60% in per capita terms (FAOSTAT, 2017b). The sector's exposure to trade over this period increased considerably, both on export and import sides. Chile became a net overall exporter of livestock products in the 2000s, but returned to net imports in the 2010s with a broadening negative balance (ODEPA, 2017a). Chile has traditionally been an exporter of sheep meat and wool and has also considerably increased net exports of pig meat and poultry meat since the early 2000s. These exports are destined to markets with different consumption characteristics and sanitary requirements – from large emerging markets such as China and Russia, to North America and the European Union. Chile is a net importer of beef and in 2015-16 it was also net-importing dairy products. A good sanitary status is thus important for Chile to both minimise domestic market risks and to ensure stable access to export markets.

Around two-thirds of agricultural establishments in Chile undertake some livestock activity (INE, 2007b).[1] The cattle and sheep sub-sectors have a distinctly dualistic farm structure with most of the herds concentrated in a small number of large operations, and numerous small establishments existing alongside (Annex 6.A1). For example, almost 70% of the total sheep number is concentrated in units with 500 hectares and more, but which represent only 2% of all holdings that keep sheep, while units below 50 hectares constitute around 80% of such holdings. The presence of many small livestock holders in these industries makes them important as a constituency to be targeted by animal disease policy. The dualistic farm structure is also observed in poultry and pig production. However, the ownership and organisation of these industries differ significantly from the bovine and sheep sectors: the numerous pig and poultry establishments are typically parts of integrated businesses that are owned and managed by the same operators.

Chilean livestock producers are a relatively aged community. Among the individual farmers, persons close to or above the retirement age (55 years and older) constitute 55%. This share is higher than amongst those who are not engaged in livestock production (Figure 6.1.A). Human capital in agriculture remains low: 77% of individual livestock farmers have only basic or preparatory education or no schooling at all, while the share of those with middle, technical or higher education is 23% (Figure 6.1.B). These educational attainments compare less favourably with farmers who do not keep livestock. For this group the persons with more advanced education levels – from middle to higher education – constitute a share almost twice as high (43%).

Contract arrangements between producers and downstream operators – up to full vertical integration in some sectors – prevail in the meat and dairy chains in Chile. All this suggests that downstream companies, through contracting and industry food safety programmes, play a key role in the establishment of sanitary standards on farms integrated in commercial chains. The majority of sheep (62%), and a large part of beef cattle (47%), are collected on the premises for retail outlets and almost 95% of pigs are delivered to slaughter houses (INE 2015a; INE 2015b; INE 2016). The poultry meat segment is concentrated, with only four companies operating in the broiler segment and three companies in the turkey meat segment. These are highly integrated companies, controlling the entire process from parent stock farms to slaughter (Hidalgo, 2016). Dairy processing is also concentrated with six companies handling nearly 90% of marketed raw milk (ODEPA, 2017b).[2] Flexible marketing arrangements, such as deliveries to auctions and sales yards, and sales to livestock traders, are important only for beef cattle: nearly 50% of animals are marketed through these channels, but only 18% of sheep and 1% of pigs.

Figure 6.1. Age and education profiles of livestock farmers in Chile

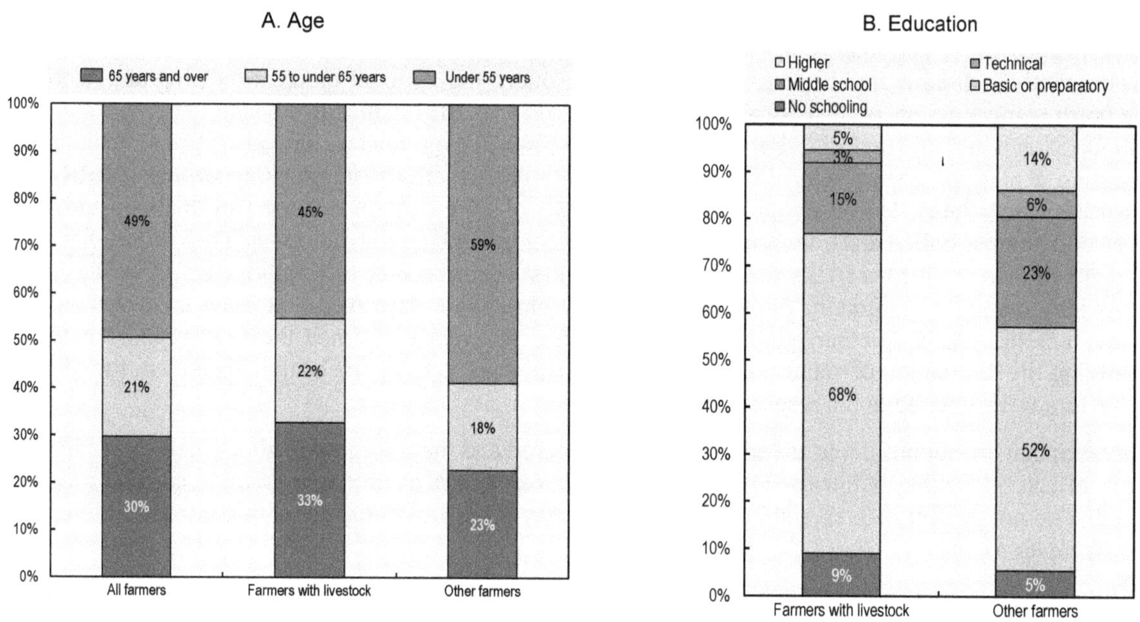

Note: This figure covers only natural persons.

Note: Only natural persons who have answered the relevant question in the survey are taken into account here. Each level of education represented includes persons who have completed their studies at that level and those who are still undertaking their studies

Source: Own elaboration based on 2007 Agricultural Census database.

Commercial product chains do not integrate very small livestock keepers, typically undertaking semi-subsistence or subsistence production. These producers raise livestock primarily for household consumption and access markets only sporadically and at local levels. Their linkages with markets are typically not well observed (or observable),[3] while the risks they present for the occurrence and spread of disease are not well informed (Chapter 2). Hamilton-West et al. (2012) provide some insights into the profile of smallholders operating outside the commercial product chains in Chile by taking the case of poultry (Annex 6.A2). The authors make a general observation that despite the different structures of the poultry sector worldwide, backyard production systems can play a major role in disease maintenance and spread because of management conditions and the lack of animal health services adapted to these production systems. They point out the need to improve the coverage of veterinary assistance and disease surveillance in backyard production.[4]

Overall situation related to livestock and animal disease risk

Chile has a favourable livestock health situation and enjoys a good reputation as a livestock product exporter for its sanitary conditions. The goal of export enhancement and a need to demonstrate good animal health and food safety status has driven significant improvements in the Chilean animal health system since the 1990s (Rojas, 2009). The overall prevention and control strategy has been strengthened, with plans developed for individual diseases, new disease eradication programmes, and an animal traceability system. Food safety has also been a major focus, closely linked with animal health. A national food safety system has been established based on international standards and involving programmes of export certification at livestock premises, official programmes for control of pathogens, anabolics, and harmful residues, as well as voluntary food safety programmes in some industries (e.g. pig meat industry). Some insight into livestock disease as a factor of production risk can be drawn from the survey of sheep breeders. Disease has been identified as one of the less frequent causes of sheep loss, accounting for 7% of lost animals, compared to the loss from predators (50%) and climatic factors (16%) (INE, 2015b).

The country is free from the majority of OIE-listed diseases, including BSE, FMD, swine fever, Aujeszky's disease, or ovine brucellosis (SAG, 2017). Chile has been FMD-free without vaccination since the 1980s after a 20-year eradication programme (Rojas, 2009), which provides Chile a significant export advantage.[5] Since 1975, the country has worked towards the eradication of bovine brucellosis: the extreme south is currently a disease free region, while others are under the national eradication program, with the extreme north being a region of "disease absence" (SAG, 2015). In 2011, Chile also began the programme for eradication of bovine tuberculosis. Between 2003 and 2007, the country has also been successfully implementing a plan for control and eradication of porcine reproductive/respiratory syndrome (PRRS) and aimed a PRRS-free status. However, an outbreak of PRRS of a new strain occurred in 2013, resulting in almost 19 000 animals culled and a launch of a new PRRS control and eradication plan. The country has seen no outbreaks of avian influenza (AI) since 2002, until the first occurrence of low pathogenic AI in December 2016, probably caused by migratory birds. Nearly 34 000 birds were destroyed and other control measures implemented (OIE, 2017). Another relatively important disease event concerned the fowl typhoid in 2015, also involving the destruction of some flock (OIE, 2017). However, only a few establishments in the pig and poultry sectors were affected in the recent outbreaks.

Diseases that are not notifiable are not officially monitored and the information about their incidence and economic effects is lacking (Chilean Government, 2016). As shown by the studies undertaken elsewhere, diseases that do not present high epidemiological concern may have substantial economic impact on livestock industry (Chapter 5).

Institutions involved in livestock disease issues within country borders

The Agricultural and Livestock Service (*Servicio Agrícola y Ganadero* – SAG) is the main institution responsible for plant and animal health in Chile. It is subordinated to the Ministry of Agriculture as a decentralised service with national outreach. SAG has 15 regional and 63 area offices, 94 border control points for plant and animal health, and 11 diagnostic laboratories. Animal health issues are under the responsibility of SAG's Livestock Protection Division, which includes disease surveillance, sanitary emergency management, sanitary information and animal traceability system, and development and implementation of disease eradication programmes. Beyond animal health, SAG's Livestock Protection Division is responsible for other important areas, such as livestock welfare, food safety, and export certification of primary products of animal origin.

The implementation of animal health programmes rests on the Official Veterinarians, Authorised Veterinarians, and the private sector. The status of Authorised Veterinarians is granted to external professionals, who conduct one or more activities within the framework of SAG's official programmes. The aim is to optimise the use of resources and expand coverage, capacity, efficiency and response capacity of SAG's services. Authorised Veterinarians annually undergo training and performance evaluation related to the programmes for which they have been certified (Chilean Government, 2016).

Chile's livestock producers and downstream operators have created various groups. National and regional farmer associations unite primary agricultural producers. Some regional farmer associations represent southern regions concentrating most of the national livestock production, such as the Agricultural and Livestock Society of Osorno (SAGO), Union of Agricultural Producers of Valdivia (SAVAL), and Union of Agricultural Producers of Bío-Bío (SOCABIO). Other groups are organised along specific segments of livestock industry: Chilean Association of Pig Producers (ASPROCER), National Federation of Milk Producers (FEDELECHE), National Federation of Beef Producers (FEDECARNE), Association of Meat Exporters (Expo Carnes), and Chilean Association of Egg Producers. The Chilean Meat Association (ACHIC) unifies companies performing slaughter, processing, imports and marketing of meat; the Association of

Livestock Trade Fairs of Chile (AFECH) groups 10 companies that run 35 auction sites accounting for over 86% of the nationwide transactions.

There is no institutionally established biosecurity partnership between industry groups and government, including any *ex ante* formal agreement on sharing of responsibilities and costs in disease emergencies. Chile's Master Plan for the Management of Health Emergencies only states as a principle an active engagement of representatives of the private sector in emergency response (SAG, 2013). SAG and its Early Response Task Group perform simulations of exotic disease outbreaks to evaluate the responsiveness of the veterinary service and carry out training in outbreak control (e.g. related to avian influenza in 2015, classical swine fever in 2010, and FMD in 2009). Producer organisations, along with the SAG's Official Veterinarians and Authorised Veterinarians, participate in these simulations (Chilean Government, 2016).

Several other examples of industry group involvement in biosecurity work can be highlighted. In the cattle and sheep segment, industry groups (SAGO, SAVAL, AFECH, ACHIC and FEDECARNE) participate in the National Beef Commission, a public-private consultation and co-ordination platform. Among other issues, this Commission considers veterinary and sanitary programmes in the meat chain (see below). The Chilean Association of Pig Producers (ASPROCER) participates in animal health programmes in the framework of the sectoral Food Safety Management System. The poultry industry also participates in the surveillance programme for avian influenza and farmer training, and in the past has been involved in the management of the 2002 outbreak of avian influenza.

6.2. Government's activity to increase its awareness about farmer behaviour

Private operators are the ultimate decision makers of farm enterprises. Evidence about farmer behaviour and their response to policy is thus a necessary input into policy making, including in the area of animal disease.

Availability of information about farmers undertaking livestock activities

As a starting point, governments require sufficient information about the number, structural and social characteristics of the livestock farming community they engage with. This information should have adequate national coverage and consistency. As elsewhere, Agricultural Census is the most important primary source of such information in Chile. The most recent one was conducted in 2007 (INE, 2007). It reports the numbers of holdings keeping livestock and total livestock inventories; individual characteristics of producers (sex, age, and education), legal status of enterprise, as well as availability of machinery and equipment, and characteristics of members of farming households. With regard to farm size structure, the publicly released data includes the distributions based on farm area (Annex A.1). The primary census data could also be used to inform about the distribution of farms according to herd size. This is of interest for developing policies that are targeted to holdings of different herd size.

The Chilean National Institute of Statistics (INE) undertakes regular farm surveys. Surveys of sheep, goat and bovine farms are done every two years in the regions concentrating over 90% of the total stocks of these animals. These surveys cover only the establishments above a certain size: the sheep survey includes farms with 60 heads and more (around 74% of total inventories based on the situation of 2007 Agricultural Census); the bovine survey includes units with 10 heads and more (90% of total inventories in 2007 Census); and the goat survey units with 20 heads and more (all units included in the 2007 Census). The issues covered have broad scope and include updates on the farm numbers and livestock inventories, individual characteristics of producers with special emphasis on the use of technical assistance and access to internet. These surveys also inquire about the technological aspects of an enterprise (herd structure, feeding, land use, availability of infrastructure, etc.), farm investments, and marketing channels. Two separate surveys of pig and poultry producers (eggs and broilers) are also conducted. They are more frequent (semi-annual) and cover farming units above a certain size and disposing of infrastructure for commercial activity.[6] Compared to sheep, goat and bovine surveys, pig and poultry surveys inquire about a relatively narrow scope of issues, such as herd management and marketing systems of enterprise. None of the livestock surveys mentioned above look into aspects of animal health, such as farmers' perceptions about disease risks, use of different practices to prevent disease, or farmer awareness of key biosecurity information sources and their use.

Beyond statistical and analytical data collected through the Agricultural Census and farm surveys, there is also the Livestock Information and Animal Traceability System (*Sistema de Información Pecuaria y Trazabilidad Animal* – SIPEC). This system generates data on livestock inventories and other livestock characteristics for the purposes of biosecurity surveillance and control and food safety. SIPEC is based on annual declarations by livestock holders and covers all livestock types. The traceability system for the bovine sector contains information by individual animal.

To conclude, Chile's statistical system maintains regular observation of producers engaged in livestock activity and generates updated information about the existence, economic and individual characteristics of these farmers. The Agricultural Census sets a minimum area or animal number threshold for the inclusion of economic units into observation.[7] The observation between the census years (over a period of ten years) is based on surveys that exclude the smallest and predominantly "backyard" farmers and also the regions where specific livestock activities have low importance. Thus, although there is substantial census- and survey-based statistical work, the observation of the smallest livestock operations is limited – a feature common to statistical systems in many other countries.

Funded research into farmer behaviour

A preliminary examination points to an overall lack of studies in Chile on farmer behaviour, including studies focussed on livestock disease management. The available publications concern general aspects of animal disease management, such as Rojas (2009) which outlines the context and development of the biosecurity system in Chile, or Max et al. (2007) which analyses the experience of the avian influenza outbreak in 2002. Some behavioural research in agriculture has been focussed on environmental issues (Roco et al., 2015; Salazar and Rand, 2016). Other research by Guarnan and Lerdón (1999), CONAF (2011) and Reyes and Lensink (2011) looked into farm typology and the specificities of the small farming segment. PMG (2015) undertook a broadly scoped survey of farmer marketing practices, use of financial instruments, insurance, organic farming, etc. All these studies touch upon farmer behaviour in some ways, but do not include livestock disease aspects.

Awareness through interaction with industry organisations and veterinarians

Chile's government has traditionally interacted with agricultural producers in various formats, both at national and sub-national levels. This is facilitated by the fact that geographically Chile is a relatively small country and with a relatively limited number of stakeholders, in particular concerning the livestock sector. Another important feature is the activity of the Agricultural and Livestock Development Institute (INDAP), subordinated to the Ministry of Agriculture that has the mandate for agricultural and rural development. It implements a wide range of development programmes targeted to subsistence producers and family farmers and deploys a large number of personnel in the field. INDAP's activity is an important channel linking government with a farming segment of small producers.

Chile's government has sought to increase public-private co-operation in recent years. In 2011, the National Commissions were created as public-private co-ordination bodies on cross-cutting issues of sectorial and (or) national importance. Among 11 such Commissions for key product sub-sectors, there is the National Beef Commission (*Comisión Nacional de la Carne Bovina*). It unifies representatives of livestock farmers, downstream operators of the meat chain, and government. SAG, as a public body in charge of plant and animal health, is one of the institutions representing government. The National Beef Commission currently works on animal farming productivity, improvement of information and co-ordination across the meat chain. Animal health issues are cross-cutting, but largely fall under the work stream related to meat export growth. This includes disease eradication programmes, exports of live animals, livestock traceability system, and the programme for official certification for livestock establishments. As a regular platform for public-private consultation, the National Beef Commission is focussed only on the cattle chain, and does not concern specific issues of dairy, pig meat, or poultry sub-sectors. In the sheep sector, several working groups operate at regional level and there is an intention to organise a nation-wide group involving producers and leaders of peasant organisations connected with INDAP.

SAG and INDAP interact with producer organisations also through *ad hoc* working groups, workshops, seminars, training courses, as well as specific livestock projects. One example is INDAP's project implemented in collaboration with farmer organisations in the region of Coquimbo. It seeks to convert small goat farmers from meat to milk production based on semi-extensive system. Biosecurity aspects are considered in this project among other issues. Another example is the project on eradication of bovine tuberculosis in the region of Los Lagos (see Section 4). Overall, the results of these *ad hoc* activities have not been analysed or systematised, however, according to SAG the concerns are addressed.

Regular contact between the Official Veterinarian (MVO) and Authorised Veterinarians exists in the framework of training for veterinarians organised on subjects of interest for SAG. The results of these activities are communicated by the MVO at national meetings, co-ordinated by the Central level. Interaction with veterinarians is also possible within sectoral working groups and public consultations on new regulations. However, there are no explicit arrangements, e.g. regular surveys or questionnaires of veterinarians about issues of on-farm disease management (Chilean Government, 2016).

6.3. Communication, information and training for farmers

Information and education influence all aspects of farmer decision making. Appropriate communication and information about disease existence, identification, consequences, costs and benefits of control and prevention programmes, responsibilities and policies, enables farmers to make well-informed decisions and ensure the diseases are managed effectively.

Communication and information

SAG is the principal provider of animal disease information. This includes communication about disease emergencies: general regulation and contingency plans for specific diseases, disease reporting requirements and export certification. The annual updates of the national sanitary situation are also provided. Another stream of SAG's information concerns compulsory disease eradication programmes, including national disease eradication plans, current actions and situation. SAG also informs about voluntary sanitary programmes, import and export legislation and procedures. All this information is available on-line at SAG's website (www.sag.gob.cl). In addition, a bi-monthly newsletter covering the most important international sanitary events is circulated to interested users in the public and private sector (Chilean Government, 2016). SAG vets are permanently present in the livestock establishments to supervise the operations, which generates a frequent flow of information about good practices from the SAG to the livestock farmers.

INDAP, through a range of its activities, acts as an important channel of information for the segment of small farming. To the extent these programmes concern livestock production, they are likely to include information on biosecurity and animal disease issues. Since 2015, farmers and other stakeholders have been involved in INDAP's activity planning. Such participatory approach can help to better identify small farmers' information gaps and adapt the provision information, including in the area of biosecurity and animal disease. However, the extent to which this is occurring and what issues are emerging is difficult to specify as INDAP's activities are significantly localised.

The websites of the national livestock industry associations – Chilean Association of Pig Producers (ASPROCER), National Federation of Milk Producers (FEDELECHE), National Federation of Beef Producers (FEDECARNE) and Chilean Association of Egg Producers – seem to provide limited and not frequently updated information, which does not cover disease management. One exception is the Chilean Association of Pig Producers, which communicates the on-going industry food safety programmes on its website, including those related to animal health (Annex 6.A3). The existence of other private and public providers of animal health information and their activities – e.g. at the level of regional or local administrations, education and training institutions and NGOs – requires further examination.

Overall, the government constantly interacts with small farmers in the framework of agricultural development assistance. With regard to larger farmers who are not covered by INDAP's programmes, it may be tentatively observed that for this farming segment animal disease information has a top-down character.

For the moment, the government has not undertaken any specific inquiry into the information needs of livestock farmers or other stakeholders and the most appropriate channels for its provision. The extent to which producers use official sanitary information and whether they find it useful has also not been investigated (Chilean Government, 2016). The targeting and adapting of veterinary and sanitary information to recipients with different profiles may be particularly relevant in the context of Chile's farming structure combining small and subsistence farmers on one side and technologically advanced and highly integrated operations on the other. For example, only 26% of cattle farmers and 14% of sheep farmers in Chile use internet (INE 2015a; INE 2015b).

Communication about livestock disease in Chile concerns mainly epidemiological and sanitary aspects. As noted in the other country studies included in this report, there is a lack of communication about the economic aspects of disease management. Economic considerations largely affect farmer disease management decisions and farmers need to have sufficient understanding about the costs and economic effects of good (or bad) biosecurity practices, both at farm level and across livestock industry and consumers. The evidence generated in that regard in Chile seems to be limited. According to the Chilean Government (2016), the official disease control and eradication programmes concern OIE-listed diseases that interfere with trade and impact economically, but there has been no systematic work on estimating the economic impacts of animal diseases. Some economic impact studies are performed in the private sector, for example, in the context of the recent disease outbreaks affecting poultry and pig producers. However, these studies do not always reach the public domain.

Education and training

Agricultural education and training in Chile is decentralised and involves a wide range of providers which have high autonomy – public institutions, foundations, universities and private companies (OECD, 2008).

Training and technical assistance have been an important component of agricultural policy in Chile addressed to small farmers. This is one of INDAP's activities, reaching out to more than a thousand users. For example in 2015, 44% of cattle producers and 43% of sheep producers received technical assistance through INDAP in the veterinary field (INE 2015a; INE 2015b).[8] SAG and INDAP develop special programmes covering, among others, biosecurity and reproductive diseases, as well as some regional programmes for traceability and sampling. The amount and the scope of training generally vary by farmer profile: subsistence producers typically receive elementary knowledge, while producers of "business profile" are offered broader and more specific training (Chilean Government, 2016). INDAP's training modules are developed on the basis of detection of local training needs, so it is difficult to generalise about the extent to which they cover livestock producers and incorporate animal health thematic.

There is an example of INDAP-industry collaboration in farmer training related to biosecurity. INDAP and poultry industry represented by Meat Exporters Association (Expocarnes) organise training for small and medium-sized farmers and the professionals from INDAP's technical teams under the thematic of poultry health and productivity. The specialists from the University of Chile, SAG, and Expocarnes give theoretical and practical courses on production and animal health, including preventive measures and rapid reporting of avian influenza.

Training for larger producers who do not qualify for INDAP's assistance is a matter of their individual initiative. Large farming enterprises can also offer training to employed staff on subjects of interest and benefit from a tax concession for personnel training – a capped income tax credit. This concession is not specific to agriculture and is available to businesses in all economic sectors.

In sum, the government currently implements no specific systematic training programme for farmers focused on livestock disease management, although this thematic is included in overall training for small farmers. Until present, SAG has not been involved in evaluation of the existing training programmes from the perspective of disease management.

6.4. Current experience with farmer compensation policy

Compensation is the principal economic instrument of livestock policy with a direct impact on producer incentives and actions to manage disease risk. Compensation is understood in this case study to be any payment or reimbursement provided to farmers within the framework of disease control and prevention programmes. This includes (i) indemnity for direct disease losses, such as dead or destroyed animals; (ii) compensation for consequential losses, such as those from business interruption; and (iii) payments for farmer *ex ante* actions, such as subsidising biosecurity investments and operations. This part examines the degree to which Chile's compensation policy stimulates or discourages producers to make adequate efforts to prevent disease and report it in a timely fashion when it occurs.

Producers in Chile have to report a disease that is subject to obligatory notification according to SAG's list – a failure to report entails fines. The national legislation does not foresee indemnities to producers in the case of disease outbreaks, whether it concerns compensation for destroyed or sick animals, or any other types of losses resulting from outbreak control measures. There are no national funds for indemnification of livestock producers based on public sources, or co-funded by producers (or industry).

Ad hoc measures

Some *ad hoc* assistance has been provided in the past and more recently. In the 1980s, producers were compensated on an *ad hoc* basis when animal destruction was involved. This was implemented in the context of either a disease outbreak, or planned measures in some disease eradication programmes. The assistance to affected farmers in some cases was in the form of supplies of live animals for restocking.[9]

In 2013-15, indemnification for culled animals was provided in the framework of the programme for eradication of bovine tuberculosis (BT) in the region of Los Rios. The objective was to encourage slaughter of infected animals. Indemnities were paid for each animal that has been detected BT-positive on quarantined farms up to January 2013, and for animals eliminated in slaughterhouses. The compensation amounted to 4 UF[10] (approximately USD 160) for adult cattle and 2 UF (USD 80) for calves.

Livestock insurance

Chile has been implementing subsidised insurance programmes in agriculture since 2000. They began in the crop sector and recently have been extended to the livestock sector. Insurance for beef and dairy cattle was introduced in 2012 and for sheep in 2015.

Livestock insurance is a multiple risk instrument: among the perils covered it includes animal death and livestock diseases. This instrument, however, does not cover the loss due to culling of animals by the order of veterinary authority and due to exotic diseases (according to SAG's statements). Conditions of insurance are similar for bovine cattle and sheep and foresee an insurance premium concession. A 40% subsidy to the insurance premium is provided and can be increased up to 65%-70% if all additional concessions apply (Table 6.1).

Livestock insurance is relatively new and is still being rolled out. The penetration of insurance is currently relatively low. In 2016, it covered 0.4% of total cattle inventories and less than 0.4% of sheep inventories. Also, the government intends primarily to assist small producers. According to Chilean Government (2016), the uptake of the insurance is constrained by a lack of experience with insurance amongst livestock producers who do not yet have sufficient "insurance culture". Another issue is the spatial dispersion of producers, who often appear to be off-site for the underwriting of a contract and its settlement in the case of accident. There is also a lack of interest among insurance companies to operate this product.

Table 6.1. Subsidised livestock insurance in Chile

Items	Conditions
Regions covered	All regions
Eligible producers	• All farmers registered with the Internal Revenue Service and payers of VAT • Farmers not registered with the Internal Revenue Service, but credit borrowers from INDAP, BancoEstado, or other institutions – in this case insured amount is capped at UF 250 (around USD 10 000).
Animals covered	Only animals in the official identification system and for which there is record of sanitary management and vaccinations.
Basic subsidy	40% of insurance premium, plus UF 1 (around USD 40) per policy, capped at UF 80 (around USD 3 200)
Additional cumulative subsidy	Basic subsidy is increased by the additional percentage points of the insurance premium in the following cases: • Renewal of policy (+10%) • Collective contracting, i.e. if insurance is purchased through institutions such as producer associations, guilds, financial organisations or downstream companies (+10%) • Less favoured areas (+5%) • Cultivation of cereals (+5%) for cattle farmers
Indemnity deductible	Value of animal at the purchase of contract, minus a deductible of up to 10% of animal value, a deductible varying according to the size of establishment.

Source: Agroseguros (2017) and Chilean Government (2016).

Other support activities

INDAP operates credit and investment programmes for livestock producers for development of farm infrastructure. These programmes may include improvements in the sanitary conditions of farms. However, this assistance does not concern direct action to eradicate diseases. The extent to which these programmes direct resources to sanitary improvements on farms is not known (Chilean Government, 2016).

In the dairy sector, there is a voluntary industry initiative to promote biosecurity at farm level. Some dairies apply an incentive scheme whereby milk producers participating in the government programmes Farm Free from Bovine Brucellosis and Farm Free from Bovine Tuberculosis receive price bonuses for delivered milk.

6.5. Conclusions

Chile enjoys a favourable animal health situation, thanks to geographic conditions impeding disease transmission and decades of successful work on disease eradication. Strict sanitary regulations and border controls prevent entry of exotic animal diseases. The efforts to strengthen national biosecurity system enabled the expansion of Chilean livestock product exports in the 2000s, while the need to maintain good sanitary reputation as an exporter necessitated continued action. The improvements in the national biosecurity in recent period were focussed on food safety and export certification systems – the work which had important implications for animal disease management. This includes the establishment of the livestock farm register and livestock traceability system, a suite of export certification programmes for livestock farms, and further disease eradication programmes. In intensive production poultry and pig meat sectors, disease surveillance was strengthened through government-industry programmes. There were also industry initiatives for better biosecurity practices on farms, e.g. in the pig meat, dairy and beef sectors.

Disease risks are always present and their probability and nature evolves, as evidenced by the most recent outbreak of avian influenza in Chile in 2017. This latency of risk requires constant improvements in the responsiveness and efficiency of the biosecurity system even with its good performance today. Increasing farmer incentives to prevent and report disease is the essential part of this task. This case study highlights several areas where further progress could be made in this regard.

Export interests largely drive animal disease policy in Chile, which focusses on commercial livestock producers supplying domestic and export markets. This farming segment is well integrated into product chains with vertical food safety controls ensured by the official national biosecurity system and industry standards. There remain small farmers who are weakly linked with commercial product chains, and whose disease situation cannot be perfectly monitored. Improving disease surveillance and prevention amongst such farmers is an issue in many countries. This does not appear to be a significant present concern for Chile, given the limited record of livestock epidemics in recent decades, but rather an issue of increased preparedness for potential risks. One essential challenge is to strengthen the incentives of small producers to early detect and report disease. The policy related to livestock epidemic compensation is an important area where individual incentives can be aligned with public objectives.

Chile's national legislation currently foresees no direct compensation of livestock holders in the case of compulsory measures to control disease (e.g. destruction of animals and movement restrictions), while non-reporting of disease entails penalties. This raises a question on whether penalties alone are sufficient to produce desired reporting behaviour by farmers. Compensation generates positive incentives to early-report disease and comply with control measures. A broader rationale for epidemic assistance is that economic impacts of livestock epidemic on farm enterprises are typically beyond the capacity of individual farmers to cope with – the argument particularly relevant in the case of subsistence and small farmers. Furthermore, livestock epidemic may endanger not only the economic activity of small holders, but their entire livelihood. Insurance could in principle be an instrument alternative to direct compensation. However, the currently existing insurance schemes in Chile do not cover diseases of high epidemiologic risk and are available only for bovine cattle and sheep. The early experience of these schemes in Chile indicates that both the supply and the uptake of livestock insurance face certain limits, even with substantial subsidy. This instrument is unlikely to expand to cover catastrophic risks.

Thus, the rationale for direct compensation of small livestock holders related to livestock epidemics warrants consideration. Chilean livestock industry stakeholders have previously examined a possibility of introducing compensation in respect to certain diseases, but this did not materialise considering the need for financial resources and also a favourable epidemiological situation. However, as discussed at length in Part 1 and the case studies for Australia and Korea, a good design can reduce the moral hazard associated with the indemnification and make these schemes more cost-effective. This includes appropriate and transparent criteria triggering the assistance and its scope (i.e. types of losses compensated), eligibility conditions, and the valuation of compensation. The underlying funding does not need to be necessarily based on public funds only and can include contributions from industry.

Chilean livestock policy could become more informed and thus more effective through increasing the bottom-up linkages within the national biosecurity system. This concerns at least several areas.

There seems to be little focus in Chile on studying livestock farmer behaviour: their risk perceptions, drivers and constraints to undertaking disease management. A preliminary examination suggests that research related to farmer disease management in general and focussed on farmer behavioural drivers in particular, is lacking. This may be due the overall perception of animal disease in Chile as low economic and social risk. However, such studies are a necessary forward-looking input into policy development, and they may warrant public support through research calls and possible funding. In addition, the regular surveys of livestock producers by the National Institute of Statistics represent a readily existing instrument to be exploited. These surveys could, beyond current topics, inquire about the issues of interest to government related to farmers' disease management.

Increased awareness about producers could help to improve the up-take and the usefulness of official animal disease information. The provision of biosecurity information could benefit from clarifying the needs and preferences expressed by producers and other stakeholders. The government may consider an investigation into the willingness of producers to use external information, their awareness about the existing information channels, which of them are preferred and actually used, and the degree to which farmers find official information relevant and applicable. The government may consider expanding the scope of information beyond the SAG-listed diseases, to also cover those which represent normal production risk, but may have substantial economic impact on farm enterprises. Furthermore, the information could be diversified to provide evidence about the costs and economic effects of disease on individual farms and rural communities overall. The understanding of potential risks and losses may encourage farmers to prevent and report disease more effectively than formal compulsion. The government could also work together with industry groups to engage them in dissemination of biosecurity information more actively than is the case today.

Increased feedback from producers to government is also required to improve farmer knowledge and skills. The scope of farmer training in livestock disease management and the extent to which they take it up seems to be insufficiently informed. An inquiry developed jointly by the veterinary and sanitary authority, INDAP, and education providers into knowledge and skills gaps of livestock farmers may be warranted to identify critical topics and different target groups to adapt current training programmes. The systematic and adapted farmer training in animal disease management is important given the small share of producers with advanced education amongst livestock holders.

The issue of bottom-up linkages within the national biosecurity system has specific implication when it concerns the small farming segment. INDAP's networks and programmes constitute an active basis for engagement with small farming populations. There is co-operation at regional level between SAG and INDAP to foster disease prevention amongst small farmers and improve their capacity to do so. However, these activities are often informal and driven by the choices and enthusiasm of people working on the ground. These practices deserve some systematic examination which could increase government's awareness, help to identify good local practices that could be applied more broadly, as well as to exploit possible synergies across regions and stakeholders.

Notes

1. This share does not account for the establishments with poultry.

2. In 2016, the individual shares of these companies were: Colún 27%, Soprole 24%, Nestlé 19%, Watt´s 12%, Surlat 6% and Quillayes 2% (ODEPA, 2017b).

3. For example, the survey of marketing channels for cattle and sheep in Chile does not cover units with less than 60 heads of sheep and 10 heads of cattle (INE 2015a; INE 2015b).

4. Several works at the University of Chile also examined biosecurity practices of small farmers raising beef cattle, goat and sheep (Lazcano Hevia, 2010; Vásquez Silva, 2008; Rojas Guajardo, 2012). These studies applied a common method: for the production systems and livestock types under investigation the sets of technical biosecurity measures were defined, i.e. kinds of biosecurity protocols. Sample farms were selected and surveyed about the extent to which they apply these biosecurity measures. The general finding is that surveyed farms practised only a small number of measures out of these biosecurity protocols. This early work by young analysts provides interesting insights into a little-researched topic related to biosecurity practices of small producers, however, it cannot be regarded as a comprehensive assessment of farms' biosecurity status.

5. Rich et al. (2005) indicate that an FMD-free status enables countries to sell products at a 10-50% premium. Furthermore, because it is difficult to distinguish between meat of an infected animal and one with an immune response to FMD vaccination, some countries (e.g. Japan) allow full market access only from sources designated as FMD-free without vaccination.

6. The pig survey covers establishments with at least 40 pigs or 20 sows and which have the necessary infrastructure to develop commercial activity. The poultry survey includes establishments with at

least 150 broilers and (or) laying hens, and which have the necessary infrastructure to develop commercial activity (direct communication from ODEPA).

7. The Agricultural Census includes establishments with the area of annual or permanent crops of at least 0.1 hectare, or with the natural pasture or forest area of at least 0.5 hectares. The Census also includes establishments having at least any of the following: 2 large adult animals; 4 large young animals; 10 small animals; 50 geese, turkeys or rabbits; 100 roosters, hens, broiler chickens, ducks, quail or pheasants; 10 ostriches or emus; or 10 beehives (INE, 2007).

8. These figures do not cover producers keeping less than 60 heads of sheep and less than 10 heads of cattle.

9. In the 1984 FMD outbreak producers received animals for re-stocking as an indemnity, while families in the mountainous regions received subsistence allowance. In the 1987 FMD outbreak, a monetary compensation was provided for destroyed animals, valued at market price (producers with genetically improved animals could receive higher compensation). In the programme for eradication of classical swine fever (1995-98), to achieve total eradication of the pathogen, Chilean Association of Pig Producers (ASPROCER) collaborated with SAG. Animals for restocking were provided to subsistence producers in the north whose animals were culled. Similarly, SAG and ASPROCER worked together on PRRS eradication project – at its final stages, the private sector partner, provided a stock of young animals for breeding. These animals were delivered for repopulation of farms that were subjected to sanitary cleaning, disinfection and depopulation measures.

10. The Unidad de Fomento (UF) – a unit of account used in Chile, equalling approximately USD 40.

References

Agroseguros (2017), *Seguros para el Agro con Subsidio del Estado* on-line, www.agroseguros.gob.cl/ganado-bovino.

ASPROCER (2017), Chilean Association of Pig Producers on-line, www.asprocer.cl/.

Chilean Government (2016), "OECD project on producer incentives in livestock disease management: Country case questionnaire", Responses to the OECD questionnaire, September 2016.

FAO (2006), *Country Pasture/Forage Resource Profiles: Chile* by Dr. Raúl R. Vera, www.fao.org/ag/agp/agpc/doc/counprof/PDF%20files/Chile-English.pdf.

FAOSTAT (2017a), *Commodity Balances - Livestock and Fish Primary Equivalent*, www.fao.org/faostat/en/#data/BL.

FAOSTAT (2017b), Production indices, www.fao.org/faostat/en/#data.

FAOSTAT (2017c), FAOSTAT database, FAO Publications, Rome, http://faostat.fao.org/.

Guarnan, J. D. and J. E. Lerdón (1999), "Caracterizacion y tipificacion de agricultores usuarios del centro de gestion empresarial de Paillaco", *Agro Sur*, V. 27, N 2.

Hamilton-West, C., H. Rojas, J. Pinto, J. Orozco, L.P. Hervé-Claude and S. Urcelay (2012), "Characterization of backyard poultry production systems and disease risk in the central zone of Chile", *Research in Veterinary Science*, Vol. 93, pp. 121–124, http://dx.doi.org/10.1016/j.rvsc.2011.06.015.

Hamilton-West, C., H. Rojas and S. Urcelay (2007), "Backyard production systems spatial characterization, the first step to assess the risk level for the introduction and spread of highly pathogenic avian influenza in the main Chilean poultry production areas", in GISVET 07, Copenhagen.

Hamilton-West, C., H. Rojas, J. Pinto, J. Orozco and S. Urcelay (2009), "Characterization of backyard poultry productions systems in the vicinity of high risk areas for HPAI introduction", in *Proceedings of the 12th Symposium of the International Society for Veterinary Epidemiology and Economics*, Vol. 12. ISVEE, Durban.

Hidalgo, M. (2016), "Chilean poultry industry, looking at the world for growth", Arkansas Nutrition Conference 2016, Rogers, Arkansas, www.thepoultryfederation.com/public/userfiles/files/Sept_8%2010%2000%20AM_%20M_%20Hidalgo_%20Chilean%20Poultry%20production_%20Looking%20at%20the%20world%20for%20growth.pdf.

INE (2007), *Manual del Empadronador. VII Censo Nacional Agropecuario y Forestal*, Instituto Nacional de Estadisticas, Chile, http://www.censoagropecuario.cl/aspectosmetodologicos/files/manual/manual_empadronador.pdf.

INE (2016), *Encuesta de Criaderos de Cerdos : Informe Preliminar Primer Semestre Año 2016.* Instituto Nacional de Estadisticas, Chile, www.ine.cl/canales/chile_estadistico/estadisticas_agropecuarias/estadisticas_pecuarias/pecuarias.php.

INE (2015a), *Encuesta de Ganado Bovino 2015*, Instituto Nacional de Estadisticas, Chile, www.ine.cl/canales/chile_estadistico/estadisticas_agropecuarias/estadisticas_pecuarias/pecuarias.php.

INE (2015b), *Encuesta de Ganado Ovino 2015*, Instituto Nacional de Estadisticas, Chile, www.ine.cl/canales/chile_estadistico/estadisticas_agropecuarias/estadisticas_pecuarias/pecuarias.php.

INE (2008), *VII Censo Nacional Agropecuario y Forestal: Tabulados Comunales*, Instituto Nacional de Estadisticas, Chile, www.censoagropecuario.cl/noticias/09/07042009.html.

Lazcano Hevia, C. (2010), "Bioseguridad en ganadería caprina en las comunidades agrícolas de Canela", Memoria para Optar al Título Profesional de Médico Veterinario, Universidad de Chile, Facultad de Ciencias Veterinarias y Pecuarias, Escuela de Ciencias Veterinarias, Profesor Guía : Dr. M. Maino Menéndez

Max, V., J. Herrera, R. Moreira and H. Rojas (2007), "Avian Influenza in Chile: A Successful Experience", *Avian Diseases*, March 2007, Vol. 51, Issue s1, pp. 363-365.

ODEPA (2017a), *Balanza histórica de productos silvoagropecuarios por sector*, Oficina de Estudios y Políticas Agrarias, Ministerio de Agricultura, Chile, www.odepa.gob.cl/balanza-de-productos-historica/#.

ODEPA (2017b), Boletín de la leche: avance de recepción y elaboración de la industria láctea Información año 2016, prepared by Ivonne López Tapia, Oficina de Estudios y Políticas Agrarias, Chile, Ministerio de Agricultura, www.odepa.cl/wp-content/uploads/2017/02/Boletin-de-la-leche-2016-anual.pdf.

ODEPA (2017c), *Fichas Nacional y Regionales, Análisis Censales y Catastros: Información Social y Productiva Según Tamaño del Productor y Localización Geográfica*, Oficina de Estudios y Políticas Agrarias, Chile, Ministerio de Agricultura, www.odepa.gob.cl/estadisticas/censos-y-catastros/.

ODEPA (2011), *Caracterización de la Pequeña Agricultura en Chile, Descripción de Sus Nnecesidades y Sus Subsectores, Evaluación de los Servicios Prestados por ODEPA a Este Segmento, y Propuestas de Mejoramientos y Nuevos Servicios e Instrumentos : Informe Final*, Estudio contratado por la Subsecretaría de Agricultura, Innovación para el Desarrollo Agrario Consultora LTDA, Ideaconsultora, www.odepa.gob.cl/odepaweb/servicios-informacion/publica/Resumen_Ejecutivo_e_Indice.pdf.

OECD (2016), "Chile", in *Agricultural Policy Monitoring and Evaluation 2016*, OECD Publishing, Paris, http://dx.doi.org/10.1787/agr_pol-2016-9-en.

OECD (2008), *OECD Review of Agricultural Policies: Chile 2008*, OECD Publishing, Paris, http://dx.doi.org/10.1787/9789264042247-en.

OIE (2017), *World Animal Health Information Database* (WAHIS Interface), www.oie.int/wahis_2/public/wahid.php/Countryinformation/Animalsituation, accessed 27 January 2017.

Paris Yon, A.L., (2008), "Practicas de bioseguridad adoptadas en grandes explotaciones de carne bovina de la zona central de Chile", Memoria para Optar al Título Profesional de Médico Veterinario, Universidad de Chile, Facultad de Ciencias Veterinarias y Pecuarias, Escuela de Ciencias Veterinarias, Profesor Guía, Dr. M. Maino Menéndez.

PMG (2015), "Oportunidades y comportamientos relevantes en mercado de agricultores", *PMG Chile Business Improvement* on-line, www.pmgchile.com/blog/?p=3185.

Reyes, A. and R. Lensink (2011), "The Credit constraints of market-oriented farmers in Chile", *Journal of Development Studies*, V. 47, 2011, Issue 12.

Rich, K.M., A. Winter-Nelson and N. Brozovic (2005), "Modeling regional externalities with heterogeneous incentives and fixed boundaries: applications to foot-and-mouth disease control in South America", *Review of Agricultural Economics*, Vol. 27, pp. 456–464.

Roco, L., A. Engler, B. E. Bravo-Ureta and R. Jara-Rojas (2015), "Farmers' perception of climate change in Mediterranean Chile", *Regional Environmental Change*, June 2015, Volume 15, Issue 5, pp. 867–879.

Rojas Guajardo, C. D. (2012), "Bioseguridad en ganadería bovina de carne de la zona centro-sur perteneciente a la agricultura familiar campesina", Memoria para Optar al Título Profesional de Médico Veterinario, Universidad de Chile, Facultad de Ciencias Veterinarias y Pecuarias, Escuela de Ciencias Veterinarias, Profesor Guía, Dr. M. Maino Menéndez

Rojas, H. (2009), "Animal disease management in a new livestock trade environment: The case of Chile", in J. Rushton, *The Economics of Animal Health and Production*, CAB International, Oxfordshire.

SAG (2017), *Lista de Enfermedades de Denuncia Obligatoria (EDO) al SAG*, Servicio Agrícola y Ganadero, Ministerio de Agricultura, Chile, www.sag.gob.cl/sites/default/files/enfermedades_denuncia_obligatoria_sag_8-6-2015.pdf.

SAG (2015), *Situación Sanitaria Brucelosis Bovina en Chile. Resultados del Programa Nacional de Erradicación de Brucelosis Bovina año 2015*, Servicio Agrícola y Ganadero, Ministerio de Agricultura, Chile, www.sag.gob.cl/sites/default/files/situacion_sanitaria_bb_2015.pdf.

SAG (2013), *Procedimiento: Plan Maestro para la Gestion de Emergencias Sanitarias*, Servicio Agrícola y Ganadero, Ministerio de Agricultura, Chile, www.sag.cl/sites/default/files/plan_maestro_SIGES.pdf.

Salazar, C. and J. Rand (2016), "Production risk and adoption of irrigation technology: evidence from small-scale farmers in Chile", *Latin American Economic Review* 2016, 25:2, doi:10.1007/s40503-016-0032-3.

Vásquez Silva, A. P. (2008), "Bioseguridad en ganadería ovina de la zona centro-sur perteneciente a la agricultura familiar campesina", Memoria para Optar al Título Profesional de Médico Veterinario, Universidad de Chile, Facultad de Ciencias Veterinarias y Pecuarias, Escuela de Ciencias Veterinarias, Profesor Guía, Dr. M. Maino Menéndez.

Annex 6.A1

Distribution of farm and animal numbers in Chile by farm land size, 2007

Figure 6.A1.A. Cattle

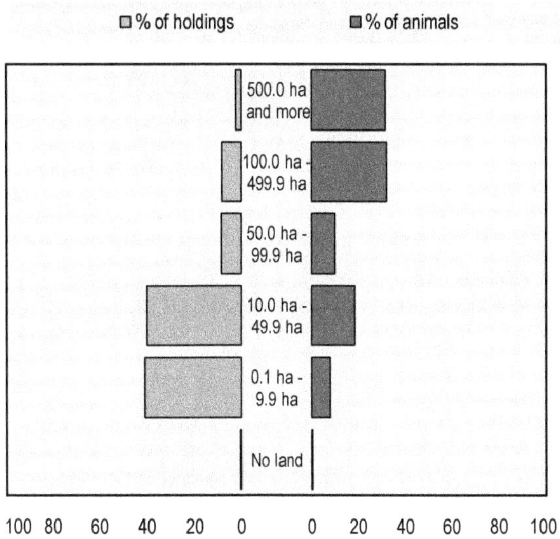

Figure 6.A1.B. Sheep

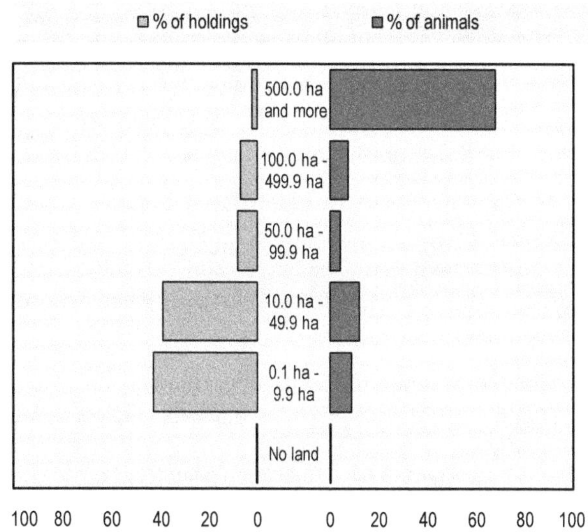

Figure 6.A1.C. Pigs

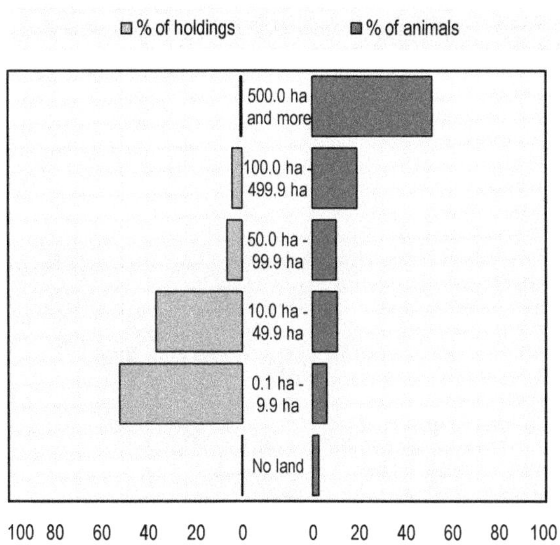

Figure 6.A1.D. Poultry

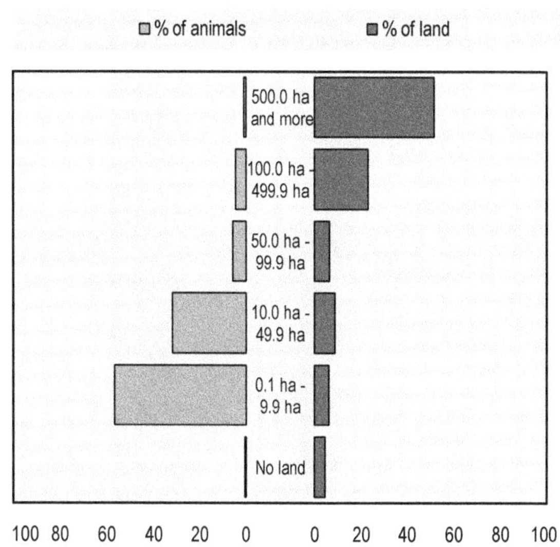

Source: ODEPA (2017c).

Annex 6.A2

Studies of backyard poultry production systems in Chile

Approximately 95% (2012) of poultry meat production is located in Chile's central zone (Valparaiso, O'Higgins and Metropolitan Region). Seven companies operate in this sector across the full poultry meat value chain exercising high biosecurity standards (Hamilton-West et al., 2012). This zone also concentrates 67% (2015) of the national egg production, but with a larger number of companies engaged in this activity (131 companies) and not all of them covering the full value chain (INE, 2016; Hamilton-West et al., 2012).

Hamilton-West et al. (2007 and 2009) estimated that 14 179 establishments with backyard production systems (further – BPS) existed in Chile's central zone which kept 418 809 birds. This roughly corresponds to below 1% of the national poultry number (FAOSTAT, 2017c).

A subsequent survey identified the main characteristics of these bird keepers, their connection with markets and biosecurity practices (Hamilton-West et al., 2012). This survey included 175 establishments and was conducted between December 2007 and June 2008. The average flock was 37 birds across all locations included in the survey, with domestic chickens representing the most common species kept in 93% of the surveyed units.

Most commonly, BPS farmers produced for own consumption and also sold products to neighbours, with only a small part directed to local markets (Figure 6.A2.1).

Figure 6.A2.1. Marketing channels for backyard poultry production in Chile: Survey results

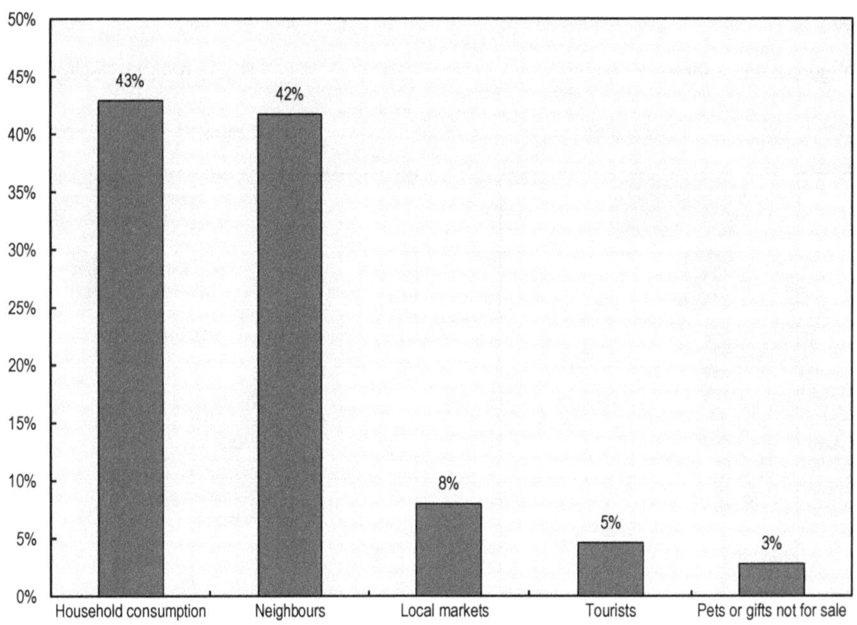

Source: Hamilton-West et al. (2012).

Almost 90% of surveyed BPS farmers used either free-range or mixed confinement (birds kept free-range during the day and in pens at night). Hamilton-West et al. (2012) note that such keeping systems increase the probability of contact between poultry of different flocks and between domestic and wild birds. In most of the surveyed BPS (98%) visitors could come into contact with backyard birds and no disinfection procedures were employed prior to entering or leaving a farm.

No BPS farmers had any formal training on disease identification and relied on own experience and knowledge exchange among neighbours. In somewhat less than three-quarters of BPS no health management of any type was performed and no treatment of sick birds or preventive measures. However, most of those who practiced some health management made recourse to veterinarians or health technicians. An official surveillance by veterinary services personnel for detection of exotic disease was carried out in 20% of BPS.

Annex 6.A3

Food safety management system in Chile's pork sector

Official programmes

Livestock Farms Under Official Certification (PABCO, for its acronym in Spanish)

National Pig Health Surveillance Programme (PNVSP, for its acronym in Spanish)

National Pathogen Control Programme

Residue Control Programme for Livestock Products

Integrated Surveillance Programme for Dioxins, Furans, and PCB's

Integrated Inspection Programme and Official Certification from the Agriculture and Livestock Service

Improved biosecurity

Best Practices at Pig Farms

Integrated Traceability System

Water and Ice Sampling at Exportation Slaughterhouses for Pork Products

Best Practices Manual for Animal Welfare for Pigs

Surveillance of Listeria Monocitogenes

Microbiological Control in Products Ready for Consumption

Country specific programmes

Pharmacological – Russian Federation

Microbiological Self-Control in Pork Meat – Russian Federation

Verification of Species for Raw and Cured Meat Products

Microbiological Self-Control – People's Republic of China

Coumaphos Self-Control – People's Republic of China

Salmonella Sampling – Sweden and Finland

Source: ASPROCER, 2017.

Chapter 7

Case study in livestock disease management: Korea

This case study begins with a contextual overview of the livestock sector and animal health situation in Korea, and then focuses on the following aspects: government awareness of producer behaviour in livestock disease management; information, education and training for producers; and producer compensation policy in Chile. The final section presents the conclusions and policy recommendations.

7.1. Overview of the livestock sector and animal health situation

Structural characteristics and economic importance of livestock production

Korea is a land-scarce country with the highest population density and the lowest availability of arable land per capita among OECD countries (0.029 hectare in 2013) (World Bank, 2016). The rapid industrialisation and urbanisation of the past decades has increased incomes (the GDP per capita has almost trebled since the mid-1990s) and shifted food consumption pattern towards livestock products. Domestic demand drew growth of domestic livestock production whose share in total agricultural output rose from only 23% in 1995 to 42 % in 2014 (OECD, 2016a), but Korea remains a net importer of livestock products, particularly beef and dairy. In 2014, domestic production covered 48% of national beef consumption, 55% of dairy products, 75% of pig meat, and 79% of chicken meat (MAFRA, 2016a). Domestic production is dependent on imported animal feed, with feed maize constituting country's top agricultural import (FAO, 2016).

Land scarcity is a significant factor leading to the overall small-scale farm structure in Korea. In 2015, a total of 1 089 thousand agricultural holdings operated in Korea (KOSTAT, 2016a) with the average farm size of only 1.5 hectares, although this represents an increase by almost 64% since 1975 (MAFRA, 2016a). Over 68% of farms have less than 1 hectare and only 8% have more than 3 hectares (KOSTAT, 2016a).

Cattle, pigs and chickens are the principal animals, with sheep representing insignificant numbers. A relatively small proportion of farm households are engaged in livestock production. Among more than one million farm households only somewhat over 53 000 keep livestock. Beef cattle are found on 7% of farms, 0.4% of farms keep dairy cattle, 0.4% pigs, and 3% chickens (KOSTAT, 2016a). Establishments with livestock derive on average 88% of their gross farm receipts from livestock activity (KOSTAT, 2016b), but many of them rely also on off-farm earnings. In 2015, the share of farm households with off-farm earnings was on average 43% across different livestock specialisations, with the lowest one (29%) observed in pig farming (KOSTAT, 2016c).

With limited land the growth in livestock output has been supported by strong increases in stocking densities (Figure 7.1). Between 1995 and 2015 beef cattle per holding increased from 5 to 30 heads, pigs from 136 to 1 679, and chickens from 928 to 5 369 (KOSTAT, 2016a). The livestock farm structure has also changed since 1995, with a shift of production towards larger farm sizes (Annex 7.A1). This process went particularly fast in the poultry sector which has become the most concentrated livestock sector and has also seen rapid development of vertical integration. In 2015, over 90% of meat chickens and meat ducks were raised within vertically integrated operations (Korean Government, 2016). Despite this apparent structural change, relatively small operations dominate in numbers across all types of livestock activities and in the beef, dairy and poultry sectors they also retain significant production shares (Figure 7.2).

Due to economic development and rural-urban migration which drew mainly on younger people, agriculture has experienced significant ageing and labour shortages (OECD, 2008). Somewhat less than three-quarters of livestock farmers in Korea are above 55 years of age, among whom those over 65 years constitute a large part (Figure 7.3). The aged structure of agricultural labour is not only the result of outflow of younger generations from rural areas. For the older-age rural population agricultural activity is also a form of a social safety net as they are not sufficiently covered by the existing pension systems. Many aged in rural areas stay economically active which contributes to the continuation of the small farming system in Korea (Annex 7.A2).

The structural characteristics discussed above indicate that farmers engaged in livestock production constitute a small part of Korean agriculture. These farmers are predominantly small-scale and in high age brackets and for many being active in agriculture is a way of social security. While livestock farmers derive most of their agricultural receipts from livestock, many of them also rely on off-farm earnings.

Figure 7.1. Changes in total livestock output and livestock densities in Korea between 1995 and 2013

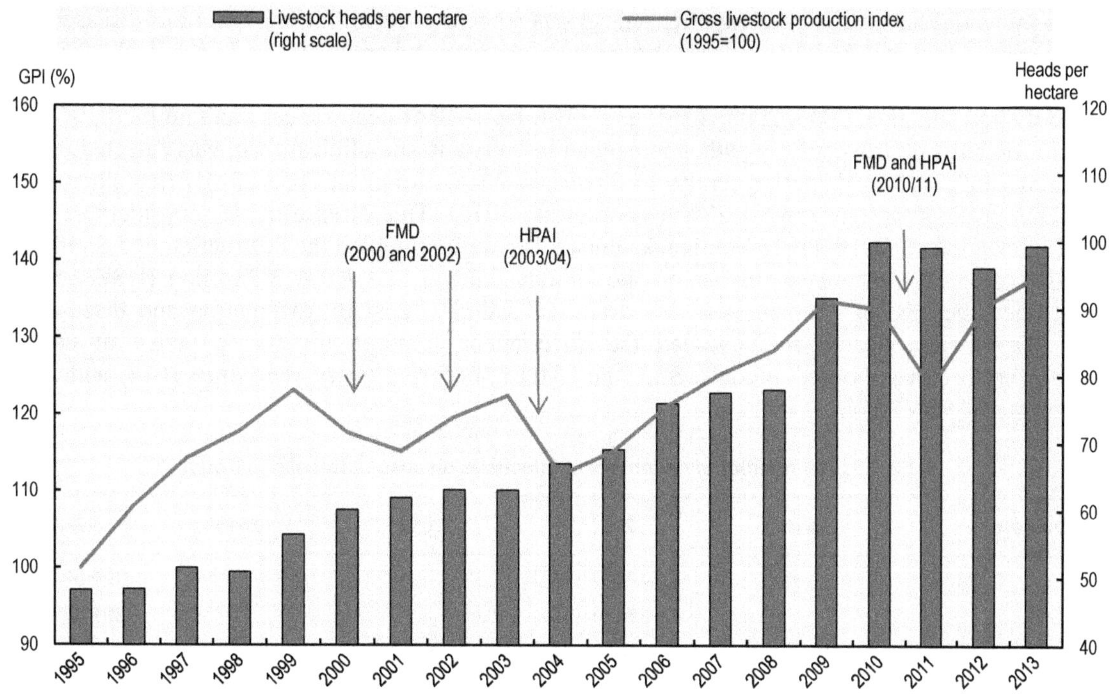

FMD – foot-and-mouth disease, HPAI – highly pathogenic avian influenza;
Note: The values of livestock densities are based on the total number for the main species (cattle, pigs, sheep, goats and poultry) divided by agricultural area.

Source: FAO (2016).

Figure 7.2. Distribution of farm numbers and livestock inventories between large and small farming segments in Korea, August 2016

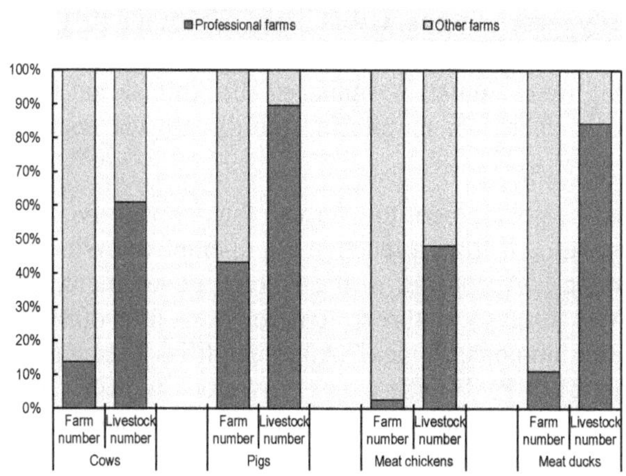

Note: The benchmark separating large and small farms is: 50 cows, 1 000 pigs, 30 000 meat chickens, and 10 000 meat ducks. The establishments with livestock above these numbers are classified as large ("professional") farms, and those below are classified as small farms.

Source: MAFRA (2016b).

Figure 7.3. Age structure of livestock farmers in Korea, 2015

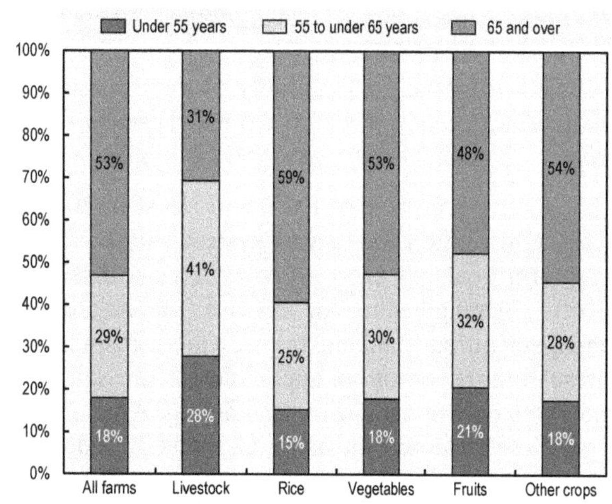

Source: KOSTAT (2016a).

Overall situation related to livestock and animal disease risk

Since the mid-2000s, Korea has experienced serious reoccurrences of highly infectious diseases, such as avian influenza, foot-and-mouth disease, brucellosis, bovine tuberculosis and classical swine fever (Table 7.1). Highly pathogenic avian influenza (HPAI) has been stubborn, with states of clinical disease notified to the OIE in 2003, 2006, 2008, 2010, and 2014. New HPAI occurrences were notified also in 2015, with 11 million birds destroyed. Low pathogenic avian influenza in sub-clinical form was detected every year between 2007 and 2010, and most recently, in 2015 and 2016. Korea had been FMD-free since the 1934 epidemic, but suffered an outbreak in 2000 (Yoon et al., 2012). This disease causes considerable financial damage. For example, in 2010-11, 153 outbreaks during 145 days prompted the destruction of 3.3 million pigs and 150 000 cattle. The estimated impact on the national budget was KRW 2.7 trillion (USD 2.5 billion), which included the cost of compensation for destroyed animals, cost of vaccination and disease control measures. This unprecedented epidemic led the government to adopt in 2011 a policy of nationwide vaccination for all cloven-hoofed animals. Still, the FMD re-occurred every year since 2014, with the most recent outbreak in early 2017.

Table 7.1. The number of major recent infectious disease outbreaks in Korea

Disease	2010	2011	2012	2013	2014
FMD	17	153 (2010-11)	-	-	188 (2014-15)
HPAI	-	53 (2010-11)	-	-	391 (2014-15)
Brucellosis	-	490	273	118	84
Bovine tuberculosis	-	257	290	321	438

Source: Adapted from Oh (2015).

Concerning diseases not subject to OIE notification and taking the most recent period only, Korea suffered large outbreaks of seven diseases in 2015 and eight in the first half of 2016. This concerns diseases such as porcine epidemic diarrhoea (PED) and chronic wasting disease (CWD). According to the Korean government, although disease occurrence has been on the decline since 2014, the subsequent deaths of piglets caused serious damage to farms. Easing of movement restrictions, the provision of livestock insurance, and other means are being applied to induce owners to voluntarily report disease. CWD broke out for the first time in six years since 2010 and requires special attention in terms of control and prevention as the data is not sufficient to prove the possibility of the disease transmitting from animals to humans. The Animal and Plant Quarantine Agency (Foreign Animal Disease Division) is in charge of monitoring the disease via research projects (Korean Government, 2016).

The reoccurrence of FMD and HPAI in 2010 have led the government to overhaul the national livestock disease prevention and control system with the focus on changing it from a reactive to pre-emptive system. A long-term goal has been set to become a disease free country. According to the Korean government, this involves strengthening of disease surveillance, improved disease outbreak control and post-outbreak management, and making farmers more responsible and autonomous. Annex 7.A3 exemplifies the changes foreseen in the system in application to prevention and control of FMD. The major "Livestock Industry Act" and "Act on Prevention of Contagious Animal Diseases" were also amended to strengthen animal disease regulation; these acts introduced a range of underlying measures discussed below.

Key institutions involved in livestock disease issues

The Ministry of Agriculture, Food, and Rural Affairs (MAFRA) is responsible for the delivery of animal health services on behalf of the Korean Government with the mandate for legislative initiative (Annex 7.A4). The Central Animal Disease Control Council is a non-permanent body deliberating on major policies related to animal disease control.

The Animal and Plant Quarantine Agency (QIA) is an executive veterinary agency implementing disease control policies and has the responsibility of veterinary research. Livestock Health Control Association (LHCA) is a public veterinary institution, performing duties of clinical examination, testing, sanitary inspections of livestock products, disinfection, and education and public relations for the prevention of livestock diseases. Central Animal Disease Surveillance Council operates as QIA's consultative platform.

Each provincial government has a veterinary service responsible for the control and eradication of diseases within the province. These veterinary services include veterinary laboratories, which carry out veterinary diagnosis, surveillance activities, and inspections of livestock products.

Livestock producer associations – the National Agricultural Cooperatives Federation (NACF), the Korean Swine Association, the Korean Poultry Association and the Korean Cattle Association – have established Joint Disease Control Units in each region, which conduct autonomous disease control activities, such as cleansing and disinfection.

7.2. Government's activity to increase awareness about farmer behaviour

Private operators are the ultimate decision makers of farm enterprises. Evidence about farmer behaviour and their response to policy is thus a necessary input into policy making, including in the area of animal disease.

Availability of information about farmers undertaking livestock activity

As a starting point, governments require sufficient information about the number, structural and social characteristics of the farming community they engage with. This information should have adequate national coverage and consistency.

Statistics Korea (KOSTAT) is the central institution producing the body of national statistics. Every five years KOSTAT conducts the Census of Agriculture, Forestry and Fisheries. It generates information on the number of farm households by type of agricultural activity, age and educational attainments of managers. It also observes the farms in terms of the value of agricultural sales, the size of livestock herds, and areas planted and harvested to different crops. Quarterly Livestock Statistics Surveys use the populations of the Agricultural Census for a more frequent monitoring of "livestock farms", defined as households which derive the largest part of agricultural receipts from livestock production. These Surveys report the number of such holdings and animals by species, and socio-economic characteristics of farms, such as gender and age of farm operators, amount of sales per holding, or farm size. The extent to which this information is used for livestock policy development requires further investigation.

There is an obvious lack of information about the households with agricultural activity but which do not fall under the official definition of agricultural holding and thus are not statistically observed. In Korea, this includes establishments with less than 0.1 hectares of land or with sales of agricultural products per year or the value of agricultural animals below KRW 1.2 million (USD 1 090). These establishments also represent certain biosecurity risks.

The re-occurrence of FMD in 2000 exposed the insufficiencies of information about the number of holdings keeping animals, their location and the numbers of animals in holdings. This prompted the government to introduce in 2003 a mandatory registration system. The establishments with cattle, swine and poultry with inventories above a certain threshold were obliged to register with local administrations and report the number of animals, the existing livestock facilities and equipment. Along with livestock farmers, livestock traders and owners or drivers of vehicles for transportation of livestock are also subject to the mandatory registration. The owners of livestock vehicles should also install a GPS device that wirelessly recognises the vehicle. The regulation has been further strengthened after the epidemics of FMD and avian influenza in 2010-11. In 2013, obligatory sanitary standards and location criteria for livestock establishments were introduced. These apply to larger farms which should receive approval by local authorities based on compliance with these standards (Annex 7.A5). Failure to comply with facility approval requirement entails a penalty of KRW 30 million (USD 27 000) and may be punished by imprisonment, while a failure to comply with the registration requirement leads to a penalty of KRW 5 million (USD 4 400).

The information from the mandatory registration and approval system is aggregated into the Korean Animal Health Integrated System (KAHIS), which is used to support disease prevention, biosecurity and control activities. For example, the creation of the KAHIS has substantially facilitated the epidemiologic investigations by enabling the analysis of big data as opposed to previous reliance on interviews.

Funded research into farmer behaviour

A preliminary examination indicates that economic research into animal disease in Korea focussed on issues of livestock insurance, in particular, the aspects of adverse selection and moral hazard (Jeong and Huh, 1998; Kim et al., 2008a). Other studies measured the economic impacts of livestock diseases and estimated direct economic losses and the associated welfare losses (Huh et al., 2001; Jung et al., 2001; Choi et al., 2002; Song et al., 2006; Woo et al., 2008; and Jeong et al., 2011). A broader behavioural research into issues of animal disease management, such as farmer risk perceptions, farmer awareness of risks and their potential effects, awareness about specific disease risk management practices, attitudes towards these practices, or attitudes towards specific (compensation) policy measures, seems to be lacking, although a further literature search is required to firmly support this conclusion. Environmentally friendly agriculture (Jung, 2008; Choi et al., 2009; Cho, 2004) and risk attitudes of rice farmers (Kim et al., 2008b) have been the main issues of interest in farmer behavioural research in Korea. Overall, livestock disease thematic seems to remain primarily a veterinary field (Annex 7A6).

Awareness through interaction with industry organisations and veterinarians

Several councils are organised in Korea for the exchange between the government and non-government stakeholders. The interaction through the channels described below is primarily focussed on veterinary and sanitary aspects of livestock epidemics.

The Central Animal Disease Control Council was created in 2002, initially to act as an advisory body to the Minister of Agriculture, Food and Rural Affairs and was also later given the task of preparing proposals for disease control policy (Box 7.1). The Council joins government officials, livestock industry representatives, experts in livestock husbandry, veterinary, medicine and environment. The creation of this body was a step towards increasing traditionally limited involvement of farm industry and other stakeholders in Korea in livestock policy development. The Council is focussed mainly on issues of disease epidemics and is accordingly structured. Five sub-councils are organised on FMD, BSE, bovine diseases, swine diseases, and poultry diseases. They review response measures to epidemics, such as the scope of movement restrictions and depopulation, whether to conduct immunisation in the case of major livestock disease outbreaks, change of vaccines, etc. Beyond the Central Council, councils associated with local governments with similar functions operate at regional level.

The Central Animal Disease Surveillance Council is the advisory platform of the Animal and Plant Quarantine Agency; while the Surveillance Councils for Animal Disease Affected Areas are held by the municipal or provincial animal disease control institutions. These councils consider operational and local issues, such as the establishment of animal disease surveillance plans, collection and analysis of information on disease epidemic, early detection of diseases, development of preventive measures, and animal disease outbreak warnings. They engage various representatives, such as the central and regional biosecurity institutions, the Livestock Health Control Association, the National Agricultural Cooperatives Federation, the Korean Veterinary Medical Association, and producer associations.

According to the Korean government it also holds consultations with veterinarian associations (Korean Pig Veterinary Society, Korean Veterinary Medical Association), veterinary universities and clinical veterinarians as part of the process for determination of disease prevention policies.

Box 7.1. Central and regional Animal Disease Control Councils in Korea

The Central Animal Disease Control Council ("Council") is a non-permanent body which deliberates on major policies that concern animal disease control, as stipulated in the Act on the Prevention of Contagious Animal Disease ("the Act"). In addition to government officials, the Council includes experts in relevant fields, such as the veterinary, livestock husbandry, medicine, and environment. The functions of the Council include:

- Formulation and implementation of measures for the management of contagious animal diseases.
- Investigation and research concerning contagious animal diseases.
- Establishment and implementation of emergency control measures for each contagious animal disease.
- Co-operation with related agencies for animal disease control.
- Formulation of quarantine measures for animals exported or imported and the products thereof and the improvement in the quarantine system.
- Other matters deemed necessary for the management and control of contagious animal disease and referred to the Council by the Minister of MAFRA or the chairperson of the Council.

The Council is currently composed of 73 members: 8 representing the government, 21 academia, 13 the livestock associations, and 31 the private sector, including veterinarians and consumer groups. Academia members represent the following fields: 14 veterinary professors, 4 medical professors and 3 are professors of economics, or agricultural economics. Members from the private sector are mostly veterinary clinicians and some are experts in law and environment, or represent consumer groups.

Source: Korean Government (2016).

7.3. Communication, information and training for farmers

Information and education influence all aspects of farmers' decision making. Appropriate communication and information about disease existence, identification, consequences, costs and benefits of control and prevention programmes, responsibilities and policies, enables farmers to make well-informed decisions and ensure the diseases are managed effectively.

Communication and information

MAFRA and the Animal Plant and Quarantine Agency (QIA) have a legal duty to notify disease outbreaks and disseminate information on the status of notifiable disease outbreaks. Information about 11 diseases, such as the date of outbreak, the kind of disease and affected farms, and the type and number of affected livestock is available in real time on the websites of the MAFRA, local governments and QIA. MAFRA maintains a website dedicated to FMD and AI. The government also collects monthly data on FMD status of pig farms according to the FMD serum surveillance plan. MAFRA and QIA are also tasked to provide detailed information about the occurrence of contagious animal disease abroad. Biosecurity information may also be disseminated through livestock industry newspapers and magazines. For direct communication, which is particularly important for small farms and aged persons in rural areas, a call centre with 188 service providers is operated by the Livestock Health Control Association, a public institution for disease prevention.[1]

Besides the information on disease outbreaks, the information on livestock disease control measures is shared with farmers and livestock stakeholders. They can obtain it directly from the websites of veterinary authorities or local governments. The government develops annual livestock health and disease control plans and manuals and provides this information to relevant public officials and people in the livestock industry. Occasionally, the government produces leaflets and producer organisations deliver to farmers and the industry. Beyond that, producer organisations publish biosecurity information on their home webpages.

There are thus various channels for communication on the epidemiological and sanitary aspects of livestock disease with farmers, directly or through their associations. However, the communication about economic aspects of disease management seems to be lacking. Economic considerations play a very important role in farmers' decisions to adopt certain behaviour. The economic information to support farmers' decisions should help them understand the cost and benefits of various disease management practices, it should provide information about economic impacts of animal disease on the farm enterprise (on profits and wealth), as well as about broader effects of potential disease outbreaks on the livestock sector as a whole, upstream and downstream industries, consumers and their local communities. Such communication could draw on a body of available research and implies the need for various studies into the economics of farm biosecurity practices and economic impact analysis of FMD and avian influenza. A number of Korean studies (cited above) measured economic impacts of livestock. Research carried out elsewhere but of relevance in the Korean context could also be mobilised to open communication with producers in the economic dimension of disease management.

For the moment, no focused surveys or studies have been undertaken into livestock farmers' information needs, the degree to which they make recourse to external information, most used and trusted sources, and the extent to which they use information from government. Another important aspect is the identification of the most effective channels and the forms of communication. Famers may not consider generic information useful and there is a need to tailor the communication according to farms of different business profiles ("professional" versus "non-professional"), specialisation, and exposure to disease risks. The predominance of "non-professional" and older age groups amongst Korean livestock farmers involves additional specifics, e.g. on-line communication may be less effective and more personalised and varied direct ways of communication may be required. Co-operation with producer associations could facilitate the identification of areas for the improvement of biosecurity communication, as well as implementation and funding of this work.

Education and training

Approximately 15% of livestock farmers in Korea have college or higher education (Figure 7.4). The dominant majority of livestock producers (82%) have only completed either middle or high school, while 3% have received no schooling. These education attainments are rather low, but compare more favourably with those in some crop farming activities (for example, rice and vegetable growing).

Recently, the government has taken an essential step to increase farmer awareness about major infectious diseases, reporting requirements, and preventive measures. In 2013, a mandatory training was introduced for farms (owners and hired farm managers) included in the livestock farming registration system. This mandatory training also covers livestock traders and owners or drivers of vehicles for transportation of livestock (Annex 7.A5).

The training themes include livestock laws and regulations, disease control and management, animal welfare, hazard analysis critical of control points (HACCP), and other optional topics. The programme includes on-site training. Livestock traders and owners or drivers of vehicles for livestock transportation additionally receive the course on livestock vehicle registration system. For the farmers, the amount of training is up-scaled depending on the size of their enterprise: smaller farmers (who only have to register their operations) undergo shorter training, while those with larger operations (who have to register their operations and receive the approval of facilities) take a more extensive training (Table 7.2). Upon completion of the mandatory programme, farmers should take a supplementary training (every two years for larger farms and every four years for small farms). A special site was created in 2015 so that farmers can take the supplementary training on-line (www.farmedu.kr).

The cost of the mandatory training is shared between the government and trainees – farmers, traders, and transporters of livestock. The government covers 70% of the training fees, with trainees contributing the remaining 30%. The government also bears the programme administration expenditures.

Figure 7.4. Education attainments of livestock farmers in comparison with other farmer groups in Korea

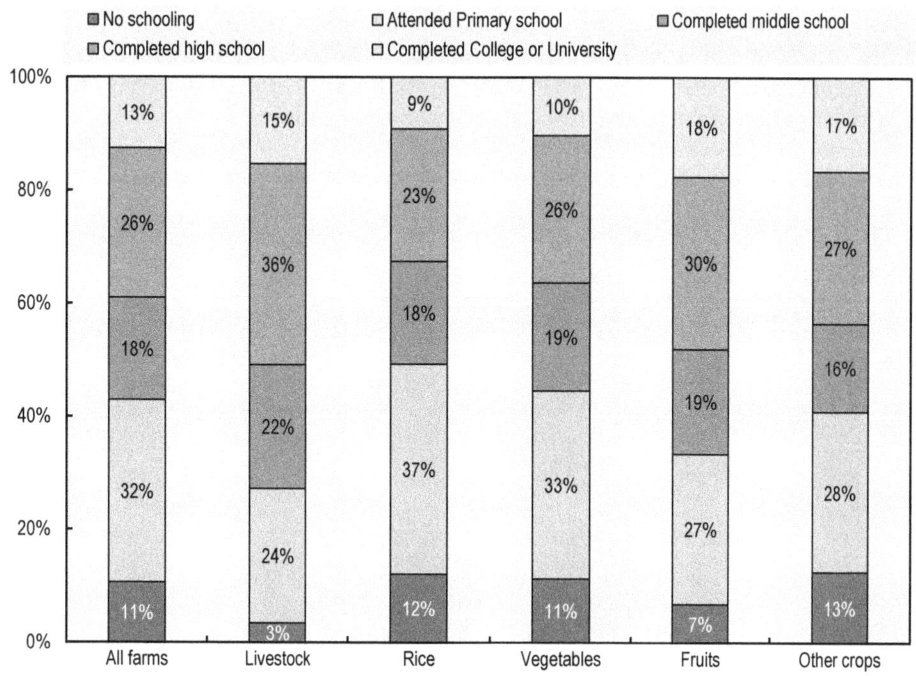

Note: livestock farms are the establishments with receipts from livestock products comprising the largest share of total agricultural receipts.

Source: KOSTAT (2016a).

Table 7.2. Mandatory training programme in animal disease prevention and control in Korea

		Mandatory training	Supplementary training
Livestock farmers	Large farms (subject to registration operations and approval of facilities)	24 hours	6 hours every 2 years
	Small farms (subject to registration of operations only)	6 hours	6 hours every 4 years
Livestock traders		- "-	4 hours every 4 years
Owners or drivers of vehicles for transportation of livestock		- "-	- " -

Source: Korean Government (2016).

Mandatory training does not concern livestock keepers who are not required to register (i.e. keepers with very small livestock numbers), poultry keepers with production facilities below the minimum size threshold (10 m^2) and also the owners of animals that are not susceptible to FMD or avian influenza. The exemption of the smallest animal keepers is driven by obviously high administration costs to engage with this group. The inclusion in the mandatory training of these micro-farmers would also involve an additional high financial burden for the government, while the willingness of these producers to voluntarily contribute to the cost of training is not clear. The exemption of the smallest livestock keepers from the obligatory training is thus an expected choice. This, however, leaves considerable risk given the assumingly large numbers of such livestock holders and the frequent re-occurrence of serious disease in recent years, such as avian influenza. It may be warranted considering alternative ways to involve this group in biosecurity training by exploring the potential for local action with engagement of local communities.

Beyond the mandatory training the government funds several voluntary training programmes. One is targeted to farms that keep cloven-hoofed livestock and thus represent a potential FMD risk. Two courses are available within this programme: a Group Training Programme on Prevention and Control Measures for Contract-Based Pig Farm Managers (about three hours) and a Tour Training Programme by region for Artiodactyla Farms (about one hour). Another voluntary training programme is aimed at prevention and control of avian influenza, and also includes several courses: "On-site Training for HPAI-affected Farms or Poultry Farms in AI-concentration Regions" and "Training for Poorly Performing Farms" based on the review and assessment results of prevention and control status of poultry operations.

Figure 7.5. Public spending on training in disease prevention and control in Korea, 2012-16

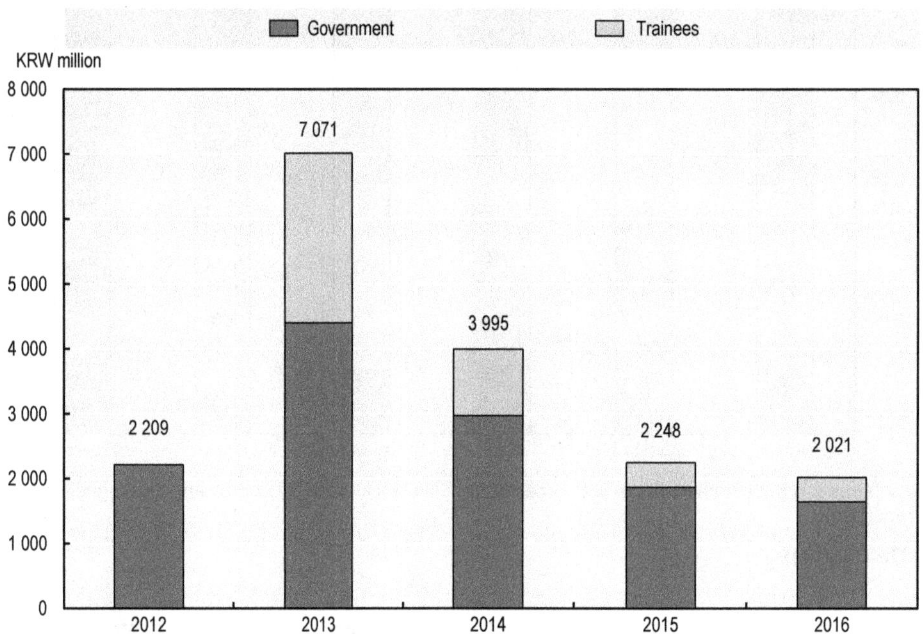

Note: the spending amounts include mandatory training only and cover all beneficiary groups, i.e. farmers, livestock traders and transporters.

Source: Korean Government (2016).

The government began the funded training programmes in 2012. The amount of spending more than tripled in 2013 with the introduction of the mandatory programme, but has been diminishing since then, reflecting the passing of the phasing-in peak (Figure 7.5). The total government spending amounted to KRW 2.6 billion (USD 2.3 million) per year in 2012-16, and varied during this period between 4% and 17% of total allocations for agricultural education and extension (as they are estimated in the OECD agricultural support database for Korea – OECD, 2016a).

The training programmes include pre-set topics. Farmer and industry opinions about their training needs have not yet been collected. Farmer and trainers' opinions about the training provided and the effectiveness of government spending have not been yet evaluated.

7.4. Current experience with farmer compensation policy

Compensation is the principal economic instrument of livestock policy with a direct impact on producer incentives and actions to manage disease risk. Compensation is understood in this case study to be any payment or reimbursement provided to farmers within the framework of disease control and prevention programmes. This includes: (i) indemnity for direct disease losses, such as dead or destroyed animals; (ii) compensation for consequential losses, such as those from business interruption; and (iii) payments for farmer *ex ante* actions, such as subsidising biosecurity investments and operations. This part examines the degree to which Korea's compensation policy stimulates or discourages producers to make adequate efforts to prevent disease and report it in a timely fashion when it occurs.

Disaster assistance for nationally notifiable diseases

Compensation policy related to infectious livestock diseases is part of the national livestock disease prevention and control policy. A range of assistance is currently in place to compensate for direct and consequential losses of livestock producers (Table 7.3). There is an explicit delineation between disaster assistance and insurable risk in Korea which is based on the categorisation of diseases into nationally notifiable and those that are not included in this list. Sixty-five livestock diseases are listed as the national notifiable infectious diseases under the "Act on Prevention of Contagious Animal Diseases". These diseases are further classified into three categories according to the degree of contagiousness and the scale of potential socio-economic losses. For each class, a specific set of outbreak control measures is established, which effectively determines the scope of potential compensation in each disease case (Annex 7.A7).

Table 7.3. Korea's support measures related to livestock epidemics

		National notifiable diseases					**Non-notifiable diseases: Insurance**
		Livestock compensation scheme	Livelihoods Stabilisation Assistance	Income Stabilisation Fund	Operations Stabilisation Fund	Fund for Stabilisation of Agro-industry	
Coverage		14 diseases in Class 1 and Class 2(1)	FMD, HPAI, CSF, ASF, CBPP, Rinderpest	FMD, HPAI	FMD, HPAI	FMD, HPAI	16 types of livestock
Financing arrangements		Costs shared between central and local governments			Financed by central government		Insurance premium co-financed by central and local governments
		80% - central government; 20% - local governments	70% - central government, 30% - local governments	70% - central government, 30% - local governments	Concessional loans	Concessional loans	
Direct losses	Culled animals	X	-	-	-	-	X
	Lost product	-	-	-	-	-	-
	Lost property	X	-	-	-	-	X
	Movement restrictions	-	-	X(2)	-	-	-
Consequential losses	Re-stocking	-	-	-	X(3)	-	-
	Partial loss of animal value	-	-	-	-	-	-
	Business interruption	-	-	-	-	X(5)	X
Household income support		-	X(4)	-	-	-	-

FMD: foot-and-mouth disease; HPAI: highly pathogenic avian influenza; CSF: classical swine fever; ASF: African swine fever; CBPP: contagious bovine pleuropneumonia.

1. Class 1: FMD, HPAI, CSF, ASF, rinderpest, CBPP; Class 2: brucellosis, tuberculosis, bovine spongiform encephalopathy, swine Aujeszky's disease, *swine influenza,* scrapie, rabies, and mule deer chronic wasting disease.
2. Losses from movement restrictions include losses from delays in livestock shipping and stocking or advanced shipping.
3. Reduced-interest loans to producers for the re-stocking following outbreaks.
4. Assistance is provided to the owners of animals slaughtered by stamping-out order.
5. Assistance is provided to agribusinesses such as hatcheries, slaughterhouses or feed companies.

Source: Korean Government (2016).

In the event of notifiable disease outbreaks, central and local governments provide various types of support to producers, and in certain cases also, to upstream and downstream businesses. This support concerns both direct losses resulting from outbreak control measures, as well as consequential losses.

The livestock compensation scheme operates for livestock keepers whose animals were ordered for destruction (Annex 7.A7). This support is provided for diseases in Class 1 and Class 2 for which culling is part of the outbreak response measures. Only 14 diseases are distinguished in these two classes that command compensation. The base indemnity rate corresponds to the market price of animals on the day it is stamped out. However, the effective indemnity rate is flexible due to the possibility of varied discounts to the base rate depending on the risk status of farm, type of disease, and compliance with prevention and outbreak control requirements (Table 7.4).

The condemned animals, whether healthy or sick, command a 100% indemnity. However, for those tested positively for FMD, AI, swine fever or brucellosis, the indemnity is discounted by 20% of the market price. This discount is meant to incentivise livestock farmers to prevent these diseases in particular. A further incentive for prevention of disease is included in the differentiation of indemnity depending on a farm's disease history: those with recurrent outbreaks in the past two years will incur a 20% and up to 80% reduction depending on the number of outbreaks. A reduction in indemnity rates is also foreseen in the event of violation of rules for preventive vaccination or failure to comply with disease outbreak control orders. Another set of discounts is intended to incentivise the early reporting of disease – delays in reporting result in reductions of indemnity rate by 20% to 40%. In the case of a failure to report the indemnity is reduced by 60%. Early reporting is also stimulated by the provision of no indemnity for dead animals. Finally, since 2015, there is a system of rewards to third parties who report the presence of suspected animals on other farms, or report other farmers violating orders on preventive measures.

Table 7.4. Compensation discounts for destroyed livestock

Discount criteria		Reduction to the base compensation rate, %
Infection with FMD, AI, swine fever, and brucellosis		20%
Unregistered, unauthorised farms		10%
Non-compliance with the recommended stocking densities of livestock		No compensation for the livestock in excess of the recommended number
Failure by contractor to ensure training in farms raising animals under contracts		5%
Risk profile of farm	2 outbreaks within 2 years	20%
	3 outbreaks within 2 years	50%
	4 outbreaks within 2 years	80%
Disease reporting	Delay in reporting from 1 to 4 days	20%
	Delay in reporting of 5 days and over	40%
	Failure to report	60%
	Early reporting (on the day of outbreak or before the appearance of symptoms)	A decrease of rates by 10% of other penalties if they apply
Prevention during "peace time"	Failure to comply with orders such as inspection, administration of medicine or injection	5%
	Failure to vaccinate for FMD	40%
	Rejection, interruption, evasion of epidemiological study	5%
Compliance with control measures	Failure to disinfect	5%
	Failure to comply with movement restrictions	5%
	Violation of temporary movement restrictions	5%
	Failure to carry out culling	5%
	Failure to carry out orders, such as burial or disinfection	5%
	Failure to carry out orders, such as movement restrictions of infected object, restriction of washing	5%

Source: MAFRA (2016d).

This current scheme has been applied since December 2015 and replaced the previous mechanism which was considered ineffective following the outbreaks of FMD and HPAI in 2014. More time is required to observe and evaluate the performance of this new scheme. However, several tentative comments about the incentive structure of the current scheme can be made.

The scheme uses around 20 different criteria that can trigger a reduction in indemnity. Farmers thus face a long list of potential penalties and may be induced to trade across different infringements. Second, a question can be raised on whether a 5% indemnity discount for the failure to comply with outbreak control or surveillance orders acts as a sufficient disincentive to such serious infringements. Third, the system with multiple penalties related to different aspects of producer behaviour may be too complex to administer. The establishment of the presence (or absence) of specific infringements takes time and may delay the payment of compensation putting farmers at a disadvantage. Alternatively, if the compliance of all the beneficiaries with all the requirements is not appropriately verified, there is a risk of unequal treatment and moral hazard. Finally, some of the penalties – compliance with registration and with livestock density regulations – are not related to particular emergency event. Although it may be operationally easier to identify and penalise the violators using the circumstance of indemnification, these infringements would be more adequately addressed through strengthening the general system of regulatory control and enforcement.

As highlighted above, the Korean livestock compensation scheme incorporates mechanisms to induce early disclosure of disease. First, farmers do not receive compensation for dead animals. Second, several brackets – "1 to 4 days", "5 days and over" and "failure to report" – are applied to upscale the penalties for late reporting. However, the use of multiple brackets may encourage a wait-and-see attitude among farmers. In particular, because a failure to report under the current scheme does not eliminate the eligibility for indemnity – other things constant, farmers would still recover from 20% of the market value of lost animals in the case of FMD, AI, swine fever and brucellosis, to 40% in all other cases. A single term for reporting disease and a denial of indemnity if it is not reported may be more effective to incentivise early disclosure. A more stringent reporting rule though requires a good level of farmer awareness about clinical signs of disease – a task which is currently being effectively addressed through the mandatory training.

Another aspect is that compensation provisions in the case of a failure to report seem to be considerably misaligned with other regulations. As already mentioned, a non-reporting farmer would be able to partly recover the cost of destroyed animals, but at the same time the "Act on Prevention of Contagious Animal Diseases" stipulates that any owner of livestock or any veterinarian who violates the obligation to report suspicious animals shall be punished by imprisonment for up to three years or incur a fine up to KRW 30 million (USD 27 000).[2] A similar misalignment concerns the non-compliance of farmers with the registration requirement: in the compensation scheme this infringement results in a 10% reduction of indemnity only, but other regulations subject it to the same criminal and financial penalty as in the case of the failure to report.

The compensation policy in Korea extends beyond losses from the compulsory culling of animals. In certain cases, consequential losses from disease outbreaks are compensated. Consequential losses can result from business interruption (e.g. buildings must be dedicated to stamping-out efforts); movement restrictions, i.e. animals cannot be moved from the property – sometimes in these cases a "welfare" slaughter is carried out; re-stocking costs; partial loss of animal value due to vaccination; or general price declines (OECD, 2012).

Several types of assistance related to consequential losses have been provided on the basis of *ad hoc* government decisions related to FMD and HPAI outbreaks:

- Income Stabilisation Fund compensated farms subjected to livestock movement restrictions for losses from shipping delay or restocking delay that lead to a fall in animal market value, or additional rearing cost.
- Operations Stabilisation Fund provided loans for restocking of farms where animal culling was implemented.
- Stabilisation Fund for Agro-Industry provides business interruption assistance to downstream operators, such as slaughterhouses, hatcheries, or feed companies at low interest rates.

Finally, consequential epidemic assistance has an equity argument in Korea: as agriculture is dominated by small farms, their business interruption could threaten the livelihood itself of livestock farmers. The Livelihoods Stabilisation Assistance can be considered as a form of social safety net in the event of several highly contagious diseases epidemics – FMD, AI, CSF, ASF, CBPP, and Rinderpest. It consists of a direct income transfer to affected households up to the amount of the average national 6-months household expenditures.

The information available since 2010 shows that the government has incurred considerable expenditures to cover losses in livestock epidemics (Figure 7.6 and Annex 7.A9). They reached an exceptional level in 2010-11 when a serious FMD outbreak occurred. The overwhelming part of compensation outlays was spent to offset direct losses of farmers from control measures. The share directed to the consequential loss assistance appears to be relatively small – it reached 2% of total compensation outlays in 2010-11 and 1% both in 2014 and 2015, with no such assistance provided in 2012 and 2013.

Figure 7.6. Loss compensation expenditures related to livestock epidemics in Korea, 2010-15

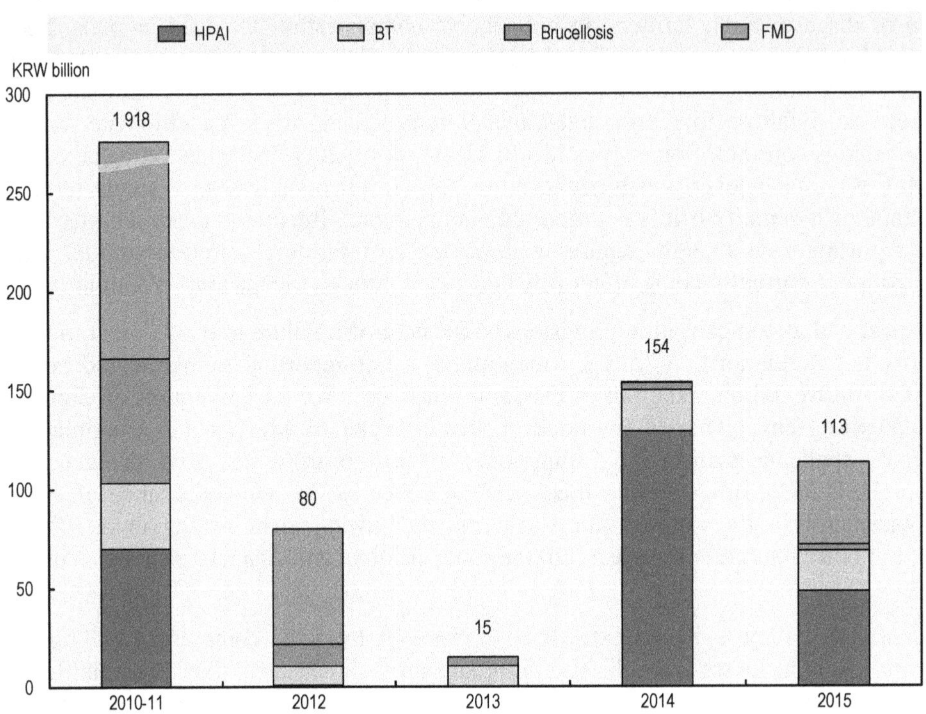

FMD: foot-and-mouth disease; BT: bovine tuberculosis; HPAI: highly pathogenic avian influenza; CSF: classical swine fever; ASF: African swine fever; CBPP: contagious bovine pleuropneumonia.

Source: Korean Government (2016).

Livestock insurance

Livestock insurance dates to the late 1990s. At the time, livestock cooperatives acted as insurers and offered government-subsidised insurance premiums. Since 2007, the government has sought to attract private companies in this activity so as to increase the quality of service. At present, several private companies – NongHyup, KB and Hanwha – offer livestock insurance and sixteen types of animals are insured.[3] The central and local governments co-finance premiums subsidies at 70-80%. Livestock diseases are among the insurable risks, but only those that are outside the list of nationally notifiable diseases. The cover includes dead animals and animals slaughtered in emergencies, as well as damage to the facilities accommodating diseased livestock and related buildings (peripherals).

The highly concessional terms led to considerable expansion of livestock insurance. Between 2011 and 2015, it increased from 55% to 91% of total livestock numbers (of 16 types covered by insurance). Over the same period, the claims-to-premiums ratio rose from 60% to 98%. The majority of claims concerned animals lost to disease and emergency slaughter; these claims amounted to 90% of the total value of claims made in 2012 and 86% in 2015.

Other assistance related to animal disease

Farmers receive subsidies for some vaccines, veterinary services, and the modernisation of livestock facilities which covers improved biosecurity. This assistance is largely focussed on prevention of FMD and avian influenza. The amounts allocated for the vaccination have increased from KRW 14 536 million (USD 12 million) in 2005 to KRW 84 801 million (USD 74 million) in 2015. Government covers all vaccination costs except in the case of FMD and circovirus.[4] The aid for veterinary services began in 2008, but has been small in terms of the number of beneficiary farms and spending amounts. The Fund for Support of the Implementation of Free Trade Agreement created in 2004, finances investments in enterprise modernisation to increase competitiveness of farmers and fishermen. The financed projects, among other components, include the overhaul and construction of new facilities to improve sanitary conditions on farms. Central and local governments and individual farmers co-finance these investment projects.

7.5. Conclusions

Korea's rising population and incomes drove domestic demand for livestock products and induced growth in domestic livestock production. Due to scarcity of agricultural land this growth was supported by a substantial increase in livestock densities. The rapid intensification of livestock production has likely played an important role in the reoccurrences of highly infectious diseases in recent periods. In certain years, livestock epidemics brought about considerable disruptions to the industry and a loss of growth.

The government responded with strong measures to address the deteriorated animal disease situation. The regulation has been significantly tightened for livestock operations, with stringent criteria introduced for production facilities, their location and livestock densities. Legal responsibility of farmers for disease reporting was increased with non-compliance leading to large financial penalties and up to criminal responsibility. Another principal step was the introduction of the mandatory training for persons involved in breeding and handling livestock, with the largest part of training costs covered by the government.

The reoccurrences of serious livestock epidemics also necessitated a revision of the previous livestock indemnity scheme, broadening of the scope of financial assistance and of the range of instruments to compensate livestock producers for direct and consequential losses.

The boundaries between different types of assistance are delineated explicitly. This is based on the classification of diseases according to the degree of contagiousness and the scale of potential socio-economic losses. Disaster assistance is provided for the nationally notifiable diseases which require destruction of livestock. The subsidised insurance addresses diseases outside the notifiable disease list. An explicit delineation between the two groups of disease risks creates clear signals to farmers about the scope of potential assistance and ensures no overlap between different types of assistance.

As in many countries, indemnification for destroyed livestock is the main compensation policy in Korea whose principal rationale is to incentivise disclosure of disease. A distinct feature of the current Korean scheme is that it foresees discounts to indemnities to discourage producer misbehaviour. This principle has an obvious logic: unless farmers face some uncompensated losses, it cannot be expected that they will change their behaviour. In this respect, the Korean compensation scheme employs a good principle to align farmer incentives to act in a socially desirable way. This also moves the compensation mechanism away from a one-size-fits-all principle to the one of adapting compensation according to individual (mis)behaviours. Nevertheless, a number of issues related to the penalty structure applied in the current scheme deserve further consideration. Overall, this comes to a possible need of simplifying and tightening the penalties so that farmers receive clearer signals about the desired behaviour and that the administration of the programme is facilitated. Also, the infringements not related to specific livestock epidemics may be more effectively addressed by strengthening control and enforcement of regulation in general, rather than by reducing compensation following the epidemic.

Other types of support related to animal disease – consequential assistance and insurance – require an in-depth analysis beyond the framework of this case study. However, several initial observations can be made. Consequential loss assistance has so far been provided discretionally and only in the cases of large epidemics of FMD and AI. Leaving aside the issue about the rationale for such assistance, a general recommendation from the OECD work on risk management is to move away from *ad hoc* assistance to the extent possible towards more explicit *ex ante* policy frameworks. The purpose here is to reduce uncertainty for both business and government. Such frameworks delimit in advance government and private responsibilities in coping with particular risks, and define criteria that trigger the assistance and its scope. The existence of explicit *ex ante* rules may stimulate businesses to develop their own crisis management strategies with an understanding of the scope and conditions for potential public assistance. *Ex ante* frameworks also allow governments to avoid budgetary decisions under political pressure at the time of crisis and allocate more spending to prevention of livestock epidemics rather than incur high costs to cope with its consequences.

Livestock insurance is a risk management instrument complementing disaster assistance in Korea, and actively promoted by the government in recent years. The effort has been on engaging large private insurers in the provision of this insurance. Substantial premium subsidies are granted to farmers to increase the uptake of insurance with the result that it covers today nearly all insurable agricultural livestock. The claims-to-premium ratio in livestock insurance has substantially increased since 2011, with the majority of claims made in respect of animal disease. This suggests that the longer-term sustainability of this rapidly expanded insurance system warrants an assessment. OECD's conceptual and empirical work on agricultural risk has shown that subsidised insurance encourages excessive risk-taking by farmers, which in the long-run may cause deficits in the insurance system and undermines its financial soundness (OECD, 2011).

Disaster assistance in Korea has so far been fully based on public funding with some parts of it co-financed by central and local governments and others fully covered by the central government. The experts (Jeong et al., 2011) proposed the organisation of biosecurity funds in Korea co-financed by livestock farms, farmers associations, and central and local governments – but this had no further developments. It may be worthwhile considering the possibility of integrating livestock producers into the cost-sharing for livestock epidemics. Several important institutional elements for a cost-sharing approach are already in place in Korea. Livestock producers are institutionalised into the commodity associations, such as the Korea Pork Producers Association and the Korea Beef Cattle Association. The Korean Animal Health Integrated System (KAHIS) contains varied information about livestock keepers and could constitute the basis for the establishment of producer contributions towards the cost-shared system.

The advantages of the public-private cost-sharing were discussed in detail in the synthesis report and the Australia case study. The key advantage of public-private cost-sharing is that it helps to optimise compensation policy by reducing moral hazard and information asymmetries within the "biosecurity contract" between private producers and government. Furthermore, cost-sharing by definition requires an explicit delineation of financial responsibilities between private and public parties, while written protocols and procedures reduce uncertainties for all stakeholders. Producer resistance to the sharing of financial burden of livestock epidemics is very likely, but there are examples of long-standing schemes with high levels of stakeholder acceptance. The country experiences show that the arrangements can vary greatly – from *ex ante* producer fees to *ex post* collections, or combining both; from flat fees to fees differentiated based on specific producer profiles (e.g. farm disease history, livestock inventories); the shared costs may cover different types of losses and involve a different distribution of financial burden between stakeholders. Thus, there is a large room of flexibility in designing cost-sharing arrangements, which allows the adaption to specific country contexts and constraints.

The current livestock disease policy seems to be driven mainly by veterinary and sanitary rationale. Whether the future policy development choice would be to fine-tune the existing instruments or to initiate new cost-sharing approaches, the Korean government should increase its engagement with producers and their organisations. The government needs to obtain better understanding of farmer behaviour if it desires to rely more on farmers' voluntary actions rather than coercion and penalties. The government may consider investing more in farmer surveys, conventional economic research and behavioural research. The scope of issues that could inform future livestock policy in Korea is broad: farmer awareness of biosecurity; how farmers make decisions about the adoption of certain practices and what the major drivers of these decisions are; how cost and investment profitability considerations affect farmer biosecurity decisions; what the financial constraints of livestock farms are and how these constraints differ across farm sizes; how farmers obtain biosecurity information and which sources they consider trustworthy; how farmers perceive their responsibility in disease management and the extent to which they are willing to act collectively in prevention and control of disease.

Gaining evidence about farmer behaviour is important not only for improving the economic instruments of policy, but also for a sustained change in individual attitudes and enhancement of social drivers towards positive behaviour. One related consideration is that the broad scope of penalties in the current livestock compensation scheme suggests that for good or bad reasons some farmers simply neglect the regulations. The government has recently introduced rewards to third parties for reporting the presence of suspected animals on other farms. This, however, poses a question about the extent to which this measure can be effective with respect to its objective and about the effects it may have in terms of trust and connectedness within the local communities. Both trust and connectedness are parts of social capital which is essential to strengthen social norms. These norms are important drivers of producer behaviour, as well as purely economic factors. Although the establishment of strong social norms for "good" behaviour takes time, it needs to be pursued and there is a role for policy through communication and "naming and shaming". To have broader responses in the Korean farming community where small "non-professional" producers represent a large constituency this communication should engage levers in different dimensions – psychological, social, as well as economic ones.

Finally, the policy problem of animal disease risk management in Korea extends far beyond the issues related to disease management as such. It fundamentally concerns the improvement of the farm structure and human capital employed in the industry. Current structural features of livestock farming in Korea present distinct challenges from the perspective of animal disease management. The rapid intensification of production over the past two decades has substantially increased the risks of occurrence and spread of disease. Although there has been an apparent structural adjustment with a concentration of production in larger units, the sector continues to be dominated by small-scale and often, non-professional, farmers. Substantial farming segments in the livestock sector may be facing constraints to undertake adequate investments in biosecurity and in better production technologies to reduce disease risks. The situation is complicated by the demographic and human capital factors when the dominant majority of producers are people of older age groups with relatively low levels of education. These groups are less likely to plan longer-term enterprise development, including investing in biosecurity.

The improvement of the livestock disease situation in Korea is therefore also a matter of structural policy to facilitate the establishment of enterprise with adequate investment-generating capacity and higher human capital. This is a long-term policy problem including several corollary dimensions. One is that current policy of high support to producers most likely has an effect of limiting structural adjustment. Another dimension is strengthening the social security for older farming generations so that the re-allocation of production factors to other operators is facilitated and occurs without adversely affecting the well-being of those who are compelled to leave agriculture. Finally, there is a challenge to ensure that the consolidation of the livestock farm structure develops sustainably and without negative effects on the environment. All these fundamental policy issues open a large research agenda on the linkages between animal disease and farm structure, social policy and sustainability and require sufficient analytical evidence for development of best policies to tackle animal disease from that perspective.

Notes

1. In 2016, 25 specialists, such as veterinarians and rearing management experts are additionally stationed at the call centre to provide consultation across wide areas including animal diseases. The number of these experts is to be increased to 40 in 2017.

2. For comparison, according to 2015 Census of Agriculture, 50% of livestock farms in Korea that had receipts from sales of livestock products had annual receipts below that amount (KOSTAT, 2016a).

3. Cattle, horses, pigs, eight kinds of poultry (chickens, ducks, pheasants, quails, turkeys, ostriches, goose, and aquarium birds), and five other types of animals (dear, sheep, bees, rabbits and badgers)

4. For FMD vaccination, large farms (with more than 50 heads of cattle and more than 1 000 heads of pigs) cover 50% of the vaccination costs, with the rest shared between the central government (35%) and local government (15%). In the case of circovirus vaccination, farms of all sizes cover 40% of costs, with the central government and local governments covering the rest in equal shares (30%-30%).

References

Cho, Wan-Hyung (2004), "Analysing producer behaviour and characteristics of environmentally friendly agricultural products", *Korean Journal of Organic Agriculture*, Vol. 12, N 1, pp. 45-66 (in Korean).

Choi, J., M. Jeong, S. Jeon, D. Sung and D. Huh (2002), *Analysis of the FMD Impact in 2002*, Korean Rural Economic Institute, Naju-si, Korea (in Korean).

Choi, Y., G. Kim, J. Lee, K. Kang and S. Yun (2009), "An Analysis of Purchasing and Using Fertilizer by Farmers", *Journal of Agricultural Extension and Community Development*, Vol. 16, N 4, pp. 687-711 (in Korean).

FAO (2016), *FAOSTAT database*, FAO Publications, Rome, http://faostat.fao.org/.

Huh, D., M. Jeong, O. Kwon, C. Yoon and J. Choi (2001), *Measures to Strengthen the Animal Disease Control System in Korea*, Korean Rural Economic Institute, Naju-si, Korea (in Korean language).

Jeong, M. and D. Huh (1998), "An analysis of the attitude to risks of livestock farmers and moral hazard in livestock insurance", *Journal of Rural Development*, Vol. 21, N 4. pp. 39-50 (in Korean).

Jeong, M., D. Huh, H. Kim and H. Lee (2011), *Measures to Improve Animal Disease Control*, Korea Rural Economic Institute, Naju-si, Korea (in Korean).

Jung, C., Y. Ryu, H. Jung, J. Kang, J. Kim and H. Jung (2001), *An Economic Analysis of Losses by Swine and Poultry Industries from Livestock Diseases,* KonKuk University (in Korean).

Jung, Jin-hwa (2008), "Farmers' Education, Technology Adoption and Income: A Case of Eco-Friendly Farming in Korean Farm Households", *Korean Journal of Agricultural Economics*, Vol. 49, N 3, pp. 71-94 (in Korean).

KAHIS (2016), *Korean Animal Health Integrated System* on-line, www.kahis.go.kr/.

Kim, T., J. Song, J. Cho and K. Jeong (2008a), "An Empirical Analysis of Adverse Selection in Livestock Insurance", *Korean Journal of Agricultural Economics*, Vol. 49, N 1, pp. 1-19 (in Korean language).

Kim, S., S. Lee and Y. Lee (2008b), "Evaluation on risk attitude of rice farmers", *Journal of Rural Development*, Vol. 31, N 1, pp. 57-75 (in Korean language).

Korean Government (2016), "OECD project on producer incentives in livestock disease management: Country case questionnaire", Responses to the OECD received from the Korean Government.

KOSTAT (2016a), *Census of Agriculture, Forestry and Fisheries 2015*, Statistics Korea, Daejeon, Korea, http://kosis.kr/statisticsList/statisticsList_01List.jsp?vwcd=MT_ZTITLE&parentId=F.

KOSTAT (2016b), *Farm Household Economic Survey*, Statistics Korea, Daejeon, Korea, http://kosis.kr/statisticsList/statisticsList_01List.jsp?vwcd=MT_ZTITLE&parentId=F#SubCont.

KOSTAT (2016c), *Livestock Statistics Survey*, Statistics Korea, Daejeon, Korea, http://kosis.kr/statisticsList/statisticsList_01List.jsp?vwcd=MT_ZTITLE&parentId=F#SubCont.

MAFRA (2016a), *Key Statistics on Agriculture, Food and Rural Affairs*, Ministry of Agriculture, Food and Rural Affairs, Sejong-si, Korea.

MAFRA (2016b), *Animal Products Traceability System*, Ministry of Agriculture, Food and Rural Affairs, Sejong-si, Korea.

MAFRA (2016c), *Livestock Disease Outbreaks and Advancement of Biosecurity System*, Report on Agricultural policies of Park Geun-hye Administration.

MAFRA (2016d), Compensation for Destroyed Livestock, on-line information, Ministry of Agriculture, Food, and Rural Affairs, Sejong-si, Korea, www.mafra.go.kr/FMD-AI/06/01_05.html.

MAFRA (2015), *Agriculture, Food and Rural Affairs Statistics Yearbook 2015*, Ministry of Agriculture, Food, and Rural Affairs, Sejong-si, Korea.

MOLEG (2016), National Law Information Centre on-line, Ministry of Government Legislation, Sejong-si, Korea, www.law.go.kr/eng/engLsSc.do?menuId=1&query=animal+disease&x=37&y=31#liBgcolor0.

Moon, H. (2002), "The Korean pension system: current state and tasks ahead", Korea Development Institute.

OECD (2016a), "Korea", in *Agricultural Policy Monitoring and Evaluation 2016*, OECD Publishing, Paris, http://dx.doi.org/10.1787/agr_pol-2016-18-en.

OECD (2016b), *OECD Economic Surveys: Korea 2016*, OECD Publishing, Paris, http://dx.doi.org/10.1787/eco_surveys-kor-2016-en.

OECD (2015), *Pensions at a Glance 2015: OECD and G20 indicators*, OECD Publishing, Paris, http://dx.doi.org/10.1787/pension_glance-2015-en.

OECD (2013), *Livestock Diseases Policies: Building bridges between science and economics*, OECD Publishing, Paris, www.oecd.org/tad/agricultural-policies/LivestockDiseasesPolicies_Proceedings2013.pdf.

OECD (2012), *Livestock Diseases: Prevention, Control and Compensation Schemes*, OECD Publishing, Paris, http://dx.doi.org/10.1787/9789264178762-en.

OECD (2011), *Managing Risk in Agriculture: Policy Assessment and Design*, OECD Publishing, Paris, http://dx.doi.org/10.1787/9789264116146-en.

OECD (2008), *Evaluation of Agricultural Policy Reforms in Korea*, OECD Publishing, Paris, www.oecd.org/tad/agricultural-policies/40383978.pdf.

Oh, S.M. (2015), *Korea's Outbreak Status of Infectious Livestock Diseases and Control Measures*, Overseas Experts Invitation Seminar on Livestock Diseases Management, Ministry of Agriculture, Food, and Rural Affairs.

Ozawa, Y., K. Chang, K. Yoshida and H. Michino (2003), "The present and future organization of Veterinary Services in Asia: the examples of the Republic of Korea and Japan", OIE *Revue Scientifique et Technique*, V. 22, N 2, pp. 499-508.

QIA (2016), *Organization of Major Veterinary Services*, Animal and Plant Quarantine Agency, Gimcheon-si, Korea, www.qia.go.kr/english/html/Animal_livestock/02AnimalLivestock_024-25.jsp.

Song, J., B. Woo, D. Huh and S. Park (2006), *An Economic Analysis of Livestock Diseases*, Korea Rural Economic Institute, Naju-si, Korea (in Korean).

USDA (2016), Production, Supply and Distribution Online (database), https://apps.fas.usda.gov/psdonline/.

Woo, B., H. Lee, Y. Hwang, J. Lee and J. Kim (2008), *An Economic Impact and Countermeasure Policies of Highly Pathogenic Avian Influenza*, Korean Rural Economic Institute, Naju-si, Korea (in Korean).

World Bank (2016), World Bank Open Data Online, http://data.worldbank.org/indicator/AG.LND.ARBL.HA.PC.

Yoon, H., S.S. Yoon, S.H. Wee, Y.J. Kim and B. Kim (2012), "Clinical manifestations of foot-and-mouth disease during the 2010/2011 epidemic in the Republic of Korea", *Transboundary and Emerging Diseases*, V. 59, pp. 517-525.

Annex 7.A1

Distribution of farm and animal numbers in Korea by farm herd size, 1995 and 2015

A. Cattle

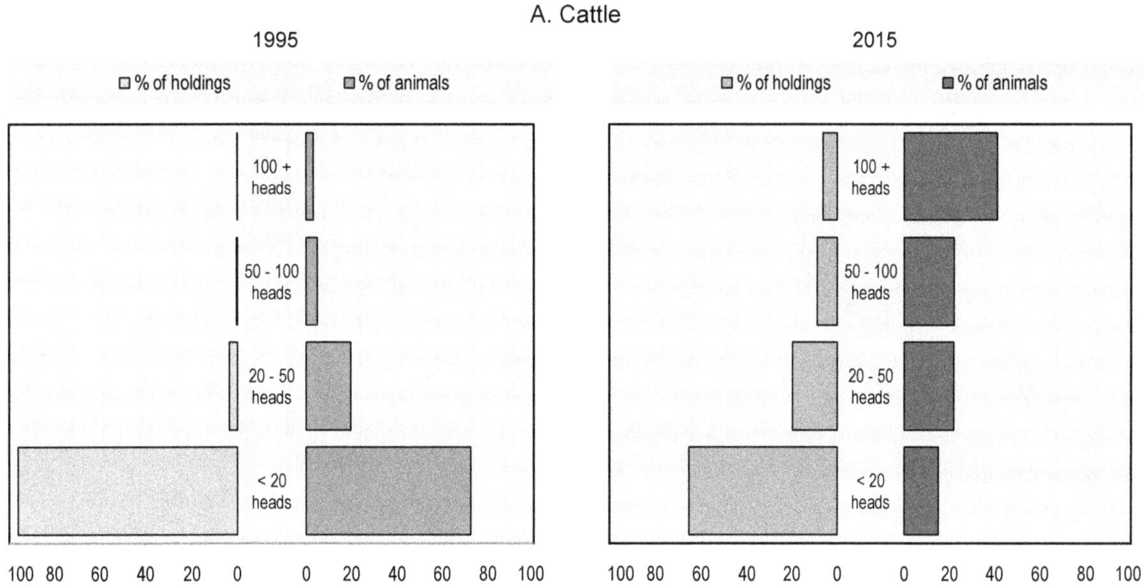

B. Pigs

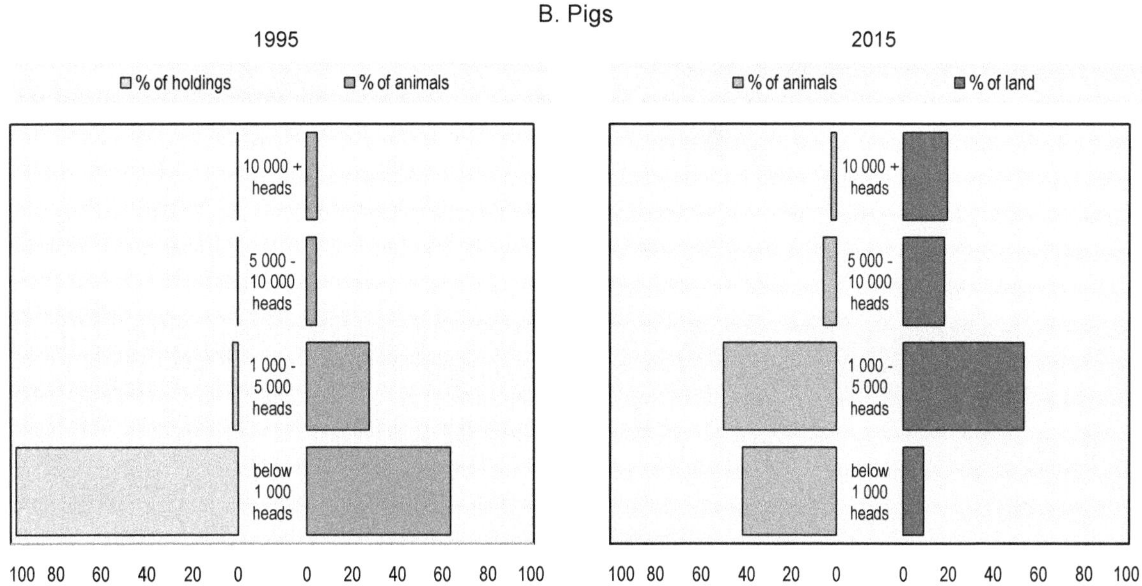

C. Chickens

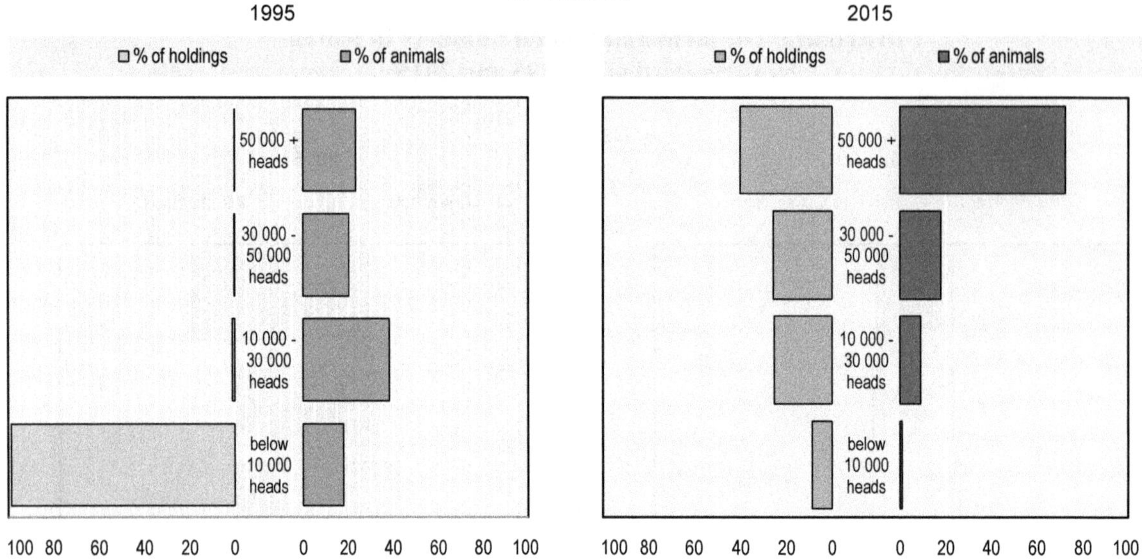

Source: KOSTAT (2016c).

Annex 7.A2

Public pension system in Korea

The relative poverty rate of the over-65 age group of Korea was 49.6% in 2013, which is almost four times higher than the OECD average of 12.6%. Their absolute poverty rate – defined as the share of persons with an income below the minimum cost of living – was 30% in 2014. The high elderly poverty rate reflects both the decline in family support and the weakness of other private and public sources of old-age income support (OECD, 2016b).

Figure 7.A2.1. Relative poverty rates in Korea and OECD average, 2013

Percentage of persons with income below 50% of the national median

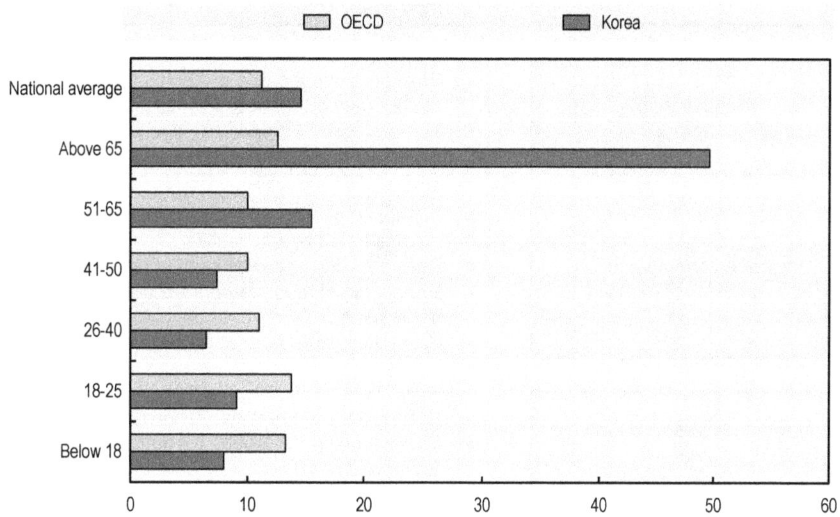

Note: relative poverty is measured by reference to median income, not taking into account household assets and liabilities.
Source: OECD (2016c).

The Korean public pension scheme was introduced relatively recently. There are two main pension schemes for the elderly: the National Pension and the Basic Pension. The National Pension Scheme (NPS), covering workers in establishments with ten or more employees, was implemented in 1988. In 1992, the compulsory coverage was expanded to firms with five and more employees. It was expanded further in 1995 to farmers and fishermen (Moon, 2002). The pension age is currently 61 with at least ten years of contributions. From 2014, the poorest 70% of those aged 65 and over can receive the Basic Pension – a non-contributory safety-net for the elderly – that pays a monthly allowance ranging from KRW 100 000 to KRW 200 000 depending on income level.

The NPS provided old-age pension benefits to 32.1% of the elderly in 2015, with pension benefits at 23.5% of the average wage.

The Basic Pension spreads resources very thinly over a large segment of the older population. The maximum benefit is equal to KRW 200 000 (USD 176) which accounted for 6.2% of the average wage in 2014. Seniors receiving no income or less than KRW 300 000 per month from their National Pension also receive an additional KRW 200 000 per month (OECD, 2015).

Annex 7.A3

New animal disease prevention and control system for FMD in Korea

Changes in the system of FMD prevention and control foresee the transition:

- From reactive to pre-emptive measures (e.g. strengthened surveillance and disinfection).
- From the veterinary-centred to a multidisciplinary approach based on cost-minimisation and utilisation of ICT.
- From measures led by the central government to cooperative activity with shared responsibility of agencies and private farmers.

Area	Measure	Actions
Institutional change	Risk management by zones	• Minimising disease spread through risk management by zones • Strengthening crisis management capacities through emergency trainings
	Clear distribution of roles between actors	• Strengthening the role of Animal and Plant Quarantine Agency as the main biosecurity agency • Expanding local biosecurity agencies and strengthening expertise and accountability
	Greater autonomy and accountability of farms	• Increased penalty for violation of biosecurity regulations and incentives for best practices • Differentiation of compensation criteria • Enhancing of management accountability of vertically integrated companies • Promoting rewards to encourage disease reporting
Efficient and Phased Prevention	Strengthened surveillance before outbreak	• Compulsory certification of vehicles transporting livestock • Strengthening the testing for antibodies at slaughterhouses • Advanced risk forecast by utilising ICT
	Rapid response	• Strengthening measures at the beginning stage (standstill, emergency stamping-out, etc.) • Strengthening regional risk management
	Post-outbreak management	• Strengthening management of affected farms and farms with low vaccination levels • Build-up of disinfection infrastructure
Promotion of Animal Health	Improvement of vaccine response	• Strengthening the quality evaluation of vaccines and localisation of production • Selection of optimal vaccines through matching testing
	Society-friendly livestock industry	• Expansion of the animal welfare certificate and strengthening the approval system • Improvement of breeding conditions, such as reducing livestock densities

Source: Korean Government (2016).

Annex 7.A4

Key institutions involved in livestock disease issues in Korea

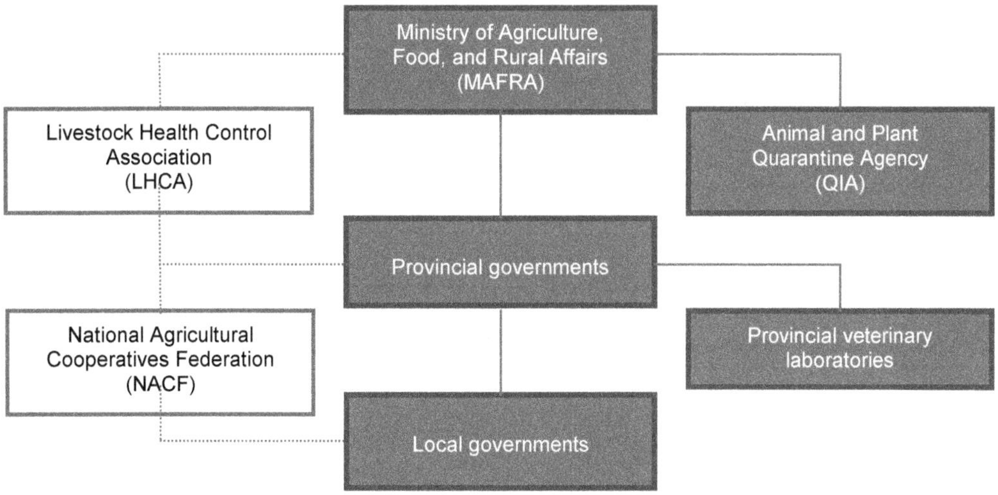

Institution	Functions
MAFRA	• Planning and coordination of vaccination and surveys for infectious animal diseases • Planning and coordination of production and quality control of veterinary biologicals • Planning and coordination of the quarantine regulations for imported or exported animals and animal products • Supervision on activities of Veterinary Medical Associations and veterinary hospital
QIA	• Prevention and control of the major animal diseases • Surveillance of animal diseases • Operation of animal diseases emergency control centre • Operation of animal diseases Surveillance Committee • Technical support with diagnostic materials providing and standardization of diagnostic methods • Educational & training programme for provincial animal health authorities
Provincial governments	• Implementation of animal disease control measures in the region
Provincial Veterinary Laboratories	• Veterinary diagnostics and disease surveillance within region • Diagnosis and Monitoring detection test of animal diseases
LHCA	• Vaccination, clinical examinations of livestock, and collection of test specimens • Sanitary inspection of livestock products • Disinfection • Education and public relations
Producers	• Livestock producer associations, such as the National Agricultural Co-operatives Federation, the Korean Swine Association, the Korean Poultry Association and the Korean Cattle Association established Joint Disease Control Units in each region, which conduct autonomous disease control activities, such as cleansing and disinfection.

Source: Based QIA (2016) and Ozawa et al. (2003).

Annex 7.A5

Approval and registration of livestock activity in Korea

Eligibility to registration and approval procedures for the establishments keeping livestock

Type of enterprise	Registration of operations required	Approval of production facilities required
Establishments with cattle and pigs:		
Farm facilities with total surface of 50 m^2 and more	Yes	Yes
Farm facilities with total a surface below 50 m^2	Yes	No
Establishments with poultry (chickens and ducks):		
Farm facilities with total surface of 50 m^2 and more	Yes	Yes
Farm facilities with total surface below 50 m^2 and up to 10 m^2	Yes	No
Farm facilities with total a surface of less than 10 m^2	No	No
All establishments with sheep and deer	Yes	No
Establishments with animals not susceptible to FMD or avian influenza (rabbits, dogs and horses)	No	No

Criteria for registration and approval of establishments with livestock: example of poultry farms

Category/ type		Establishments eligible for registration only	Establishments eligible for approval of facilities
Facility/ Equipment requirements	Livestock raising facility	Structure with easy flow of wind and ventilation	- Special livestock raising facility existing - Ventilation n system
	Egg storage facility (laying hens)	None	- Egg storage facility - Insect-, heat-resistance facility, ventilation - Temperature adjustable facility (air conditioner) for eggs
	Sterilisation facility	None	- Disinfection facility for automobile - Gate bar at the entrance - Walk-in disinfectant spray for clothes - Log for automobile and visitors - Disinfectant mat at the entrance of livestock farms
	Disease control	None	- "Authorized personnel only" sign at the entrance - Hedge or fence to control the entrance of visitors, automobiles - Storage for medicines, sterilized equipment and others
Recommended unit area for breeding		- Laying hens (cage·floor): 0.05 · 0.11 m^2/per hen(*) - Meat poultry (windowless poultry house): chicken: 39 kg/m^2; ducks: 0.246㎡/a duck	
Location requirement		None	Reject approval within 30m from roads and within 500m from slaughter house or feed factory
Training requirement		Initial minimum training: 6 hours Addition training: 6 hours (every 4 years)	Initial minimum training: 24 hours Addition training: 6hours (every 2 years)

(*) For establishments eligible for registration only: 0.042㎡ for laying hens (cage).

Source: Korean Government (2016).

Annex 7.A6

Economic studies related to livestock disease in Korea and other behavioural research

	Livestock disease studies	
1.	Study title	Jeong, M. and Huh, D. (1998) "Analysis of risk attitudes of livestock farmers and moral hazard in livestock insurance", *Journal of Rural Development*, Vol. 21, N 4. pp. 39-50 (in Korean language).
	Summary	Livestock farmers' attitudes to risks of animal loss and moral hazard in the livestock insurance scheme are studied based on a survey data.
2.	Study title	Kim, T., Song, J., Cho, J. and Jeong, K. (2008) "Empirical analysis of adverse selection in livestock insurance", *Korean Journal of Agricultural Economics*, Vol. 49, N 1, pp. 1-19 (in Korean language).
	Summary	Adverse selection that may exist in livestock insurance programmes in Korea is analysed empirically with a pig producer's preference model and survey data. The results indicate that there exists adverse selection in the disease insurance contract. Some approaches to address adverse selection are presented such as introduction of compulsory insurance or differentiated insurance premium reflecting risk levels of individual farms.
3.	Study title	Huh, D., Jeong M., Kwon, O., Yoon, C. and Choi, J. (2001) *Measures to Strengthen the Animal Disease Control System in Korea*, Korean Rural Economic Institute, Naju-si, Korea (in Korean language).
	Summary	Economic costs of animal disease are estimated using the data between 1980 and 2000. The economic costs of diseases are estimated to vary for the cattle sector between KRW 824 billion and KRW 2 750 billion, for the swine sector between KRW 688 billion and KRW 1 095 billion, and for the chicken sector between KRW 154 billion and KRW 855 billion. Measures to strengthen the animal disease control system are proposed, such as reorganisation of control institutions; strengthening the role of the private sector; enhancement of the efficiency of quarantine system; development of a standard disease control procedure; establishment of an information system for contagious diseases; and pooling of veterinarians and livestock-related experts.
4.	Study title	Jung, C., Ryu, Y., Jung, H., Kang, J., Kim J. and Jung, H. (2001) *An Economic Analysis of Losses by Swine and Poultry Industries from Livestock Diseases,* KonKuk University (in Korean language).
	Summary	This study estimates economic costs of governments and producers related to livestock diseases, including government expenditures for compensation scheme, decrease in production value due to reduced farm gate prices and loss of export revenue. To reduce these, the authors propose an improvement of disease monitoring system to strengthen disease prevention.
5.	Study title	Choi, J., Jeong, M., Jeon, S., Sung, D. and Huh, D. (2002) *Analysis of the FMD Impact in 2002*, Korean Rural Economic Institute, Naju-si, Korea (in Korean language).
	Summary	The study analyses the economic impact of 2002 FMD epidemic in terms of its effects on supply and demand of livestock products and consumers reaction. A cost-benefit analysis of vaccination and stamping out decisions is made.
6.	Study title	Song, J., Woo, B., Huh, D. and Park, S. (2006) *An Economic Analysis of Livestock Diseases*, Korea Rural Economic Institute, Naju-si, Korea (in Korean language).
	Summary	The study employed an economic analysis model and livestock statistical data to measure the economic impact of livestock diseases per year. It found that losses of cattle farms can vary between KRW 500 million to KRW 67 billion. The losses of pigs and poultry farms are estimated KRW 5.3 billion and KRW 800 million, respectively. The losses of the livestock sector from PMWS (Post-Weaning Multisystemic Wasting Syndrome) and calf diarrhoea are estimated at KRW 18 million and KRW 28 million, respectively.

7.	Study title	Woo, B., Lee, H., Hwang, Y., Lee, J. and Kim, J. (2008) *An Economic Impact and Countermeasure Policies of Highly Pathogenic Avian Influenza*, Korean Rural Economic Institute, Naju-si, Korea (in Korean language).
	Summary	An economic impact of HPAI of 2008 is estimated covering the upstream, farm production and downstream stages. The study finds that economic loss from the outbreak of HPAI exceeded KRW 630 billion. The authors also reviewed the current animal disease surveillance system of Korea. Introducing an early warning system for HPAI is important to reduce a potential loss. To establish an early warning system, several systemic changes are recommended, such as maintaining breeding record and strengthening incentives for early reporting.
8.	Study title	Jeong, M., Huh, D., Kim, H. and Lee, H. (2011) *Measures to Improve Animal Disease Control*, Korea Rural Economic Institute, Naju-si, Korea (in Korean language).
	Summary	The study analysed the economic impact of FMD and HPAI, and suggested a variety of policy measures to improve the animal disease control system. The suggestions include increasing the number of staff and expending the quarantine facilities in ports and airports; improving the ability of regional biosecurity agencies; installing farm border fences and vehicle disinfection facilities; creation of bio-security funds by all stakeholders; and introduction of livestock permit system.
	Other studies related to farmer behaviour	
9.	Study title	Jung, Jin-hwa (2008) "Farmer education, technology adoption and Income: a case of eco-friendly farming in Korean farm households", *Korean Journal of Agricultural Economics*, Vol. 49, N 3, pp. 71-94
	Summary	The effect of farmer educational attainment on agricultural income, focusing on the allocative effect of education in association with technology adoption is analysed with the agricultural census data. The results indicate that education of both farm manager and family member raises the probability of technology adoption and farm managers' education attainment raises agricultural income by reinforcing the income effect of technology adoption. The author concludes that promoting farmer education is a good policy that can lead to technology adoption and speed up the diffusion of new technologies.
10.	Study title	Choi, Y., Kim, G., Lee, J., Kang, K., and Yun, S. (2009) "Analysis of the purchase and use fertiliser by farmers", *Journal of Agricultural Extension and Community Development*, Vol. 16, N 4, pp. 687-711 (in Korean language).
	Summary	This study was conducted to examine and compare farmers' purchase and use of fertilisers. Data were gathered from a total of 326 farmers across the country. The findings include: first, 70.6% of greenhouse horticulture farmers, 89% of upland-cultivating farmers, 76.3% of fruit-growing farmers purchased fertiliser in Nong-hyup (a farmer cooperative organisation); second, only 54.2% of the greenhouse horticulture farmers, 60.2% of the upland cultivating farmers and 70.4% of the fruit-growing farmers recognized optimum levels of fertiliser application. However, about half of farmers do not comply with optimum level of fertiliser, which means that there exist a significant gap between their behaviour and belief.
11.	Study title	Cho, Wan-Hyung (2004) "Analysing producer behaviour and characteristics of environmentally friendly agricultural products", *Korean Journal of Organic Agriculture*, Vol. 12, N 1, pp. 45-66 (in Korean language).
	Summary	Farmer social and economic behaviours and the characteristics of environmentally friendly agricultural products are examined based on the surveys on 341 farmers producing quality-certified environmentally friendly agricultural products. The author suggests policy implications, such as diversifying sales channels and strengthening farmer education and communication.
12.	Study title	Kim, S., Lee, S. and Lee, Y. (2008) "Evaluation on risk attitude of rice farmers", *Journal of Rural Development*, Vol. 31, N 1, pp. 57-75 (in Korean language).
	Summary	The study examines risk attitudes of Korean rice farmers based on responses about risk sources using an attitudinal scale approach. Economic, social, personal, and environmental sources of risk are considered in the measurement of risk attitudes. The results show that rice farmers are more likely to manage risks associated with the timing of farming practices, the amount of fertiliser, drainage management and flooding controls and pest and weed controls. Rice farmers who are younger and more educated, and who have more income and larger size of farming land are more aggressive in managing their exposure to risk.

Annex 7.A7

National notifiable diseases in Korea and response measures

Disease class	Disease	Control measures
Class 1	Cattle plaque, contagious bovine pleuropneumonia, FMD, plaque of small ruminants, blue tongue, rift valley fever, lumpy skin disease, sheep pox, vesicular stomatitis, African horse sickness, African swine fever, swine fever, swine vesicular disease, Newcastle disease, HPAI and others that are equivalent to the aforementioned	• Quarantine/detection of suspicious animal/stuff • Movement restriction of contaminated farm owner/family/workers • Access control to contaminated area of people/animal/vehicle • Access control to livestock facilities of people/animal/vehicle • Prohibition on taking out of animal/stuff from contaminated area • Restriction on pasturing animals • Order to close livestock facilities • Order to suspend business to livestock related business • Stamping out (6 diseases)
Class 2	Anthrax, blackleg, brucellosis, tuberculosis, Johne's disease, BSE, Q fever, swine Aujeszky's disease, Japanese encephalitis, Teschen disease, scrapie, glanders, equine infectious anaemia, equine viral arteritis, canine infectious disease, equine infectious uteritis, Eastern and Western equine encephalitis, Venezuelan equine encephalitis, pullorum, fowl typhoid, fowl cholera, rabies, mule deer chronic wasting disease and others that are equivalent to the aforementioned	• Quarantine/detection of suspicious animal/stuff • Access control to contaminated area of people/animal/vehicle • Prohibition on taking out of animal/stuff from contaminated area • Restriction on pasturing animals • Order to close livestock facilities • Order to suspend business to livestock related business • Stamping out (8 diseases)
Class 3	Bovine ephemeral fever, bovine akabane diseases, chicken mycoplasma disease, LPAI, foul brood and others that are equivalent to the aforementioned	• Quarantine/detection of suspicious animal/stuff • Prohibition on taking out of animal/stuff from contaminated area • Restriction on pasturing animals • Order to close livestock facilities • Order to suspend business to livestock related business

Source: MOLEG (2016).

Annex 7.A8

Livestock compensation scheme in the Korean Act on Prevention of Contagious Animal Diseases

Incentive aspects	Modalities
Scope of compensation	Compensation to livestock holders is payable for livestock slaughtered by the stamping-out order. Animals that died before the order are not compensated. Objects incinerated or buried in complying with the veterinary authority's order in the suspicion to be contaminated with pathogens of animal diseases are reimbursed.
Consequential losses	In the case of FMD or AI, concessional loans may be provided for re-stocking to farms (Operations Stabilisation Fund) and for business interruption to agricultural businesses (Fund for Stabilisation of Agro-industry companies).
Cost-sharing	The compensation is fully borne by the central, regional, and local governments. The central government covers 80% of the compensation and the regional and local government cover the remaining 10%.
Rules for valuation	For incinerated or buried objects, the value is assessed on the basis of the market price at the time of disposal. For livestock, market price of animal slaughtered is based on the farm gate price or wholesale price monitored by producer associations or NACF (National Agricultural Co-operatives Federation) on the day of stamping-out. If not available, the value is based on the price immediately prior to the implementation of measure.
Assessment of compensation payment	The amount of payment is established by a payment assessment team, created by local administration. The team comprises five members, including a local government official, a member of producer organisation, a member of Provincial Veterinary Laboratory and a veterinarian. The amount of payment is assessed by all the team members considering farm gate price and wholesale price and the average value of estimations of all team members is applied to the final assessment.
Discounts and penalties	In the case of FMD, AI, brucellosis, and CSF the indemnity is reduced by 20%. Reductions to compensation are applied in the case of reporting delay, non-compliance with rules for preventive measures, farm disease history and other criteria (see Table 7.4).
Timeframe for compensation	After a livestock holder requests compensation claim to the local administration, the latter should submit it to the regional administration within 2 days. Following a 15-day review of the claim, the regional administration will notify the decision. Local administration will then pay out the compensation to livestock holder.

Source: MOLEG (2016).

Annex 7.A9

Government expenditures on emergency animal disease events in Korea, 2010-15

Year	Disease	Species	Total expenditure		Direct loss of culled animals	Of which		
						Operational support	Price support	Consumption measures
			USD million (1)	KRW billion	KRW billion			
2010-11	Brucellosis	Bovine	55.6	62.9	62.9	0	0	0
	Tuberculosis	Bovine / Deer	29.4	33.3	33.3	0	0	0
	FMD	Artiodactyla	1 548.6	1 751.5	1 725.6	25.9	0	0
	HPAI	Birds	61.8	69.9	66.4	3.5	0	0
2012	Brucellosis	Bovine	9.8	11.1	11.1	0	0	0
	Tuberculosis	Bovine / Deer	8.6	9.7	9.7	0	0	0
	FMD	Artiodactyla	51.5	58.3	58.3	0	0	0
	HPAI	Birds	0.7	0.8	0.8	0	0	0
2013	Brucellosis	Bovine	3.9	4.4	4.4	0	0	0
	Tuberculosis	Bovine / Deer	9.3	10.5	10.5	0	0	0
2014	Brucellosis	Bovine	3.1	3.5	3.5	0	0	0
	Tuberculosis	Bovine / Deer	18.4	20.8	20.8	0	0	0
	FMD	Artiodactyla	0.4	0.5	0.5	0	0	0
	HPAI	Birds	114.1	129.1	127.2	1.9	0	0
2015	Brucellosis	Bovine	2.7	3.0	3.0	0	0	0
	Tuberculosis	Bovine / Deer	18.2	20.6	20.6	0	0	0
	FMD	Artiodactyla	36.8	41.6	41.1	0.5	0	0
	HPAI	Birds	42.5	48.1	47.5	0.6	0	0
Total expenditures								
2010-11	-	-	1 695.5	1 917.6	1 888.2	29.4	0	0
2012	-	-	70.6	79.9	79.9	0	0	0
2013	-	-	13.2	14.9	14.9	0	0	0
2014	-	-	136.1	153.9	152.0	1.9	0	0
2015	-	-	100.2	113.3	112.2	1.1	0	0

(*) For all years, the exchange rate for 2015 is applied (USD 1 = KRW 1 131).

Source: Korean Government (2016).

ORGANISATION FOR ECONOMIC CO-OPERATION AND DEVELOPMENT

The OECD is a unique forum where governments work together to address the economic, social and environmental challenges of globalisation. The OECD is also at the forefront of efforts to understand and to help governments respond to new developments and concerns, such as corporate governance, the information economy and the challenges of an ageing population. The Organisation provides a setting where governments can compare policy experiences, seek answers to common problems, identify good practice and work to co-ordinate domestic and international policies.

The OECD member countries are: Australia, Austria, Belgium, Canada, Chile, the Czech Republic, Denmark, Estonia, Finland, France, Germany, Greece, Hungary, Iceland, Ireland, Israel, Italy, Japan, Korea, Latvia, Luxembourg, Mexico, the Netherlands, New Zealand, Norway, Poland, Portugal, the Slovak Republic, Slovenia, Spain, Sweden, Switzerland, Turkey, the United Kingdom and the United States. The European Union takes part in the work of the OECD.

OECD Publishing disseminates widely the results of the Organisation's statistics gathering and research on economic, social and environmental issues, as well as the conventions, guidelines and standards agreed by its members.

OECD PUBLISHING, 2, rue André-Pascal, 75775 PARIS CEDEX 16
(51 2017 10 1 P) ISBN 978-92-64-27947-6 – 2017

www.ingramcontent.com/pod-product-compliance
Lightning Source LLC
Chambersburg PA
CBHW061215240926
51846CB00006B/1230